ABOUT THE AUTHOR

Martin Wilson is an experienced management consultant who has been running his own company, Solidus, for 16 years. Although he started as an information systems specialist, he now works in the customer care field and on strategies for new technology and change that work with the needs of the people in client organisations.

Martin has worked with organisations of all sizes, from small owner-run businesses to government departments and multinational corporations. He has also worked in most industrial and commercial sectors, as his skills are generally applicable. Increasingly his work is in competitive markets with blue chip clients who need to use customer care to achieve an edge in their market.

He also worked for a large international firm of accountants and business advisors, where he was heavily involved with leading multidisciplinary consultancy teams facilitating the changes in the UK's National Health Service.

Martin is an established writer on business topics, having published in both magazines and books. *Creating and Developing a Consultancy Practice* is his third book, and he already has others in mind.

CREATING AND DEVELOPING A CONSULTANCY PRACTICE

Martin Wilson

Oak Tree Press
Dublin • London

Oak Tree Press
Merrion Building
Lower Merrion Street
Dublin 2, Ireland

A catalogue record of this book is
available from the British Library

ISBN 1-86076-044-9

Printed in Ireland by Colour Books Ltd.

CONTENTS

Dedication

Alison, David and Alexandra,
my supportive family.

ACKNOWLEDGEMENTS

When I first became a consultant, I had little background in professional consultancy. I had worked in a computer software house, but there the approach was very different. So I had to learn a lot of lessons the hard way and by reading around the field. I was fortunate in that I had run a small business before, and so I possessed many of the basic skills. However, I wish that I had been given some guidance, as I would have avoided many mistakes and progressed more rapidly. My hope is that this book will bridge some of the gap for future generations of consultants.

Until you write a book, it is difficult to appreciate how many other people are involved apart from the author. There are the editors, designers, sales and marketing people and others at the publisher, all of who help shape the book and try to prevent the author making a fool of himself. Then there are many others who contribute to the content. There are all those clients who trained me in the art and science of consultancy. There are those colleagues, past and present, who have done likewise and who provided information, anecdotes and comments on my ideas and on the structure of this book. I could not have written it without them.

There are two people in particular whom I have to thank. One is my father, Peter, who has been of great assistance with all my books and who, with his father, Harry, encouraged my interest in the English language; I hope I have done them justice.

The biggest single contribution was made by my friend and colleague, Tim Stretton. We have spent a lot of time debating ideas and approaches to consultancy, much of which has been incorporated into this book. Tim also had the onerous task of reading my early drafts and making helpful comments. For that I am very grateful, because it is very easy for an author to lose sight of what is good and to feel that it is all gibberish. Tim kept me straight with candid comments and support.

But at the end of the day, I have to take responsibility for the final result. I attempted to do justice to the help I have received, but any failings and errors are mine. My most sincere thanks go to everybody who has helped in any way.

Finally, I must acknowledge the support of my wife, Alison, and my children, David and Alexandra. They tolerated my absence with the computer with good grace and genuine interest in progress. Thank you.

Martin P. Wilson
Nottingham, December 1997

CHAPTER 1

INTRODUCTION

Many people see becoming a consultant as a way of achieving high earnings with considerable personal freedom. Realistically it is not possible to achieve both. Many consultants earn little more than middle managers; only a very small group are high earners by any standards. The rest earn a good salary through working long hours and being responsive to their clients' needs — that usually means less rather than more personal freedom! However, all consultants have to make decisions about the balance between earnings and their private lives; any immediate family should also be involved in the decision as they will be affected.

Many technical specialists assume that, because they are genuinely experts in their field, they will make good consultants. Unfortunately that is not always so. Even specialist technical consultants need a wide range of skills other than technical competence. Similarly, success as a manager does not automatically qualify someone as a consultant, because management and consultancy are very different and require different capabilities and personal styles.

Successful consultancy is more about people skills than technical knowledge and ability. Of course, any prospective consultant must be competent in their specialist field. But to achieve success as an independent, or even as a senior consultant in a large firm, you must have strong 'people skills'.

As a consultant who wishes to be successful, you also need marketing and sales skills, as you will be required to win new work. You will also need to be a good administrator and project manager, as you will be responsible for the performance of other consultants who provide support to your clients.

TARGET READER

This book has a wide potential readership. First, it aims to meet the needs of anyone aspiring to be a consultant. You should read it well before starting out to ensure that you are well prepared and have the required background. Such an in-depth reading will give the would-be consultant time to research the market and develop the skills that will be needed when they go out on their own. An ill-prepared adviser without the right talents will damage themselves and more importantly their clients — to the detriment of all consultants.

Second, many practising consultants should benefit from this book, especially those who do not have experience of working in a large professional practice. All consultants should go back to basics from time to time and re-examine their motivations, personal objectives and skills, and whether they are still able to meet the needs of clients. By doing so, they will refresh their approach to the benefit of their practice and their clients.

There are many reasons why individuals move into consultancy. Often, it is not through any great desire to do so, but because they need to earn a living and, on the face of it, consultancy seems an easy way of doing so. Hopefully, this book will show that it is not as easy as it seems, but will provide a framework for those who are determined to try out the role of business advisor. A lot of unsuitable people have wasted their redundancy cheques or pension lump sums on half-hearted attempts to become consultants. In many ways, I hope this book is as successful in dissuading those without the skills or desire from trying to be consultants as it is in helping the rest to get started. Facing up to the fact that one is not cut out to be a consultant is not failure, but trying to be one without the aptitude is. I wish anyone who decides against being a consultant every success in whatever else they choose to do — they will be a lot happier than they would be if they pursued the wrong career.

That said, it is a highly rewarding career — financially, intellectually and socially. If it is for you, you will wonder why you did not make the move earlier and you will not be able to imagine doing anything else.

OBJECTIVES

All good consultants make the objectives for any project clear at the outset. I do not intend to depart from that sound approach in this book. So I will now set out what I am trying to achieve with this book. We will return to these objectives at the end to test whether we were successful.

Broadly, the objectives for this book are to:

1. Debunk some myths and stereotypes about consultants;

2. Set the new consultant on the right track;

3. Provide all advisors, new or established, with some fresh ideas;

4. Refresh the approach of experienced consultants;

5. Allow anyone considering working as a business advisor to decide whether the profession is for them and whether they have the skills and motivation to be successful.

STRUCTURE OF THE BOOK

Creating and Developing a Consultancy Practice is divided into three parts:

Part 1 — Is Consultancy for You?

Chapter 2 briefly sets out what a consultant is and what the implications are for the individual and their family. It also considers the consultancy role and the rewards that can accrue if one is successful. Finally, it considers the risks of being a business advisor and the demands placed on the consultant.

Chapter 3 explores the personal and family issues of being a consultant. It discusses motivation, the skills required and the commitment needed for success from both the individual and their family. Finally, it covers the reality of setting out on the road to becoming a consultant.

Chapters 2 and 3 contain self-assessment questionnaires to help the reader who may be considering a career in consultancy to determine whether it is for them.

Part 2 — The Nature of Consultancy

Part 2 explores what consultants do and how they do it. Chapter 4 looks at styles of consultancy, the specialist knowledge that can be offered and the key skills required to work as a consultant in almost any business-related discipline.

The consultancy process itself is considered in Chapter 5. It sets out the basic steps in most consultancy projects. It also examines the skill areas with which all consultants should be comfortable. Of course, it can only give a flavour of how consultancy is performed. All consultants work differently, clients have different needs and each specialism has its own unique characteristics. However, there is an underlying common thread which this chapter illustrates.

Part 3 — The Business of Consultancy

This final part is concerned with the business aspects of consultancy and the organisation of a practice.

Chapter 6 sets out the marketing aspects of consultancy. Without successful marketing and a supporting sales effort, no consultancy practice will win work. Without work you are not a consultant. The chapter shows how to identify possible clients, what they want, what you can offer and how you can bring them together. Most new consultants struggle with finding customers and underestimate how long it takes to build a viable client base. As this chapter stresses, this is a non-stop process — and it is hard work. But it can be done if you have the desire and the motivation.

Chapter 7 looks at the issues of understanding and managing your costs so that you can set fees at a level that will reward your efforts and that clients will pay. The bases for charging are widening all the time, with day rates being overtaken by fixed-price and even results-based fees. The reader is guided through the options and when to use them.

Estimating the work involved in a project is an important element both of successful proposals and making a profit from doing the work. This important area is discussed in Chapter 8.

Chapter 9 deals with handling the sales process. This is a distinct area to marketing; it is an essential skill area for any consultant who aspires to run their own practice or to achieve senior positions in large consultancy firms. The chapter covers the process of consultancy sales, but it does not go into great detail with regard to general skills, as they are well covered in many other books dedicated to the subject.

Having won a client, it is important to keep them happy, as they will provide future work, either directly or through recommendation. Chapter 10 considers quality — what it means in a professional or technical environment and the wider requirements of customer care.

Chapter 11 is about the nuts and bolts of running a practice with specific application to professional advisory service businesses. It does not cover basic business administration such as book-keeping, as anyone providing business advice should ensure that they are comfortable with running a business before they start advising others how to run theirs (even if this advice only covers certain technical issues). All business advice, however technical, should be related to the business benefits that it provides — this requires a *good* understanding of all aspect of business.

From time to time, most small consultancy practices (and large ones for that matter) go through difficult times when new work does not seem to come in. Chapter 12 discusses some of the things that the independent consultant can do to help manage such circumstances.

Throughout the book, there are questionnaires and associated analyses, action plans, check lists and case studies to illustrate the issues. The case studies are included for both explanation and diversion — most of us like a bit of gossip!

There is a final summary (Chapter 13), relating everything that goes before to the original objectives and pulling it all together.

HOW TO USE THIS BOOK

There are two anticipated approaches to using this book. First, it can be used as a workbook to be read from start to finish. By doing so, the fledgling consultant will develop a framework which will get them off on the right foot in their practice.

For the more established business advisor and for those who used this book to get started, it will provide a reference work. I hope it will be used to regenerate ideas when readers are unsure of where they are going or why. All of us go through such periods of uncertainty or lose sight of the basics. By coming back to this book, the reader should be able to regenerate their thinking and produce fresh ideas as to how to take their practice forward.

But all readers will have to add their own experience and knowledge to the concepts and approaches in this book. As already suggested, it provides a structure, but it does not, and cannot, provide all the answers. That is what makes running a consultancy practice such an interesting and hopefully rewarding career.

SUMMARY

All consultants should be familiar with the practical basics of planning and running a business before even contemplating embarking on a career in consultancy. How can you expect clients to take you seriously as a business advisor if you are not competent in the most basic business functions? This book therefore does not cover book-keeping and other business management — there are many other books and courses available on those subjects. These can be used in conjunction with this book if needed; it is certainly recommended that all new consultants should check their knowledge and understanding.

Creating and Developing a Consultancy Practice covers three main areas: what is a consultant and why become one; the process of consultancy; and finally the marketing, organisation and administration of an effective consultancy practice.

Good luck. I hope you avoid some of the mistakes I made when I started out on a career in consultancy. But above all enjoy it — I still do after more than 15 years in the business.

PART 1

IS CONSULTANCY FOR YOU?

Chapter 2

What is a Consultant?

The title 'consultant' is used rather freely by all sorts of people in all sorts of ways, so we first need to define what we mean by the word for the purposes of this book. In many industries, 'consultant' has become the favoured replacement for 'executive' as in 'Sales Consultant' or 'Personal Communications Consultant' — read as salesman or mobile telephone salesman.

This book is about business consultancy rather than advisors or providers of services to individuals. The latter may well benefit from studying this book, but there are particular issues in such a role that this book does not set out to address.

So as our starting point: what is a consultant? For our purposes a consultant is someone who gives advice or provides expertise, specialist or otherwise, to businesses or other organisations. This definition will be extended as we develop the concept of the business advisor's role.

OBJECTIVES

The aim of this chapter is to enable the reader to:

- Challenge the myths and stereotypes that surround the consultancy profession;

- Understand the pressures and demands faced by consultants, especially independent consultants and those running small firms;

- Face their own motivation for becoming a consultant and appreciate how that fits with the demands of being a consultant;

- Be aware of the potential risks and rewards facing the starting consultant and the continuing challenges that the profession presents;

- Extend such issues to their impact on the lifestyle that the reader will face as a consultant.

We will examine these issues in more detail in this chapter and, in future chapters, provide a basis for further consideration of the reader's aptitude, desire and commitment to becoming a consultant.

CONSULTANTS — ROLES AND RESPONSIBILITIES

So what is a consultant, what do they do? As a starting point it is easier to define what a consultant is not. A consultant is not:

- A director

- A manager

- Contract staff

- An interim manager or any other form of temporary staff.

Understanding this is important as it can have an impact on how you work as a consultant and the responsibilities that you carry. In the worst case you could be regarded as a shadow director — with serious implications, especially in the event of the client going into liquidation. In such a scenario you could be disqualified from acting as a director in any company (including your own) or even be made bankrupt with all that would mean for the rest of your practice and your personal life.

A consultant is primarily an advisor, although many take on some of the roles above from time to time. Perhaps the key difference between a consultant and someone acting as a freelance expert can be found by answering the following question: who is responsible for managing the work on a day-to-day basis? A consultant is essentially self-managing on projects for which they are engaged, obviously within an agreed project plan to meet the client's needs. Their routine work will not be supervised by the client's directors or managers, although key elements and the final results of the work will be accepted, or not, by the commissioning manager before appropriate payments are made.

A freelance technician on the other hand will work as part of the client's team, and the work they undertake will be assigned, monitored and managed by the client to ensure that the approach adopted fits with the client's standards and culture. Often a freelance will be paid by the hour rather than by results, although there are exceptions.

Similarly, although a consultant may advise, they should not usurp the responsibility of client management to make decisions. A consultant should guide the client to the best options. The client should make the final decision based on that advice and their own knowledge and judgement. After all, they will have to run the business afterwards.

PERSONAL MOTIVATION

A key aspect that any aspiring consultant should address is your own motivation for becoming a consultant. There are many common reasons but some include:

- Arrogance

- Redundancy or early retirement

- Disability

- Family reasons

- Greater personal freedom

- To share and increase your knowledge

- Variety of work

- Expectation of getting rich.

Let us explore these, and others, in more detail and consider how they fit with the reality of being a consultant. As we will see some are valid reason but many are not a good basis on their own at least for attempting to become a consultant.

Arrogance

> I am better than my boss — and everyone else for that
> matter — so I am going to become a consultant. Then they
> will listen to my ideas. I am going to tell them what to do
> and they will listen and obey.

I am afraid consultancy does not work that way — a consultant
has to achieve results often against the scepticism of clients and
their staff. Unlike a manager or director, a consultant has absolutely no authority due to their position, so they cannot impose
anything on the unwilling. Therefore a consultant has to achieve
results by persuasion, strength of argument, their personal enthusiasm for their ideas and the clearly demonstrated benefits they
will bring to the client. In that respect, it is not much different to
the in-house member of staff — the only difference is that the client is paying a lot of money (usually) for those ideas, and that
tends to result in more consideration being given to the consultant's ideas. But it also means that such ideas will have to be more
than the obvious, as the client will want to be convinced that they
are getting value for money from the consultant.

Redundancy or Early Retirement

Many people consider becoming consultants when they are made
redundant or retire early. It is seen as an easy way of replacing
lost earnings. As I hope this book will show, this it is not necessarily the case for many people. Most successful consultants see
consultancy as a vocation — they cannot really envisage doing
anything else. Without that commitment, few people will stay the
course because the demands are so high.

Most potential consultants taking early retirement or becoming redundant will tend to have had (longish) careers as managers
or perhaps as functional specialists, and will therefore have the
skills and mind-set appropriate to such a role. As we will see, consultants need a set of skills that are substantially different to those
of traditional managers. Some people, although they will nomi-
nally have been managers, will in practice have worked as internal consultants; such people will be better placed to become consultants, but they are rare. One of the most difficult tasks I have is

explaining to some acquaintances, who are well established in their careers as managers, what I do and why clients use me.

Unfortunately many such people embark on a forlorn attempt to be consultants, and when the redundancy money has run out they give it up as a bad job. They will rarely blame their lack of proper preparation or their unsuitability. In the meantime, they may well have bought work by charging fees that are too low to be supportable, and in some cases still given poor value to their clients. By so doing they will have done harm to the profession as a whole. But worst of all they will have hurt their families and themselves, and their confidence will have taken a beating at a time when it was already at a low ebb. Hopefully, this book will persuade some of these people to look for more suitable opportunities.

A few survive, give real value and prosper. They will make mistakes but they will learn and be better consultants for it. Perhaps this book will help them to achieve results more quickly and with less pain.

Disability

Some forms of consultancy can provide a route to a fulfilling career for those who are often at a disadvantage in traditional employment. However, as with anyone entering the consultancy profession, the right skills and drive are needed. Some forms of consultancy can be undertaken remotely and at times of the day or night that suit the consultant, but selling is still usually face to face. As we explore later consultancy is as much about relationships as about technical skills, and for that reason alone client and consultant usually have to meet.

Family Reasons

Similarly, those with the right skills can often fit their consultancy practice around family commitments such as caring for elderly parents, young children or invalid partners. As we discuss elsewhere, income and flexibility have to be balanced. But providing advice is often about research and analysis, which can be done at a time and place to suit the consultant. I know of consultants who arrange their work around the school day and holidays. They ar-

range their appointments so that they are usually only out between 8.30 a.m. and 3.30 p.m. and they have mainly desk work
during the school holidays. This is not always possible, but it does
mean that they can minimise the need for third-party child-care.

It will require excellent time management and a strong will.
Clients will frequently want you to work to their timetable, however inconvenient for you. Will you be able to say 'no' to the client? Remember, they are the ones who pay the piper and call the
tune!

It comes down to being clear about the objectives that you
have for your career, as an individual and as part of a family. A
career as an independent consultant may allow you to achieve the
balance between work and home that you want.

Greater Personal Freedom

If consultancy can allow you the flexibility to meet family needs,
then it can also allow you to meet personal needs. However, as
with all such matters, there are trade-offs: if you want to use consultancy to allow you to pursue other interests then you may have
to compromise earnings, job satisfaction or regularity of income.

I have worked with technical specialists who were keen rock-
climbers and mountaineers. They used to work on a project for
say, six months, and then spend the rest of the year climbing, often in far-flung places such as the Himalayas. However, occasionally they would have problems finding new work on their return,
so they would have periods without an income. But for them it
was worth it as it allowed them to do what they really wanted.

Client loyalty will only remain strong if it is tended and you
meet their needs. If you take long periods away from your consultancy practice, you will effectively be a start-up each time you
return. That will limit earnings, personal development and eventually job satisfaction, as the work available to you will be limited.

However, if personal freedom means having the time to play
golf during the week, or to travel for a couple of weeks every few
months, then a successful consultancy practice can be developed.
Indeed many consultants do just that rather than retire — they
just spend increasing time on their other interests. As I said, being
a consultant is often a vocation and therefore many are reluctant

to give it up completely while they are fit enough to carry on. Often their clients will not let them!

To Share and Increase Your Knowledge

Knowledge is a major element of the vocation of a consultant. It is certainly my principal motivation after earning enough to keep my family comfortable. I am simply curious and want to know why organisations work in the way they do. I suppose I could have been an academic, and might yet become one, but I need the practical involvement. I would be unhappy with an entirely theoretical role. I need to test my ideas and I can only do that by operating as a consultant and working with my clients.

I learn new things from each and every assignment, however apparently mundane. That increases my knowledge and I hope makes me more useful (and therefore valuable) to clients. The process works both ways, but I cannot envisage life without continual learning.

Having gained knowledge, most consultants are like me and want to use their knowledge in a practical way. And, of course, by doing so they extend their own knowledge and understanding of their field. That is where the motivation originates.

Variety of Work

One of the main attractions of consultancy for me is the variety. I have always been interested in business, management and how it all works. So every new client is a new experience, even if the work is much the same. There are always new challenges.

As with any occupation, there will always be routine work that can become dull. With consultancy you can always look forward to a new client and new projects.

It also directs my learning. My parents (and some teachers) always encouraged me to learn, to find out, to be interested in the world around me. They gave me the skills to learn — I do not generally need courses as I am better at learning than being taught. That is not to say I know it all — far from it. Personal development through learning is not something I do because I am told I should. I do it because I am driven by habit and personality to do so. I simply could not stop.

Expectation of Getting Rich

The most successful consultants can indeed become very wealthy. But, as with most professions, it is only the relatively few who achieve the highest earnings. Many more make a good living but often it is not much more than they might have achieved in employment. A considerable number do not do very well at all and are worse off than they would have been in a more mundane job.

Success is not easy in any field, however you define it. To achieve real wealth from consultancy you need talent, luck, commitment and drive, insight and then more luck. That is the same whatever career you wish to pursue — the skills set may not be the same but the broad headings are.

And high-level success almost invariably means sacrifices, at the level of your personal life, your relationships, even your health. You must be prepared to take risks and suffer the consequences, and then to bounce back and try again. Most successful people, in most fields, have had bad times. Success is rare at the first attempt and consultancy is no more a quick and easy route to wealth than any other business venture.

REWARDS

Potentially, the rewards for consultants can be almost as high as one wants. However, achieving the highest levels requires very specialised high-level skills that are in great demand, combined with great marketing and sales ability, backed up by a lot of luck. Even then it will not be achieved overnight and will take an almost complete dedication to success — social and family life will need to come in a very distant second place.

Most established and committed consultants earn good incomes, usually at least comparable with directors or top managers with the same specialist expertise working as an employee in a sizeable organisation.

But there are also many who only earn middle management salaries and struggle to do that on a consistent basis. They tend to be the people who lack the drive or the requisite skills, especially the sales and marketing abilities which are so essential to success in any business.

RICHNESS

It is not all unremitting hard work. Above all a consultancy career leads to a richness of life. Not necessarily in financial terms, although the rewards can be excellent, but rather in the experiences that you will have as a consultant.

I certainly find it exciting — the thrill of winning new work, of turning around a client's problems or achieving the client's objectives.

It is a career that allows you as an individual to make choices on both your own behalf and for your clients. Few other careers allow such flexibility.

The people you will meet, whatever your relationship with them, will enrich your life and experience. You will be constantly surprised by people. Many will become friends and very few will leave you without adding to your understanding of the world.

Those people will involve you in stimulating intellectual battles, usually in a friendly way. But your abilities will be challenged, and by rising to those challenges your skills will be developed. Above all, your life will be enriched. You will widen your horizons and be aware of so much more than people who live much narrower lives. Mind you, it will mean that you will have to work hard at humility, as it is all too easy for the wide experience to make you appear arrogant!

A friend and colleague, Tim Stretton, summed it up when he said that 'it is the pure sheer bloody enjoyment' of the consultancy life that still attracts him to it.

RISKS

The risks are certainly manageable and need be no more than you are prepared to take. However, there will be some element of a direct relationship with rewards — the higher the desired rewards, the higher the risk.

Compared with the risks of earning the same income from manufacturing or trading, the risks are low. There is no stock, premises are not essential and the equipment is quite modest for many consultancy specialisms. Because of this, and with properly structured contracts, a busy business consultancy can quickly generate substantial cash balances.

Uncertainty of income is a major problem and always will be. It is a particular problem during the early days of any business. Consultancy is no different. The small practice dependent on one or two clients is very vulnerable because even one client leaving or a single missed contract may represent a substantial reduction in total income. Also, the small firm is in great danger as it is very easy to neglect marketing and sales when business is good. Consequently when the current work is completed there is no new project and a potentially fatal gap emerges before new work is found.

Consultancy is fairly unusual in the business world in that it is almost impossible to build an order book or schedule work to be started when time permits. Once clients have made a decision they invariably want the consultant to start straight away. However, later on we will explore ways of achieving some element of work scheduled to start in the future.

The independent consultant and the small firm are also at risk from illness to key personnel. This is a particular problem for consultants because, as we will explore later, clients buy the individual, not the firm. So it is often not possible to substitute a colleague or a third party. Furthermore, if the work is well under way, it is difficult for a consultant new to the project to come up to speed. At best, the project is going to be delayed, with an inevitable impact on cash flow.

DEMANDS

There are many demands on consultants which work against the achievement of the greater personal freedom desired by many of those who enter the profession.

- Clients' demands — some think they own you and will *demand* your time at whatever time of day, or even night, suits them.

- Client expectations can also create pressures, even when the client is trying to be reasonable. This is particularly likely where the client does not understand the nature of consultancy. The experienced consultant will manage client's expectations from the start so that the consultant can actually deliver satisfaction to the client.

- There could be a lot of travel, and the need to stay away, especially if you are a high-level specialist or working in an industry sector where there are relatively few geographically spread potential clients. The higher the fees you wish to earn, the more likely you will have to travel, unless you are based in a major metropolitan centre such as London or Paris. Business travel sounds glamorous but bear in mind (especially in conjunction with the next paragraph) that such travel is not a holiday. You may well be visiting exciting places but will see little or none of them because you will be working — the client will not want to pay for you to be a tourist!

- Long hours are often inevitable, especially where travelling is involved. Much of that travelling time will be wrapped around a full working day at the client's premises. There will also be demand to produce work quickly as you will need to do the work when the client wants it; often this will conflict with the needs of other clients, so reports and the like will be written late at night, over weekends etc. Again, the higher the fees, the higher the client's expectations and the more likely that you will need to work unsocial hours.

- Uncertainty of income. By the very nature of project-based consultancy many, perhaps most, independent consultants suffer from the problems of famine and feast. When they are busy, it is difficult to keep the sales effort going so that when a project finishes there is no paying work to replace it. That is very stressful and we will explore ways of mitigating the problem later in the book.

LIFESTYLE

The consultancy lifestyle is often perceived as glamorous but, like many such professions, it masks a lot of hard work and difficult personal decisions. Success requires a balance to be drawn between the ambition and one's domestic or social life. Consultancy by its nature demands that the balance be drawn closer to work than for many other careers. The higher the desired rewards, the less time and commitment available to home life.

However, it is possible to use consultancy to achieve greater freedom, but it will require the consultant to accept reduced rewards. Reducing travel, hours and, possibly, the variety of work will allow that greater freedom, but with a reduction of potential income. Again, we will explore this later, but one should not simply accept lower rates if one does not wish to work full-time. Indeed the reverse should be true, as will be shown in Chapter 7, 'Fees, Pricing and Costing'.

It is up to each consultant to make that decision, and the earlier it can be made the better.

SELF-ASSESSMENT QUESTIONNAIRE

This is just a small test to help you explore your attitudes towards and motivation for becoming a consultant. Work your way through this questionnaire before you look at the answers and explanation at the end of the chapter.

Why do you want to be a consultant? Score each one in the range zero to ten where zero is complete disagreement and ten is complete agreement. Note your scores for all the questions before looking at the analysis at the end of the chapter.

1. I want high financial rewards.

2. It is an easy way to earn a living.

3. I want to share my substantial knowledge and experience.

4. I am good in a crisis.

5. No-one wants to employ me.

6. I am too old to get another job.

7. I want to get away from office politics and concentrate on my technical skills.

8. I do not like routine — I need variety.

9. I want to widen my skills.

10. I want to avoid responsibility.

11. I want the glamorous life, travel, fast cars, expensive hotels and meals . . .

12. I am going to make sure that my ideas are used.

13. I want to travel and meet people.

14. I enjoy an intellectual argument.

15. I like solving problems.

16. I think the new ideas are wrong so I will do things in my old way — that is, a better way.

17. I don't know what else to do.

18. When the going gets tough I get going — I enjoy a challenge.

19. I want to be loved.

Now look at the interpretation at the end of the chapter to see how you fared and whether your expectations are reasonable.

PLANNING

As a prospective consultant you need to know what you really want out of your career and what you are prepared to put into it. Only by being clear about your personal needs and ambitions can you plan to achieve them. You also have to be honest about your strengths and weaknesses.

Personal objectives and aspirations can vary widely. Some new consultants simply wish to earn a top-up to their pension; others may wish to build a reputation, to become a 'guru' in their field. For others, money may be the principal motivation, while others simply want to earn enough in two days so that they can spend the rest of the time on the golf course, climbing or looking after young children or elderly relatives. All can be accommodated with appropriate planning. But such objectives need to be stated and the implications understood and documented.

To achieve your ambitions you will need to assess the risks involved and the commitment you are prepared to make. And it is just as important to ask: what are your friends and family prepared to sacrifice to help you achieve those ambitions?

CHECKLIST

1. *Are you in a job? — Stay in it!*

   At least until you are properly organised, with enough paying work to make it worthwhile giving up a salary. When you have decided you are going to be a consultant, use the time in paid employment to prepare thoroughly for your new adventure.

   Use the library and study resources available to you to develop your knowledge and skills. If you are working towards consultancy as a long-term goal, make sure you get relevant training and seek out opportunities with your employer to add practical experience to that training. If possible, try to actively take on more demanding roles that will further your experience — if necessary do so without requiring the promotion or salary increase that usually goes with them. The aim is to be in a position to be successful as a consultant in the long-term, not to achieve modest short-term financial gains. But accept the cash if it is available! And if you are cut out to be a consultant you will probably find that you enjoy this approach to your work rather more than when you were adopting the average employee attitude of merely doing what was expected. You might even end up staying!

   I took that approach and stayed on for an extra 18 months as I kept getting promoted and being given more challenging roles. It was invaluable experience when I did go out on my own.

2. *Start preparing now.*

   Do not wait until you have left your present position. There is a lot you can do now. Apart from planning, you can start earning fees, assuming that your employment contract does not prevent this. In any case you can start networking, talking to potential clients, suppliers and associates. Start thinking like a consultant and use your weekends and evenings to make the launch of your new business as successful as possible.

   If your social and domestic life does not come under pressure in the transition period between what you are doing now and the launch of your practice, then you are not working hard enough on your preparation. If you are not prepared to put in that effort now, you do not have the personal commitment that you will need to be successful as a consultant.

3. *Assess your current financial position.*

What are your current living costs? What assets do you have or could you realise if necessary to fund your practice. Include everything, even if at this stage you would not be prepared to use it as risk capital.

4. *List your personal objectives.*

Some of these may be financial but many will be lifestyle aspirations. As part of this exercise establish how much time such ideals will require — time that will therefore not be available to your consultancy practice. There may be a cost to all or some of these personal ambitions — quantify them.

5. *Determine your minimum financial needs.*

Do not underestimate your expenses. At this stage just establish the personal budget on which you could just about get by if you give up your social life and the little (and especially the large) luxuries that you enjoy. This will give you a base line below which you cannot afford to fall — your new consultancy practice will have to cover those costs and the practice expenses at least.

We will use this in Chapter 10 when we look at business planning and setting fee levels.

SUMMARY

As a would-be, or perhaps as a struggling, consultant you should examine what is involved in being a consultant. The responsibilities are different from that of the manager, and a consultant has to be able to get things done in an environment where they do not have direct authority. That means you will need good interpersonal skills to encourage and motivate people at all levels.

A consultant is a self-managing practitioner whose primary responsibility is to advise. To be able to advise means that there will also be investigative, analytical and problem-solving roles to adopt. A consultant does not take decisions on behalf of a client — that is the directors' and managers' responsibility — but leads the client to take the necessary decisions and actions for the organisation.

A consultant should understand their own personal motivation for becoming a consultant, as many reasons for doing so are founded on a false perception of what a consultancy career is like. Consultancy is too demanding a career to drift into because other options seem closed. A professional advisor who is not whole-hearted about what they do will not do justice to their clients or themselves and will ultimately fail. But it is possible to achieve high earnings through long hours and hard work, or to work less, but still hard, and allow time for other personal objectives. Some forms of consultancy can be fitted around disability or the role of parent or carer — but as always it needs commitment and organisation to be successful.

I obviously believe that consultancy is an interesting, rewarding and fulfilling career — I have been doing it from choice for more than 15 years. But you do have to be committed and determined — it is not an easy route to high financial rewards. As in all fields, the rewards only come from hard work and dedication and acceptance of the demands that are placed on you, your family and friends.

Do not drift into consultancy — plan your move by working through the following chapters.

INTERPRETATION OF QUESTIONNAIRE

Start with a score of 100, and then you will need to add or subtract your scores to individual questions as follows:

1. **Do nothing with this score** — it is neither a reason to be a consultant nor a reason not to be.

2. **Subtract** — It is not an easy way to earn a living — success in any field requires commitment and hard work.

3. **Add** — If you have good experience then there is likely to be a need for consultancy and a valid reason to become a consultant.

4. **Add** — You need to be able to keep your head when faced with problems and similar pressures.

5. **Subtract** — If no-one wants to employ you then is it likely that they will want to use you as a consultant?

6. **Subtract** — As with question 5, if you are apparently unemployable, is your experience appropriate to current business needs? You may face the same resistance either as a consultant or as a potential employee.

7. **Subtract** — Your relationship as a consultant will be different but you will have to face many non-technical issues. Consultancy is a personal service, not simply a technical one.

8. **Add** — Many consultants get bored with routine management and prefer the variety that consultancy can offer.

9. **Add your score for question 9 if you scored less than 4 for question 1 and subtract if you scored 7 or more for question 1** — You cannot have both high rewards and a lot of time for other interests.

10. **Subtract** — You cannot avoid responsibility as a consultant. You will have to live with your recommendations and to justify them.

11. **Subtract** — Consultancy will not provide a playboy (or girl) lifestyle. Even if you do travel and stay in expensive hotels you will not usually have time for much sightseeing or partying. Indeed, as often as not you will simply use your hotel for sleeping!

12. **Subtract** — It does not work like that. If you were not able to 'sell' your ideas as an employee you will probably do no better as a consultant.

13. **Add** — You are getting to the joy of consultancy — it is about being interested in what you do, the places you go and especially the people you meet.

14. **Add** — Consultancy is an intellectual challenge, albeit applied to practical ends.

15. **Add** — That is why consultants are employed.

16. **Subtract** — A consultant needs an open mind and a willingness to accept that their ideas may not be right. Consultants need to look forward by using the best of the past that is still relevant, combined with new ideas and ways of doing things.

17. **Subtract five times your score** — If you do not *want* to be a consultant, if you choose it simply for lack of having anything else, then you should not even think about it further.

18. **Add** — Consultants need to be able to dig in and make positive things happen, however difficult the challenge. They need to make the best of the situation.

19. **Subtract** — Consultants are professional scapegoats. In general the best that can be hoped for is to be respected.

Now consider your score:

Less than 100. Do not even think about consultancy, or at least not until you have more experience and more understanding of the role of consultants. Perhaps you should redo the questionnaire after studying this book.

101 to 124. You might be tempted to try consultancy but you probably won't achieve the personal satisfaction or the financial rewards. There are probably more suitable careers for you.

125 to 150. You are probably marginal, but if you have the skills and the determination, then you might be able to make a reasonable living — but will you enjoy it?

More than 150. Assuming you have the right skills and experience then you should be able to succeed as a consultant. But it will still be hard work — you will have to really want it to happen.

CHAPTER 3

PERSONAL ISSUES

In this chapter we will explore the personal skills and attributes that you will need to succeed as a consultant. The more of these you have the easier it will be to establish your consultancy practice and the more you will enjoy it. If you lack key skills it will make success that much more elusive, and even if it comes you may well not enjoy the work or the lifestyle. So consider this chapter very carefully and be painfully candid about your capabilities.

OBJECTIVES

The aim of this chapter is to allow you to:

1. Establish whether you have the personality and personal attributes that are needed by consultants;

2. Determine if you have the key skills that you will need;

3. Identify what personal development you might need to strengthen those skills;

4. Ask whether you have the health, drive and commitment to take on the burden of starting and running a consultancy business;

5. Ask your friends and family whether they are prepared to accept your changed lifestyle and to support you in your efforts;

6. Make a considered and formal decision about your future in consultancy.

APTITUDE

Most would-be consultants are very surprised when I largely ignore their technical skills when talking to them about a future as a professional advisor. Such skills are important, very important, but they are not the most important factor in likely success as a consultant.

Consultancy is people-oriented in whatever field of advice you operate. I recently had a conversation with a friend who is embarking on a career in consultancy after early retirement. He had won his first assignment and was telling me how he was looking forward to it as he liked the people. I was able to tell him that in my experience that was usually the case. Clients buy the person, not their technical skills — those are taken for granted — so there has to be some chemistry between client and consultant before the assignment is awarded. By the way, my friend will be successful as he is an outgoing character, very likeable, and before retirement he was working as an internal consultant and troubleshooter. He is also well connected in his industry and he has been running businesses in parallel with his professional career. And he makes time to take on a very active community service role and an active social life. It is such energetic and determined people that you are up against!

This means that good interpersonal skills are absolutely fundamental to success in consultancy. Ask friends and family how *they* see you in this respect — ask them to be brutally honest and do not get cross if they are! If you do not like people, get irritated when they do not see your point immediately or do not tolerate small talk, then you may well find consultancy difficult. Before you become a consultant you need to sell your service — without a client you are not a consultant. Selling needs those interpersonal skills.

That does not mean that you have to become the stereotype of the oily or aggressive salesman — in fact the best salespeople are nothing of the kind. But you do have to be able to put strangers at ease and get them to like and respect you.

Consultants need to be disciplined — they need to work alone and to deliver on their promises whatever it costs them personally.

Being tough-minded is a valuable, if not necessary, aptitude for all consultants. You will need it to force yourself to meet deadlines when you do not even feel like working. It will stand you in good stead when the going gets difficult, whether because of awkward and unreasonable clients or through shortage of work. Being tough-minded will enable you to dig into your inner reserves and respond effectively in a crisis. You need that strength of character that used to be called moral fibre, which will prevent you giving in when the going gets tough.

Good health is another prerequisite if you want to earn the high rewards. Clients will expect results whatever your circumstances — that is what they are paying for. As we have already found, consultancy can involve long hours, travelling and potentially, loneliness. You must have the physical stamina to be able to stand up to it.

Active management of your health will therefore serve you well. Sensible exercise is an important part of stress management, as is a sensible diet. It is all too easy when busy or working away from home to neglect both. To do so may put your wellbeing, that of your family and of your clients at risk. You also need to find forms of relaxation and stress management that you can do anywhere, as you may well spend time working away. It will not do your financial rewards much good if your body lets you down! That is where being disciplined and tough-minded comes in again.

Finally, you will have to be a self-starter. You must be someone who makes things happen. Many consultants are driven personalities who find it difficult to switch off and relax. You need that sort of determination and energy to make a success of any business, and consultancy is no different.

But do find time to relax and put work completely to one side. When I worked for a large firm of advisors I worked hard to avoid taking work home. Instead I would work late, go in at weekends to do work that I could have brought home. It had two benefits: one was that when I was at home I was able to give my family time and to give myself space. The second benefit was that it reduced my stress due to guilt. All too often I have taken a case full of work home and it just sat throbbing in the corner making me feel guilty and raising my stress level — and I never get as much done at home as I had hoped. It is more difficult now as I work from home, but I do have a separate room, so I can close the door on my working life.

COMPETENCE

The key judgement that any advisor can make is whether they are competent to take on a particular project. A consultant is employed in part for their judgement and that decision is the first test. You have to be prepared to say to a client 'I cannot do that work', but as we see later when we talk about managing the relationship, it should be followed with '. . . but I know someone who can' or 'I will help you find someone who can'.

Do not under any circumstances take on work for which you do not have the skills. You will only harm your own reputation, the client's business and the reputation of your profession. Reputation is valuable and fragile — protect it at all costs. You have to be able to say 'No', even if you need the money it might bring.

A consultant's specialist skills should be at a high level, even though their work for clients will often be at a much lower level. That depth of background is important to ensure that recommendations are based on a thorough understanding of current issues and future strategy. This, combined with your decision on whether or not to take on a particular project, means you should not expect to work at the edge of your expertise very often.

A friend and colleague was unhappy; he felt that he was not giving his clients value for money because he was using so little of his skills and experience. But I pointed out that he was giving good value because he was giving his clients what they wanted and needed. In most cases they could not have handled or understood his high level expertise; it would have been inappropriate.

So to a large extent, clients will take a consultant's expertise for granted, and would not be able to assess it effectively in any case. If they could, would they have been looking for third party help?

Therefore the key skills that will make a consultant are the (so-called) people or inter-personal skills. To be effective a consultant needs to like people and to get along with them. No one can develop a rapport with or even like everybody, but a would-be consultant has to be able to do so with most people. Talking to many consultants reveals that they generally get work from people with whom they can establish some sort of rapport — it is very rare to get a project from a client who dislikes the consultant, even in a technical consultancy specialism. If you do not like people you are unlikely to be a success as a consultant.

Indeed if you do not get on with people you are unlikely to be successful with the last two essential areas of competency, marketing and sales. Whilst marketing does include a substantial proportion of desk-based analytical work, it also involves talking to would-be customers to find out what they need. Without a genuine interest in the customer, no business will be successful. Marketing is in large part an analytical function, only partly concerned with the glossy promotion that is often loosely described as marketing. We will explore the marketing mix in detail in Chapter 6.

Finally, selling skills are essential for any business; yet, with marketing, it is the main area with which many potential consultants struggle most. Many new consultants come from functional disciplines other than marketing and sales and have little or no experience of them. Indeed, many consultants do not enjoy the marketing and sales aspects of running their business — there are parts of it that I positively hate (like cold-calling on the telephone). But they have had to come to terms with it in order to concentrate on the aspects of consultancy that they do enjoy.

Unlike most other functions, consultancy sales cannot really be delegated, as the client 'buys' the person, not the firm or even the consultant's skills. A senior consultant has to sell, even if they work for a large practice. So selling skills have to be part of a consultant's armoury. The good news is that to a large extent they can be learned especially if you are someone who likes people. But it is better if you have learned those skills before you start out on your own — you need to be able to sell your consultancy services from day one.

COMMITMENT

Success in any new business needs total commitment. Consultancy is not only a business, it can be a total lifestyle.

Unless you are a complete loner — in which case you will probably not have the necessary personal skills — other people will be affected by your move into consultancy. So you should consider the impact on them and whether they will make the sacrifices and give you the support that you will need.

Your family will have to understand and be comfortable with your commitments. They will have to recognise that you may be less available to them than at present, more irritable or distracted and that, in the short term at least, the family may be financially worse off. If they do not or cannot share your commitment then you will have problems. Starting and running any new business is stressful enough without having problems at home. So you and your family need to explore the full implications of your new career and be clear that they appreciate them and will share them.

Similarly, your friends will have to accommodate a change in your social life and relationships. You may not be able to give as much time to shared activities as in the past and indeed may not be able to afford the lifestyle you currently share. As with your family, you will need them when the going gets tough — they are an important part of your life and should not be cast aside thoughtlessly. You will need to relax, so make sure your friends will be still there when you do. Make sure they understand why you may be less available and that you still value them.

So are you and the people closest to you fully committed to your new life? If you have any doubts then you will have to work hard to make sure that commitment is there *before* you start. Without it you will fail or destroy your life outside work.

SUPPORT

So you have friends and family who understand your plans and the implications for their relationship with you. But it should go beyond that. Do you have their active support and encouragement? With any business you need all the support you can get.

This support can take many forms. Family or friends may actually assist with the business, or at least be there when you need them to discuss ideas or provide moral support. But you also want them to keep their ear to the ground and let you know of anything that may be of interest where they work, through other contacts or their own specialist and industry knowledge. You are going into the knowledge business so all information is valuable even if you choose to take no action.

Existing contacts are extremely important, as we will see when we look at marketing in Chapter 6. They will be part of your resources by supplying information and even by providing referrals to potential business. They may even put work your way themselves. You never know when you will need your contacts, so stay in touch and nurture the relationships. Let them know what you are doing and they will let you know what level of support you can expect — do not push it too hard, just get a feel whether they will continue to give you support appropriate to the relationship.

Professional associates will be a valuable resource in a variety of ways. They may provide specialist help on your projects and you on theirs, thus widening the scope of projects that you can both take on. They will be a valuable source of market intelligence and even cross-referral of new business.

Existing clients are of course valuable, but you may face a dilemma in seeking support or work from them. If the relationship comes about from your previous employment as an advisor, then you may be constrained from approaching them by the terms of your previous employment contract or severance package. The last thing you want is to get into a legal battle with your old employer — it will be expensive and too much of a distraction. You may be able to agree that you should take some clients with you, especially if your old employer will struggle to retain such clients once you are no longer available.

Bear in mind that you may wish to work with your old employer. Since I left my last job, I have agreed terms with several offices of the firm to provide specialist expertise that they do not have to their clients. As a result I have worked for clients I could not have reached otherwise, and I have the prospect of more in the future.

SKILLS

So what skills do you have?

Technical and Specialist

Your technical and specialist skills have to be of the highest order. There must be no question marks over your competence in the fields in which you are going to offer advice to clients. If you have any doubts, pull back from becoming an independent advisor until you have been able to address the weaknesses. You owe that duty of care to your clients.

However skilled you are, there will be limits to your expertise and you must be aware of these if you are going to be able to make that key judgement about your capability to take on each project that you are offered. Do not fight shy of admitting that you do not know — but use it as a spur to find out.

As well as knowing your limits, you must also know how to push those limits further out. Remember you will not have a boss suggesting that you go on training courses. You will have to take personal responsibility for keeping your knowledge current. I am staggered by how many, apparently experienced, consultants seem indifferent to new thinking and developments in their field. I cannot conceive of being so uninterested in my work that I would not constantly try to learn more. From time to time I see 'consultants' who know less about their specialism than some of their clients!

Creativity

Peter Drucker said in the *Harvard Business Review*: 'Every organisation — not just businesses — needs one core competence: innovation' ('The Information Executives Truly Need', *Harvard Business Review*, January–February 1995).

I believe this to be especially true of business consultancy. Real competitive advantage comes from large changes rather than incremental improvement. Incremental improvement is important as it maintains the competitive status quo and consolidates competitive gains. But simply copying existing best practice for your clients condemns them to being perpetual followers and to steady decay. And the same is true for your own business.

So creativity, I suggest, is an important ability for a consultant who aspires to be a giant in their field. Work at it — like all skills it is a combination of basic talent and constant practice. You may not become a Leonardo da Vinci but you can improve your creativity. Work at it. Matthew Arnold, the leading athletics coach, said in a BBC radio interview that he frequently saw youngsters with more physical talent than Colin Jackson, the champion hurdler, who never earned a fraction of his success. They simply were not prepared to work hard enough — the difference, Arnold said, was that Jackson, even as a youngster was disciplined and determined to succeed. He was prepared to do what it took to *earn* his success and that is true in all fields — the best simply will not accept that they cannot improve their performance. They will always do just a little bit more training, put in a little more effort than everyone else to make the most of their basic talent.

Business

As an independent consultant or the principal of a consultancy practice, you are first and foremost in business. You therefore must possess basic business skills and you should not start your own business until you have the essential skills and knowledge.

So what are the key business skills and to what level should you have them? The latter is an easy question to answer. You must possess these skills to a level that will allow you to hold a sensible, albeit non-specialist, conversation with the top people in the relevant functions at your client company. In other words, you must be able to speak the same language. I would argue that this applies whatever type of advice you provide. You *must* be able to put it in a business context and understand the broader business implications of your advice. Clearly this means that, generally, you need higher level expertise if you are dealing with multinational organisations than if dealing with small owner-run businesses.

If you regard consultancy as a profession — whatever you believe that to mean — then you should operate the rest of your business as professionally as you undertake your client work. The two are inseparable.

Marketing and Sales

Bringing in business makes marketing and sales a key skill. You need to possess those skills before you start your new consultancy practice. If you have no experience of these roles then you are not ready to start your consultancy business, because you need to be able to do your marketing to find your first clients and use your sales skills to sell them your services. Until you have done that you are not a consultant but an unemployed would-be consultant!

If you are in employment, try to move into a role where you will get exposure to good marketing and sales people. I learned an enormous amount by working in a technical support role to a sales team selling computer systems. It meant I had to learn to translate the features of our products into benefits to the potential customer and to understand how we could use our products and services to meet the customer's expressed, and implied, needs. I was fortunate in that I worked with some very professional sales people and I learned a lot just watching them.

But even with that experience, doing it all for myself was a major challenge and I soon discovered that theory and practice could be very different. You will not be wasting time getting that experience and the more front-line experience you can get in pro-fessional marketing and sales organisations the better.

Personal

As has already been discussed, a consultant needs a whole raft of personal skills to succeed as a professional advisor. They include:

- People skills such as the ability to get along with strangers and find common ground. A key ability is to be sensitive to what people are really saying; often the words and the message can be very different. A consultant does not need to be gregarious — although many are — but they need the ability to quickly develop a rapport with a stranger. If you do not like people or company, you will probably struggle as a consultant.

- Self-development skills are essential for a successful independent consultant, as you will have no manager undertaking personal appraisals or doing training needs assessment. You have to be able to see your own weaknesses and take appropriate action to correct them. That may involve training courses, but a key skill for all consultants is the ability to learn by using a multitude of other sources: experience, books, journals and personal research. You should be someone who is always looking to improve their knowledge and understanding — a consultant cannot stand still, otherwise their knowledge will be overtaken by that of their clients.

- Do you work hard? You need to have the ability and natural tendency to work hard — the pursuit of excellence should be your aim. But that search should be tempered with pragmatism so that you do not lose sight of what the client needs and can actually use.

- Passion, or even obsession, can be a useful personality trait in consultants if it is linked with a practical bent. Passionate people generate excitement which drives them and motivates the people they meet. Be excited by what you do and your clients will share it, to your mutual benefit.

- Persistence is absolutely essential. Sticking at the job until you get the results you need is a key to success. It will come into play in promoting your business and selling your services. It means that you will deliver what clients need whatever the odds, and from that will derive a reputation for reliability and ability that will stand you in good stead as your business develops.

FORMAL QUALIFICATIONS

Formal qualifications are not needed to be a consultant in many fields. There are exceptions, such as accounting and the legal profession, where it is essential. And there are many others where it may be expected — in engineering, for instance, where clients will require a Chartered Engineer. However you should be familiar with practice and qualification requirements in your own technical field — if you do not, you are not ready to become a consult-ant.

Qualifications can be useful as they demonstrate a certain level of training and intellect. But it was summed up for me by a junior consultant who said that an academic qualification has a shelf life of about eighteen months — after that it is what you have done with it that matters. You have to add experience to academic study quickly if it is to be of more than passing interest in a consultancy (or indeed any business) career.

SELF-DISCIPLINE

Much has already been made of the importance of commitment and hard work. However, the need for self-discipline goes further than that.

Firstly, there is the need to be sufficiently self-disciplined to do the difficult or hard tasks rather than making a show of being busy by doing the easy things. This means that if there is a diffi-cult decision to be taken or unpleasant findings to be passed on to the client, it is done and not avoided or otherwise postponed.

A very important part of self-discipline is to make time for family, friends and oneself. It is very easy when time is money and one is busy to view leisure time as lost earnings. Holidays suddenly appear several times as expensive because of the lost fees. This is a dangerous attitude to adopt, as it will ultimately have an impact on your relationships and your health.

When relationships and health suffer, work performance also suffers. So, as you expect to be in consultancy for the long term, you need to achieve a balance between work and leisure. I try to avoid working at weekends — to achieve this I may have to work longer hours during the week. But I then get a clear weekend to enjoy an active social life with family and friends, to support my son's sporting activities and my daughter's school and other events. Sometimes, of course, it is not possible but then I make it up by taking time off during the week for a round of golf or what-ever I need to relax.

By doing so, my life is more varied than simply being a con-sultant. Rest allows me to work better.

SELF-ASSESSMENT QUESTIONNAIRE

This is not a strict, psychologically checked test. It is simply intended to give you a feel for whether you possess the right personal skills and attributes for becoming a consultant. Anyway if you really want to be a consultant you will probably ignore it if it doesn't give you the results that you want! All I can hope is that it may make the hesitant think twice before pursuing a career that they know in their heart they are not equipped to follow.

Work through the following statements, giving each a score between 0, for total disagreement, and 10, for total agreement, as you believe they apply to you. Do not look at the interpretation at the end of the chapter until you have completed all questions. With this type of exercise your first impressions are likely to be the most reliable — do not agonise over your answers or try to second-guess what they mean. You need an honest assessment of your suitability, not an answer that is engineered to tell you what you want to know.

1. I understand business and finance.

2. I am not very outgoing and find it difficult to meet new people.

3. Crises do not upset me. I just get on with sorting out the problems.

4. I am good at managing my time.

5. I avoid conflict at all costs.

6. I tend to get homesick or lonely when I am on my own.

7. I am a good researcher. I know how to use a library and sources of information.

8. I do not talk about business and management with friends and colleagues in social situations.

9. I am interested in people and what makes them 'tick'.

10. I need a clear definition of the tasks that I need to undertake.

11. I enjoy solving problems, and I am good at it.

12. I read the business pages of a 'quality' newspaper and other business magazines, and watch business programmes on television.

13. I keep my weight in reasonable bounds and I take regular exercise.

14. I read non-business, non-fiction as a leisure pursuit.

15. I worry about problems that I cannot do anything about.

16. Business and management processes hold little interest for me.

17. I can accept criticism and use it to improve my performance.

18. I am easily distracted from the task in hand.

19. I can sensibly discuss most business functional areas (marketing, finance, manufacturing, etc.) at a senior level.

20. I am not particularly passionate about my specialist field.

21. I have a lot of business contacts in senior positions.

22. I have never worked in a sales or related position.

23. Colleagues rarely seek my advice outside my main function.

24. I always honour promises — whatever it costs me personally.

25. I have in-depth expertise in my specialist field.

26. (a) My friends and family support my move into consultancy. (b) They understand the implications for them.

27. I show the pressure I am under to outsiders.

28. I am not prepared to make personal and financial sacrifices to get my consultancy career off the ground.

29. My technical expertise is unquestionable.

30. I am an innovator and produce creative but workable solutions to challenges.

31. I know the limit of my competence.

32. I tend to jump to conclusions.

33. I stick at a job until it is properly completed.

34. (a) Work is my over-riding interest.
    (b) I have few interests outside work.

35. I know what qualifications are needed to be a consultant in my field and I have what is needed.

36. I have access to on-line services and routinely use them to find information.

37. I read quickly and accurately.

38. I have, or can obtain, the necessary equipment and facilities (laboratory, workshop or whatever) that I will need to operate as a consultant in my specialist field.

39. I am comfortable speaking in public on my specialised field and how it relates to business success.

40. I know my way around my local business and technical libraries. And I have access to them.

41. I am not a fluent writer. Writing and language do not come easily to me.

42. I have worked successfully as a project manager.

43. I get easily irritated by office politics and other peoples' attitudes.

44. I need to be loved.

45. I have many associates with complementary skills in my specialist and related fields.

Now interpret your responses using the rules at the end of the chapter. Do not fudge the results. You need to be honest so that you can work on your weaknesses and capitalise on your strengths.

REALITY

What is the reality? It is not as glamorous as it is often portrayed. There is a lot of rejection — do not forget, you are selling yourself most of the time. There will be demanding clients and clients with unreasonable expectations. There will be bureaucracy from the tax man and other government agencies. There will be worries when cheques do not come in when expected or when you fail to win crucial projects. There will be projects where you misjudge the amount of work involved and have to work through the night or over weekends. There will be boring projects and awkward or un-cooperative clients.

And holidays. Holidays will never be quite the same; because you will be aware of the value of your time you will see holidays as double expense. There will be all that income you could have earned and the actual money you spend on the holiday — it can take the pleasure out of holidays if you let it! For my own part, I at least try to take the 'scenic route', time permitting, when travelling to meetings.

Whether or not you aim to be a high-earning consultant you will face the prospect of working long hours. To get the top rewards you will spend a lot of time travelling but it is not like being a tourist — you will travel, visit the client and your hotel room and not much else. I spent several months travelling to Edinburgh once a fortnight and I saw less of the city and what it has to offer than most tourists would see in a day!

Even without the travelling, the new business will take a lot of time if it is to get off the ground. So at the start you should be prepared for long hours of analysis, planning, letter writing and administration. Once you have some regular clients you may be able to reduce your time commitment. But there will always be non-chargeable work that you will have to do: administration, selling, marketing and personal development, to list but a few.

But it is not all doom and gloom. I have been in it for more than 15 years and rarely think about doing anything else, because there are always interesting people to meet and exciting, challenging projects that I want to work on. In such cases I will work long hours and give up my free time because the work interests me and I get paid well for it. Who could ask for more?

There is huge personal satisfaction in seeing that your work has made a difference. I enjoy nothing more than visiting a client months or years after I finished a project to find they have taken the ideas from that work forward successfully, developing it further and making more of it than I ever envisaged. Over the years I have worked with many people whose careers were going nowhere and as a result of working together I have helped them raise their sights and realise that they could really achieve much more than they had ever thought.

ACTION PLAN

This action plan is about preparing yourself to become a consultant. Assuming you have come through the self-assessment questionnaire as and are satisfied that you possess the best resources for success, then the next steps are to:

1. Recheck the Self-Assessment questionnaire — have you been brutally honest with yourself? If not, repeat it — do not be soft on yourself.

2. Make a list of your personal strengths and weaknesses. Get friends and family to check it — accept their views with good grace. Better to be hurt a little now than to waste a lot of time or money in the future.

3. Review the questionnaire from Chapter 2. Do the two results support each other?

4. Make a list of your skills, experience and knowledge. It will be useful when you come to develop your marketing plans.

INTERPRETING THE SELF-ASSESSMENT QUESTIONNAIRE

Start with a score of 100 and add or subtract your scores as instructed below. Do not adjust your scores from your first impression!

1. **Add** — Whatever your specialism you need to be able to put it into a business context. You need to be able to understand the cost–benefit and return-on-investment needs.

2. **Subtract** — This may cause you problems if you are not comfortable meeting new people. Consultants need to be able to relate to people and establish a rapport quickly.

3. **Add** — An important skill as the client may well be buying your time to solve their problems — you cannot afford to go to pieces in such circumstances.

4. **Add** — Time and diary management must be at a high level for anyone who aspires to be successful as a consultant.

5. **Subtract** — A consultant will certainly need to handle conflict. Often a consultant will need to challenge a client's long and deeply held beliefs and must not shirk from doing so when necessary.

6. **Subtract** — A consultant may well need to travel especially if they want to work at a high level or in highly specialised areas. That may involve working away from home, possibly for extended periods. Even without travel, a consultant will often have little support from client staff and must be tough-minded enough to cope with such situations.

7. **Add** — A consultant cannot know everything and therefore the ability to find information or gain new knowledge is a prerequisite.

8. **Subtract** — A consultant has to be interested in what they do. They need access to people who have a suitable background and a shared interest in relevant issues who can act as a sounding-board or source of different viewpoints.

9. **Add** — Consultancy is very much about people. A consultant who is not interested in people will suffer and be less effective than they might otherwise be. You will also miss out on much of the richness of the consultancy life.

10. **Subtract 3 times your score** — As a consultant you *must* be a self-starter. Your client is paying a lot of money for your time so you have to be able to start providing benefit early in the relationship. There will be no one around to tell you what to do or how to do it — you will have to be self-sufficient. That is true even if you are working in a large consultancy practice.

11. **Add** — You need a high score here as this is frequently why clients retain consultants.

12. **Add** — As well as a deep technical expertise you also need a good wide business understanding in which to ply those technical skills.

13. **Add** — Good health is important in any role but as consultancy can be stressful, with all the health consequences, then it is particularly important. You should be self-disciplined to actively manage your health and avoid the temptation to eat and drink too much, especially when living in hotels.

14. **Add** — A consultant needs a wide background to develop rapport with clients. You therefore need wide interests so that you can find common ground with clients and their staff. In addition, a broad knowledge is also important for supporting creativity which is about connections, often with lessons from apparently unrelated fields. You never know what may be useful.

15. **Subtract** — You must be able to put out of your mind those things that you cannot influence. As a consultant, you will be expected to address client's problems, which means that you will face more difficulties than most managers. You need to be able to manage the stress and avoid inflicting undue pressure on yourself. You cannot afford the luxury of being an emotional 'worrier' — you need to be more calculating.

16. **Subtract 3 times your score** — Whatever your technical discipline, you need to have an interest and understanding about how business and management works as clients will expect you to apply your technical expertise to meet business needs.

17. **Add** — Continuing development is essential and well-meant criticism is a valuable spur. You should seek criticism so that you can improve your performance. You will also need to be able to handle unjustified or negative criticism with controlled good grace. Remember that as a consultant you will often be used as a professional scapegoat.

18. **Subtract** — As already pointed out, a consultant has to be a self-starter with good self-discipline. You have to achieve results whatever distractions or problems are put in your way.

If you do not have that self-discipline and concentration then you will struggle to achieve long-term success as a consultant.

19. **Add** — You will need to work with the heads of specialist areas in client firms; and an understanding of the issues that they face will stand you in good stead both in winning work and earning the client's trust when on assignment.

20. **Subtract** — Then why are you doing it? You need to be able to communicate your enthusiasm to clients and their staff. If you do not believe in what you are doing, why should the client?

21. **Add** — Good contacts are invaluable. They will not necessarily provide work directly but they can be a source of referral or introduction to potential clients. In addition closer contacts may well be able to provide advice, support and information.

22. **Subtract** — Sales skills will be especially important in the early days of your independent consultancy career. Sales skills will always be important for a consultant in a senior position.

23. **Subtract** — This suggests that you are not rounded or do not communicate your broader vision very well. Both of these are important facilities for any consultant.

24. **Add** — Clients expect no less, and that is as it should be.

25. **Add twice your score and subtract 10** — If there is *any* question about your technical ability then you should not be considering becoming a consultant. You owe it to your clients to give them quality service which you cannot do if there any difficulties with your technical expertise.

26. (a) **Add but only if the score to (b) is over 7** — Without their support the pressures will be increased. (b) **Add** — because they must understand that you will be less available to them and probably have less energy when you are.

27. **Subtract** — You must be tough-minded and be seen to be so. Clients will not have confidence if you show lack of confidence or the uncertainty that comes from being under pressure.

28. **Subtract 10 times your score** — If you are not prepared to make that sort of commitment then you should not be starting a business of any kind. To get a new business off the ground then some sacrifices will be necessary, at least in the short term.

29. **Add** — If you have any doubt about your technical ability then at the very least you should seek an independent assessment from people whose judgement you value. If there is still doubt then you should try to become a consultant.

30. **Add** — If you want to be more than a journeyman consultant then you will need to innovate in and around your technical area.

31. **Add your score if it is over 7 and subtract twice your score if it less than 6** — The key judgement a consultant has to make before starting any project is whether they have the skills, competence and resources to do the work full justice.

32. **Subtract** — A good consultant keeps an open mind until they have sufficient evidence to come to properly considered conclusions. Only then should any solutions be proposed.

33. **Add** — A consultant has to make things happen and deliver on promises. You must adopt a professional approach which means ensuring that all work is properly performed.

34. (a) **Subtract** — A consultant needs to be enthusiastic about what they do. And they may well appear single-minded, but you also need to be well-rounded. (b) **Subtract** — To develop a rapport with other people you will need to be able to find common ground, which only comes by having wide interests.

35. **Add if your score is more than 7. If the score is 7 or below then subtract 10 and add the score** — A consultant must know the regulatory framework in which they operate; if they are not able to establish that then they do not have the research capability to make a success of consultancy.

36. **Add** — A consultant should be comfortable with appropriate new technology and research tools, particularly computers

with word-processing and spreadsheet software, and with using on-line services as a research facility.

37. **Add** — A valuable facility is the ability to read quickly and accurately. It makes the job that bit easier.

38. **Add** — You must be able to afford to buy the facilities that you need. You will also need to be able to build the facility from your starting point — will you be dependent on accumulated material and data?

39. **Add** — A valuable ability as most consultants will have to stand up in front of audiences to explain their findings and solutions. These audiences will often be knowledgeable and challenging — it is not a place for the uncertain public speaker!

40. **Add** — Essential are the research facilities offered by such libraries; as is the ability to use them effectively. Librarians are helpful, but knowing how a library is organised will make a consultant a more effective researcher.

41. **Subtract** — Reports and proposals are an inevitable part of a consultant's work, so you need to become comfortable using the written word. Not everyone will become fluent but all should work at being able to write concisely, clearly and, ideally, reasonably quickly. Writing takes a surprising amount of time, even for accomplished writers.

42. **Add** — An essential skill for most project management disciplines. It is essential if you are using a consultancy team or external suppliers.

43. **Subtract** — You will need to work around the client's politics and the attitudes of their staff. You cannot afford to show your irritation or you will lose control of the situation. Work on becoming a 'people' person.

44. **Subtract twice your score** — As a consultant you will be a professional scapegoat. You will also need to tell clients things they do not want to hear and for which you will not be thanked. The most you can hope is for their respect, but to be loved will be very much the exception rather than the norm.

45. **Add** — Access to associates who provide complementary skills and quality review can only improve the services that you can offer. That will strengthen your practice. They will also provide sounding boards for your ideas.

Now consider your score.

SUMMARY

In this chapter we have explored the skills and aptitudes that you need to be successful in consultancy. We have determined that the key skills are much wider than the technical field in which you intend to offer advice.

The main aptitudes and skills are all people-related. Consultancy, especially as an independent, can be a tough career and good health, ability to work hard, tough-mindedness and persistence are essential prerequisites. But if it can be coupled with a genuine interest in people and a passion for what you are doing, then success is much more likely.

Technical skills have to be well-honed and at a level that they do not become an issue in discussion with clients. If clients raise the issue of technical competence, they probably feel that you have not shown the depth of understanding that they expect. In my experience, clients only ask about technical skills when they have cause to believe that the consultant has shown a lack of understanding of the issues in the discussion of the problem.

The key judgement a consultant has to make on each new project is 'Am I competent to do this work properly and in the best interests of the client?' If the answer is 'yes', then all well and good but if the answer is 'no' then they should turn the work down. However, we will explore in later chapters how to handle such circumstances to the benefit of both the client and the consultant's reputation.

If you have scored low on the self-assessment questionnaire, then you should seriously question your suitability to be a consultant. Remember, it is not failure to admit that a particular career is not for you. But it is failure to embark on a career for which you are not equipped and which ultimately makes you, or your family, unhappy.

PART 2

THE NATURE OF CONSULTANCY

CHAPTER 4

STYLES, SKILLS AND SPECIALISMS

Consultancy is a varied profession and each consultant will approach it in a different way. Their style will reflect their personality and the skills they offer will be based on their experience, training and interests. The services they provide will be based on personal judgement of the market with due regard to the consultant's style and abilities.

As a new consultant you will need to find your own consultancy personality that will meet the needs of clients. This chapter provides a framework on which to base your own ideas.

OBJECTIVES

This chapter will help you understand the consultancy and other business advisory roles that you could adopt. It will allow you to:

1. Appreciate the style of consultancy that you might adopt;

2. Understand the many consultancy skills that you may be required to offer;

3. Understand the variety of specialisms that are covered by the generic title 'consultant';

4. Decide whether you should specialise in an industry or geographical region or in some other way.

CONSULTANCY STYLES

Consultancy is a very personal service at the point of delivery. Even in large firms with well-defined approaches and methodologies, each consultant will bring their own personality and expertise to bear, with the result that each person will stress different aspects of the firm's style. In small consultancies, the style will be almost totally defined by the individual consultant for their own projects but within a business and marketing strategy it will be defined by the practice as a whole. And of course the solo consultant will do their own thing entirely.

It should not be forgotten that clients will have an influence on how the consultant approaches the work. The client's needs will suggest a particular approach that will then be modified by the skills and resources available internally at the client firm. Only then will the consultant bring their own preferences to bear on the approach that is finally adopted.

So the style used will vary from consultant to consultant and from client to client. It will also vary with time. But most of all it will adapt to meet the needs of each particular project. The consultant has to be flexible enough to adopt many roles, often at the same time!

Advisory

This is, for me, what consultancy is about. It is about sharing expertise and advising and supporting clients in defining and achieving their objectives. Consultants advise, managers take decisions on their own judgement of their own knowledge and the consultant's advice. As a consultant I may not agree with the final decision but if I have advised and argued the case for the various options and the client still wants to take what I see as the 'wrong' decision I will support them — especially if they have thought through their decision. I will even support them with advice on how best to make it work if I am asked.

It is rather like the following quote from S.G. Tallentyre, usually attributed to Voltaire:

> I disapprove of what you say, but I will defend to the death your right to say it (Tallentyre, *The Friends of Voltaire*, 1907).

I may not agree with a client's decision and I will record the fact. But I recognise that it is their responsibility to manage their organisation and to live with the consequences. I can only advise and try to ensure that they take their decision based on sound knowledge and careful consideration of the options and their likely consequences.

Facilitative

A lot of the work I have done in the recent past — and I suspect this is a growing part of consultancy — is to work with a client to enable its staff to undertake some piece of work. It is similar in many ways to being a mentor but the focus is usually on a group who have to achieve a particular set of objectives.

An important aspect of acting as a facilitator is to keep one's own ego in check — the consultant is not there to *do* the work but to enable others to do so. It is about skill and knowledge transfer, not by traditional teaching or training methods but by working alongside the people who are to be developed. It is about taking a questioning approach and allowing the client staff to *find* their own solutions by means of the facilitator asking open questions such as: 'Why do you think it is doing . . . ?' rather than 'Could it be doing . . . because of . . . ?'. With the first approach, the person being questioned has to find causes or reasons by using their knowledge — and by asking questions of the facilitator. With the second, the questioner has provided a possible solution or cause and the responder requires less understanding and no problem-solving skills. More is learnt in the first case, but it may take a little longer to get there.

I try to provide skills and knowledge transfer in most of my work. Sometimes this is not possible, because I am brought in to get a quick result, which the existing staff do not have the time or perhaps the skills to achieve in the time allowed. In that case a facilitative role would be inappropriate. It is a personal approach that some consultants do not favour because they feel it reduces the likelihood that they will be asked back to do further work. I do not subscribe to the view that making the client dependent is good business. It may be in the short term, but the client will resent it and switch to someone with a more enlightened approach as soon as the opportunity arises. I find it means that, as the client develops, I have to do less of the routine work and am used on the bigger, more strategic elements. I enjoy the work more and my contribution becomes less generic and more personal, so the customer gets more from me. Everyone is happy and the relationship prospers.

Operational

This form of consultancy is concerned with operational aspects of the organisation's affairs. It is perhaps the most traditional of business advice, as it addresses the broadest management and technical issues affecting the way the organisation operates.

This can include, amongst other factors:

- Financial advice — costing, strategy, corporate finance, etc.

- Planning — business, financial, strategic

- Marketing

- Information systems and technology

- Management and organisational development.

Business Services

Consultancy has recorded enormous growth rates in recent years — often much faster than those of their clients. Many commentators have argued that this is unsustainable. However, the commentators have misunderstood the nature of much of that growth. The growth has been in business services rather than what I regard as genuine consultancy. But because it has been provided by traditional consultancy businesses it has been treated as consultancy income.

The management of a client's computer centre or providing software development is not, in my opinion, consultancy. It is sub-contracted business services in the same way as cleaning or catering services. Such work may come out of cross-selling by advisors, but it is not consultancy. I would go further and say that much of the change or project management work is not consultancy either. Often the consulting firm will provide a complete team to manage a project for the client; if that team is taking day-to-day management decisions on behalf of the client, they are not consultants but interim managers or sub-contract service providers.

It appears that it is in these areas where a lot of criticism of consultants originates. I strongly believe that this should be excluded from the figures for consultancy fees and the growth of the industry. These services encourage the growth of small specialist, 'boutique' consultancies who aim to do one thing well rather than being all things to all clients.

Some may feel that I am arguing a purist point here but I believe this view provides the independent consultant with a great sales edge. Because the small practice does not, cannot, provide these sub-contracted services, they can genuinely claim to be offering advice that is in the best interest of the client. They cannot be accused of trying to sell their facilities management, software development or other business services on the back of their advice. There is no conflict of interest involved. They can claim to be more honest in their approach; at least they can be seen to be giving independent advice.

Stereotypes

There are many stereotypes of consultants and like many such generalisations there is a considerable element of truth in many of them. Usually they are based on an old-fashioned view of the profession, but there are consultants who still operate in such ways and fit the stereotypes, much to the irritation and frustration of their clients and their more enlightened colleagues. There is a joke which goes like this:

> There was a solicitor, an estate agent and a consultant marooned on a desert island. It was small with few creature comforts and nothing with which to make even a simple raft. But within swimming distance there was a much longer coastline with lush vegetation and fresh water tumbling over waterfalls into the sea. The coastline belonged to the mainland, or at least to a much larger island.

The three of them sat there arguing about how to get to the greater comfort and safety across the narrow stretch of water. Although all three were capable swimmers, the discussion centred on who should make the crossing and how. You see, there was a snag. The waters around the island on which they sat were clearly infested with many large sharks. The triangular dorsal fins cut the surface of the water as they chased their prey in the straits that separated the two coasts.

All through the day and night they discussed the probability of surviving the swim with such risks. The solicitor and the estate agent were adamant that they would not try it even though the lack of food and water was making them steadily weaker. Soon they would be too weak even to attempt the crossing. Eventually the consultant could stand the discomfort no longer and announced that, whatever the others were going to do, he was going to make the crossing.

As morning dawned the consultant walked down to the water's edge and strode out into the sea. As he did so the sharks came closer and their numbers grew. Eventually the consultant started to swim and the sharks closed in.

But to the surprise of the solicitor and the estate agent the sharks did not attack. Instead they formed into two orderly lines; the pair left behind watched the consultant swim down the lane formed until he reached the other side. The estate agent turned to the solicitor and asked: 'Why did they do that?' The solicitor sighed and replied: 'Professional respect'.

OK, it is corny but it sums up how many people view consultants. But like any vocation or profession there are good and bad eggs. Consultants are people and reflect the best and worst of society. So enjoy the jokes at your expense; do not take them personally. Even when jibes are aimed at you personally, remember that the person making them could do what you are doing if they had the skills, the drive and the bottle. Who is showing the greatest strength of character? In my experience, consultants do not face that problem too much but it is a common problem for contract staff who have to do the same work alongside permanent staff who are not getting paid as much as the freelancer. Consultants tend to work at higher levels and in less easily comparable roles.

ROLES

At different times and on different jobs consultants will take on a wide variety of roles. Each consultant will need to use most of the roles detailed below at some time in their careers, so you should be familiar with them and seek to develop appropriate skills.

Advisor

As we have already said, the prime role of any consultant is that of advisor. The consultant should not be making decisions on behalf of the client — that is a manager's responsibility. Many consultants forget this, but it is dangerous as it exposes them to more risk of claims for damages.

Troubleshooter

It is not uncommon for consultants to be brought in when the client has tried and failed to address problems. This often means that matters are worse than they might have been if advice had been sought earlier. You will therefore have to move quickly and come to some initial conclusions without being able to undertake detailed analysis. In fact, you need to identify action that must be taken as the analysis is performed — it is not a case of jumping to conclusions or making knee-jerk reactions to the problems. Such an approach may well be the reason for the client's current difficulties.

Troubleshooting therefore implies a consultant who can think quickly and clearly in pressure situations, often with limited information. It is important to take courses of action that will improve matters without closing off other options that may arise as the problem becomes better understood. It is about balancing the need for action against the risks of that action. That balance will be constantly changing as understanding develops and new problems materialise. So troubleshooting is in large part a highly intellectual exercise but it also requires organisational or project management skills. But above all it needs people management skills, because as a troubleshooter, you will need to quickly gain the support and trust of people so that they will get behind your action plan.

Not all consultants have the experience or the skills for this kind of work — it may therefore not be for you. As this book stresses, a consultant is engaged for their judgement and the most important judgement you must make is whether you are competent to take on the offered work. It can be exciting work if you enjoy it, but it can be highly stressful if you do not. If you are in the latter category and like a more ordered and perhaps contemplative approach then do not accept troubleshooting assignments.

Facilitator

An increasingly common role for a consultant is that of facilitator. This can take many forms, from simply leading a meeting or workshop to providing support on a major change project. The role is, as the name suggests, to enable or facilitate the achievement of a desired objective by the client. This does not mean doing the work itself, but providing guidance and encouragement, passing on skills or whatever else is needed to allow the client's staff to achieve the required results.

Clients are concerned that the skills used on a project walk out of the door when the consultancy team leaves. This was very common with more traditional consultancy projects; many clients are therefore now concerned with skills and knowledge transfer. The best way to ensure such a transfer is for the client's people to do the work alongside or under the guidance of the consultant. That way, the in-house staff have actually done the work and have developed the skills to continue the implementation into the future.

Facilitation can also have financial benefits for the client as it means a lot of the relatively low-level work is not done by expensive consultants. Also, if facilitation is effective, the involvement of the consultant will decline as the local people develop. As the project progresses the consultant will be needed less and less, until they are only used on an occasional basis as a sounding board.

Mentor

A mentor requires a very similar set of skills to those of a facilitator, except that the mentor's role is usually provided to an individual rather than to a group. Also, the mentor is called upon when the client needs support rather than in a more formal process or series of meetings. Mentoring usually takes place over an extended period and the nature of the role will change as the mentored individual develops.

Conscience

Often I find I have to act as the client's conscience and tell them how it really is. One of the most challenging instances was when I was called in by a director to work with her department to improve their communications and team working. I had to start by interviewing everybody to understand the dynamics of the department, so that I could organise a follow-up workshop to address some of the key issues. It soon became clear that the director was the main problem as far as communication was concerned — the rest of the team were mutually supportive and got on fine. The problem was how to tell the director of my findings and to make recommendations about how she could modify her behaviour to improve matters. But there was a concern that she would have to authorise my invoice — how willing would she be to do so after I had told her a few home truths?

She disagreed with much of my argument in a quiet way and accepted some points. We agreed how we were going to structure the workshop and I presented my bill (which was paid on time). It was obvious during the workshop that she had in fact taken on board my messages and was working very hard to change her naturally abrupt style. The workshop went very well; the feedback I got from her staff subsequently was that she had tried to change but over time had slipped back into old ways. Changes in behaviour need regular reinforcement and it is in this situation that I would recommend the client and I have frequent meetings to review progress and to further refine the behaviour until it becomes habitual. She chose not to accept mentoring support and so the new behaviour did not become established through regular reinforcement.

Project Manager

A consultant almost always has to act as a project manager if only for your end of the project. You have to make sure the appropriate resources are properly deployed at the right time and that promised deadlines and costs are met.

But that is often the role clients demand of consultants (although by my definition, that may not be strictly consultancy, but management). Nevertheless it is a role most consultants will take on at some time.

Teacher or Trainer

Most consultants will, as part of their role, act as a trainer or teacher from time to time. The role is different from that of mentor as it is more formally structured and scheduled. It is also more often limited in duration or period.

Advocate

An advocate represents another person's interests usually because they do not have the capability, for whatever reason, to do so themselves. In consultancy, this can often arise when conducting organisational reviews or in other forms of human resource consultancy, but it can arise in almost any situation that involves people.

An individual or group may not have a voice that is listened to by management and therefore they are not given due regard in planning and managing change. In such circumstances the consultant should make sure that everyone is fairly dealt with. This can happen in many forms of change management, which means that any consultant could face the need to act as an advocate.

It is therefore an important skill which requires the consultant to be sensitive to the implications of their proposal and what effect they will have on individuals. You should always be conscious of the effect of your work on other people and their families. Being seen to be fair and reasonable should always be an important objective of any project. It has a knock-on effect on whether you will get support from others who will suffer less as a result of changes. The fairer you are with the disadvantaged groups, the easier it will be to take everyone else along with the changes.

Negotiator

Acting as a negotiator is a common role for a consultant; it starts with establishing the terms of reference with a client. Those who are involved with procurement on behalf of clients, or who act as troubleshooters or project managers will need strong negotiating skills — without them, you will not be effective. You will need to negotiate both internally within the client firm and externally with third parties.

You will not be an effective consultant if you cannot negotiate, as clients will dictate the terms for any project. From then on, you will be under your client's thumb. If you do not have negotiating skills, then find a job that will allow you to develop them at someone else's expense before you set out on your career as a consultant.

Sounding Board

Often the client will already have ideas about the way forward but simply does not have the confidence to implement them without sharing them with a disinterested third party. Often it would be inappropriate to share fears, new ideas or the like with (perhaps junior) colleagues. It may be seen as a sign of weakness or a failure of leadership to do so. It may simply be for confidentiality reasons if, for example, it involves major change and possibly redundancies.

Often the mentoring role develops into providing a sounding board as the individual client manager becomes more confident in their skills but still needs the comfort of sharing their ideas with someone who will give them an honest opinion without making judgements about their competence. Indeed, it may allow a creative manager to share ideas that are too radical for most of their colleagues to consider dispassionately. It is in this situation that a knowledgeable outsider can be very helpful as a sounding board. Between, them the client and consultant can work ideas up to a state where concepts can be shared more widely — the unworkable ones will have been weeded out so that only the best go forward.

Agent Provocateur

Sometimes a consultant will need to be deliberately provocative. This is an approach that must be used with care but a consultant has to be prepared to challenge the status quo and may sometimes need to do so in a confrontational way.

On one occasion, we had a very vigorous argument with the senior members of a client organisation about some recommendations we had made. We were challenging some fundamental values held by the senior managers and asking them to justify them and to refute our alternative framework. The meeting went on for a long time and there was much passion on both sides and by the end we still could not agree. But everybody had clarified their own thinking and the client team adopted the broad thrust of our suggestions, but reworked them to fit with their values and beliefs.

After the meeting we went for a meal and had a very pleasant evening. The chief executive had enjoyed the intellectual challenge and debate and recognised that he was much clearer about his preferred approach. We had therefore fulfilled our role in producing a clear answer to the problem that the client could, and would, deliver. It did not matter that it was not entirely our preferred solution. The client has to believe in the solution; otherwise they will not see it through. If, as in this case, they understand why they are doing something and are passionate in their belief, more often than not they will be successful. Despite the heated argument we remained good friends and still meet on an occasional basis and know that if they need consultants they will give us a call.

Scapegoat!

As a consultant you will have to accept that you will often be used as a professional scapegoat!

Sometimes you will be brought in so that difficult decisions, such as laying off staff, can be blamed on you even though the client management knew what was needed. They simply were not prepared to carry the responsibility for saying so. This sort of use of consultants is not uncommon, especially where there is a blame-laying or at least a risk-averse culture in the organisation.

No one wants to be seen saying the 'wrong' thing, so they get a consultant to do it; and they can blame the consultant if it turns out badly. And it often will, because such clients will fudge the difficult decisions during the implementation. Watch out for them: they are not pleasant clients to work for and they will not give you credit if you do a good job — the credit will be theirs. In such a situation you carry all the risks without the benefits.

Even if you do a good job on a conventional project which the client genuinely appreciates, you will be blamed by many managers and staff for any problems that surface in the six months or so after your work is finished. You may even be held responsible for problems on projects in which you had no part. That goes with being an outsider who is no longer working with the client, and you should not take it to heart. In any case you should be able to judge how well your work went and how the client felt about the results.

This is all a natural defence mechanism by those who are still there. Unless you genuinely got it badly wrong, the client will still value your work. Although they may pay lip service internally to the 'accusations', they will not really accept them. They will simply be a convenient fiction — it is all part of the game. The real test is whether the client stays in touch and uses you again; that is the real measure of how you are regarded.

SPECIALISMS

There are almost as many consultant specialisms as there are consultants. Each consultant will possess their own mix of specialist skills and knowledge with their own industry interests and understanding. So the nature of your specialism is fairly unimportant as long as there is a demand for it and customers who are prepared to pay for it.

Remember, consultancy can be a fashion industry. There are many firms that will jump on the latest management fad and call their services by that name. It may well be exactly the same as what they were doing before, dressed up with the new buzzwords. If you concentrate on the benefits that your services provide to clients you will not need to get hung up on what it is called — clients will just ask you to do what is necessary and you will just get on with it!

So if you are worried about what to call your service, then you have missed the point. Concentrate on what it does for the client's business performance and why they need it.

But we will consider some of the bigger consultancy specialisms and some of the services they include. It will soon become clear how impossible it is to define the totality of consultancy services.

Information Management and Technology

All three levels of information-related strategy (management, systems and technology) offer wide opportunities for consultancy support. I would not include aspects such as programming, project management, computing services, facilities management or training and help desk services under the heading of consultancy.

Information consultancy particularly includes strategy planning for the management and use of information, associated support systems and technical strategy for providing the underlying infrastructure. All sizes of organisation need support in these areas, but the strategic approach frequently requires the consultant to educate the possible client before they can sell these services to them. Indeed, this is the case with a lot of consultancy.

But information system consultancy also covers a wide range of functional areas, including training needs assessment, change management, communication and organisation development. It was through those connections that I was able to develop my wide-ranging cross-functional approach. I actually started my professional career as a computer programmer, which gave me access to all aspects of the organisations for which I worked.

There is demand for people with technical skills, but there is also a growing need for people who can work across the divide between information technology and the other functional areas within the business. Consultants who can relate technology to business benefits are always in demand.

Marketing

Marketing is central to most organisations, and as a result, many projects have a marketing dimension. Many other consultancies that do not regard themselves as marketing specialists will have an element of marketing in their services. Marketing should be a core competency for any business, as it has an impact on almost every other function within the organisation.

Marketing strategy is a key part of an organisation's strategic and business planning. The strategy is often supported by consultants who will facilitate its implementation or address particular aspects on behalf of the client.

Product design and development is often supported by marketing expertise to help test customer reaction to possible new products. This will often be to support the designers and technical specialists in product development. There are successful consultancies who major on the product development element of marketing strategy and will cover both the technology and the marketing aspects of new products. Indeed, they will take the project from concept to launch before handing it over to their client for ongoing sales and manufacturing.

Promotion strategy will vary from pure marketing strategy work to the sort of advice and support provided by many advertising agencies. Indeed agencies have been widening their scope to provide integrated services across a large part of marketing in general, and the promotional side of marketing in particular.

Pricing strategy is a key part of the marketing mix and it is an area where external advice may be used, especially by the smaller client who has less in-house marketing expertise. But as with any aspect it should really be considered as part of the overall marketing strategy and business planning.

Consultancy is often used to plan the way the product reaches its customers. This again is an important part of the marketing strategy, but will also extend into operational areas such as logistics. This confirms the need for consultants, whatever their specialist expertise, to have a well-rounded business understanding. Consultants have an essential role in bridging the artificial gaps between these many business functions.

Finally, once the customer has bought the product or service, suppliers need to know how well it meets customer needs and whether customers are happy with the whole experience of dealing with the supplier. Outside specialists are routinely used to research and evaluate customer views and especially customer perceptions of both the company and the product. Such customer satisfaction surveys need to be independent to get customers' candid views — most people are reluctant to be critical when talking to employees of the supplier.

Business Process Reengineering

Business process reengineering (BPR) consultancy should be essentially facilitative. It is about helping the client to find their own answers. A consultant should not provide solutions, but should encourage the client to challenge the norm. In that way they should come up with innovative ideas that the consultant can help the client implement.

Change management is central to any business process reengineering exercise. Many of the solutions should come from the bottom up rather than being driven down from senior management. As with any change programme, the management should have a vision and a strategic framework which can be shared with staff. The staff should then be able to identify better ways of providing the product or service. Just sit in a staff canteen and listen — you will hear any number of discussions suggesting how the business could run better.

The other area in which a consultant can help is to support and encourage a cross-functional approach to the reengineering. Indeed, a major plank of BPR is to eliminate many of the handovers that occur to accommodate the essentially arbitrary functional separation of tasks in the business process.

On top of that, there are additional functional consultancy opportunities within business process reengineering, such as risk assessment, option and investment appraisal, project management and other implementation support.

Finance

There is more to financial consultancy than accountancy, but much financial consultancy is provided by traditional accounting firms. Some are well equipped to do so but many have a limited view of what constitutes financial strategy. This sort of problem is not confined simply to accountants; it is a common problem with many technical specialists when they move into consultancy. They tend to see everything in terms of their technical skills rather than in broader business terms.

Indeed, it is noticeable that finance directors in large public companies are increasingly more likely to be financial analysts, perhaps with an MBA, rather than qualified accountants. This is because they are concerned with the financial aspects of a *business* strategy, not with accounting controls. The latter technical role is left to the financial controller who will almost certainly be a qualified accountant (at least in the UK).

Corporate finance, acquisitions, loan structuring and policy are the meat and drink of the financial strategist's function and are the main areas where financial consultancy support is required. They are areas where organisations do not have a need for permanent expertise. It is a classic case of consultancy requirement — comprehensive high-level expertise is needed for a particular purpose and may then never be required again. It is so specialist that it is unlikely that the in-house staff would get sufficient experience to be fully competent, so it is very proper to use external consultants.

Taxation is an area where the dividing line between the traditional accountant's role and that of the consultant is blurred (and often meaningless). Most tax consultants are accountants who have specialised in tax, usually one particular aspect of tax such as international, inheritance or value added tax. They tend to operate in a narrow field but with a very deep understanding of that field — often as good or better than most of the people who work for the tax authorities. It is not an area which one can move into from outside; all the best practitioners I know in this field have built their expertise in specialist functions with either a large accountancy firm or one of the tax authorities.

There is an occasional need for forensic or investigative work where fraud or other malpractice is suspected. Often this will require similar skills to those of an auditor or an insolvency practitioner. In these days where computers are the norm, investigators will need or have access to detailed technical computing expertise. They should also have a good understanding of what is required to preserve evidence, as such matters could lead to prosecutions.

And all that without considering the traditional role of accountants in accounts preparation, audit, etc.

Quality

Quality has been a major consultancy specialism for many years. It has emerged from the cultural and management issues of consultancy through total quality management and *Kaizen* imported from Japan. It has also evolved from ISO 9000 and quality assurance procedures and compliance.

This means there has been a major growth of consultancy practices offering advice and support in all of the above areas. However, clients are becoming more selective and are increasingly moving towards those who have real expertise, not just an understanding of how to achieve particular accreditation. Clients want access to the experience of their competitors and other industries rather than standard solutions, as they are seeking to make their quality systems work for them in providing real business advantage instead of simply getting the badge. They want to change the culture in their organisations so that it drives quality.

This culture stems from sharing experience and best practice with everyone within the client organisation. This means that a major part of quality-related consultancy is about training and other needs assessment. Today's businesses are moving into an even more strongly customer-focused approach that more closely integrates the various business processes. Total quality management and ISO 9000 are still valid, but tend now to be part of a much larger picture.

Change Management

In the 1990s, change management in various guises — business process reengineering, the learning organisation and others — has been a major thrust of many consultancy portfolios and it will continue be so for the foreseeable future. Indeed, change management is an essential part of many consultancy projects; why use a consultant if not to make changes?

The above specialisms all have roles to play in creating change, but even more in supporting change.

Training

Most consultants provide training from time to time. Training has also become a major form of consultancy in the last few years as the value of aligning staff development with business objectives has been appreciated. As a consequence, many human resource functions have grown in importance as a consultancy specialism. There has been substantial growth in training needs assessment and the subsequent delivery of highly focused training.

There has been a knock-on effect in other advisory fields as the training element has been added to many projects. Since consultancy is concerned with change, the need to equip staff to cope with new circumstances means that they need training and other forms of personal development. This occurs at all levels within an organisation, up to and including chief executive. Traditionally, directors would not be included in training but this has changed as directors themselves have realised that they need support in keeping up with the rapidly changing business environment.

All consultants should work on their teaching and training skills, as it will be a necessary part of their work for the foreseeable future. At the very least, you will always be creating change and change has training requirements — you should have defined that need, determined the cost of training and then included the costs and benefits in the option and investment appraisals.

Few consultants will be able to avoid providing training — if there are fees for it, why should they?

Industry

A consultant can act as an expert in an industrial sector such as the oil industry or retailing. You would usually, but not necessarily, have a secondary functional specialism (in marketing, for example).

In the past I have worked with many such industrial specialists, and to some extent I was one myself for a while. I have worked with a housing association specialist who was a former treasurer and finance officer of different associations. When I was part of a team at a large consultancy, bidding to provide services in the electricity industry, we used a specialist electricity industry consultant to familiarise ourselves with the issues facing the electrical power generation and distribution sector.

All industries will have advisors with specialist knowledge of that sector. Some will have made their career in the industry before becoming consultants; others, like me, will have gained their knowledge and expertise through providing advisory services to organisations within the industry.

Geographical

There are many consultants whose main selling point is their knowledge and experience in particular geographical markets. They may offer general business advice but in the context of doing business in Eastern Europe, Africa, the Far East, or wherever. They can advise on business practice, regulations and cultural issues relating to their specialist region.

To be effective they will usually have had substantial experience working and living in the particular area and are maintaining and updating that expertise by continuing to work there. Some may be tempted to try to offer advice of this sort based on an intellectual exercise and research. I would discourage you from trying that approach, as the subtle but essential knowledge will only come from prolonged personal exposure to the culture and bureaucracy of the region of interest. If you have recently lived and worked there at a suitable level, it will be a valuable extra string to your consultancy bow, so you should seek to exploit that experience.

Outsourcing and Facilities Management

Many organisations have begun to focus on their core functions and to buy in the rest from sub-contractors. Many of these subsidiary functions have been moved out to third parties or 'outsourced'. These are often provided by the larger consultancies; this has given rise to what appears to be a rate of growth of consultancy that cannot be supported in the long term. Similarly, many of the traditional in-house functions such as information systems are managed by external suppliers, often the large consultancy firms again. It is my personal view that these are business services, not consultancy, and should be treated differently by the statistics (see our earlier discussion about what constitutes consultancy).

Consultancy is growing, but not at the meteoric rate suggested when these business services are included. I have confidence that professional advisory services for business will continue to provide an important part of an organisation's development. The pace of change is such that businesses cannot hope to keep all the expertise it needs in-house, nor should it attempt to do so as it would prove ridiculously expensive. What is more, the people concerned would be under-exploited and would get bored. Bored staff tend to be disruptive . . .

The List is Endless . . .

At the end of the day, almost any expertise can be provided as consultancy. The question that the prospective consultant has to ask is: 'Will there be enough work?' The more esoteric the specialist skills being offered, the less likely that there will be enough — or at least the harder it will be to sell. The danger with important but unusual services is that the sales cycle can involve a considerable amount of education about the need for the service and the service itself. This makes the sales process lengthy and expensive and you will almost certainly achieve a lower strike rate than with more conventional services.

Also, because of the longer sales cycle there will be cash-flow implications — you will need to be able to stand the extra working capital that will be necessary. That is, unless you can simultaneously do other work that pays back rather quicker. But in the end the rewards should also be higher to justify the extra effort, and the more specialised nature of the work will mean less competition — the law of supply and demand.

Just because no-one is offering the advice does not mean that there is no demand. It may be an important niche that no-one else with the right skills has recognised. But be cautious — check out that there is a demand (not just a need) and that you can sell into that market before you put all your eggs in one basket. If you have identified a genuinely new opportunity you must be prepared to face competition once you have become visible and demonstrated that there is a market. Other consultancy firms, many without the right skills, will jump on the bandwagon, so you will have to have a strategy for coping with that competition.

SUMMARY

There are a wide range of consultancy styles or approaches. Many are advisory, whilst others are designed to enable clients find their own solutions. Others are technical or operational in nature.

There has been a tendency for larger consultancy firms to move into providing outsourced services under the banner of 'consultancy'. In reality many of these services, such as computing services, logistics management and others, are not consultancy but operational business services.

Consultants take many roles. Most consultants will take on most of them at various times. Indeed, they may take several different roles on the same project at different times or in varying circumstances. Many involve training or education, whilst others are more technical and hands-on. From time to time, consultants will also take on management roles in support of their clients. All consultants must assume that an important role is as scapegoat!

The specialist advice offered by consultants is as wide as business and industry itself. It varies from highly technical functional expertise, through industrial expertise to geographical or market knowledge. The nature of the advice within each of these areas is as wide again. If there is a need for particular expertise within business and other organisations, there will be consultants who offer that advice.

So even if your expertise is highly specialised, it is likely that someone, somewhere will be offering advice in that field. Whether you can find clients will depend on your marketing and sales abilities. You must use skills other than your technical ones to determine success.

.

CHAPTER 5

THE CONSULTANCY PROCESS

One cannot be prescriptive about consultancy, but the basic approach is similar in almost any field. In this chapter I suggest one model, but I recognise that every consultant will differ, at least in detail, and some fields may be significantly different. Use this as a starting framework, but twist, bend and pull it into a shape that suits you and your clients. Make sure that, if you do make changes, you do so for good and properly understood reasons.

OBJECTIVES

This chapter will allow the reader to:

1. Understand the generic consultancy process;

2. Appreciate how their own specialist services will fit it into that general framework;

3. Add any additional steps appropriate to their services.

THE PROCESS

A generalised example of the consultancy process is set out in Figure 5.1. Within your own field, there may be specific additional steps. You should develop your own approach to suit the type of work you do, but make sure you include the important points from the general model. All consultancy work should have clear and measurable objectives; otherwise, how will you or your client know whether you have delivered what you promised? You need to know so that you can ask for payment and the clients need to know before they sign the cheque.

```
                    Agreement to Proceed
                            ↓
                    Brief from Client
                            ↓
                    Initial Survey
                    Needs Assessment
                            ↓
                    Data Collection  ←──────────────┐
        ┌──────────┬───────┴────────┬──────────┐    │
   Analogy    Deconstruction    Analysis    Research │
        └──────┐   └───────┐  ┌───────┘ ┌──────┘    │
              Interpretation &                       │
              problem-solving                        │
   Creative    ┌───────┴───────┐                     │
   Ideas → Creativity &      Synthesis               │
          Innovation                                 │
              └───────┐   ┌───┘                      │
                  Define Options                     │
                            ↓                        │
Investment Rules &      Option Appraisal ──── More   │
Required Returns →                          Information
                            ↓
                       Recommend
                            ↓
                    Report Presentation
                            ↓
                    Costed Action Plan
                            ↓
                        Approval
                            ↓
                    Implementation &
                    Monitoring
                            ↓
                        Sign-Off
```

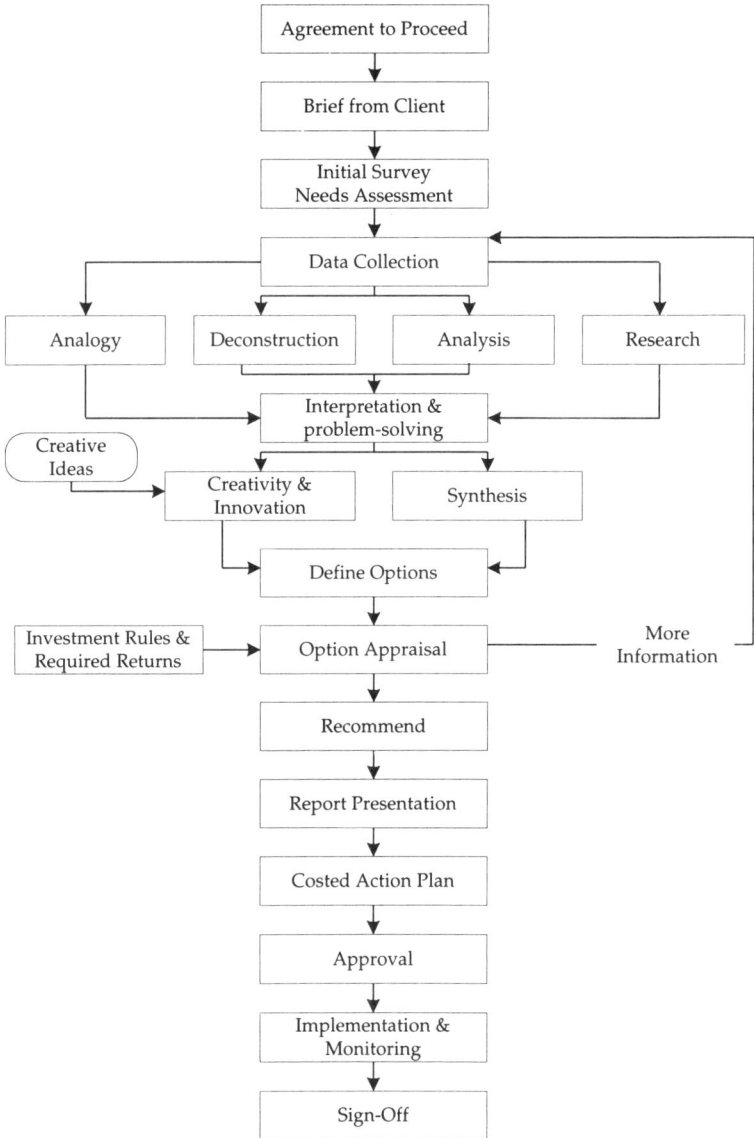

Figure 5.1: The Consultancy Process

PRE-PROPOSAL

Consultancy starts with the first contact. Even though that will be part of the sales cycle, it will also be necessary to use your consultancy skills to start the collection of information. This will enable you to make the key judgement — 'Am I competent to meet this client's needs?' — and to start to build a picture of the issues and approaches that are likely to be successful, firstly to make the sale and secondly to achieve a good result for the client.

Initial Contact

As a consultant, and a salesperson, you are on duty from the initial contact with the client. You need to be collecting information all the time to better understand how you can help your client to improve relevant aspects of their business. Similarly, you need to show a professional front from the start and respect the prospective client's time and interests. Do not leap in, but use the first contact to find out why the potential customer called you (for example, if they were referred to you by a mutual contact) or why they might feel it appropriate to give you further time to make your case (for example, if you contacted them by direct mail).

Early Meetings

The early meetings will be considered in more detail in Chapters 6 and 9 when marketing and selling consultancy services are explored in detail. The first meetings are as much about developing rapport and mutual trust as about finding out what is required to meet the client's needs.

Early meetings should be used to listen rather than expound on your own ideas — you need to understand what the real issues are. It is not unusual for a consultant to spend a lot of time talking about one set of problems whilst merely alluding to the real difficulty. You need to be perceptive to spot the underlying challenges and nudge the prospective customer into talking about them. This ability to guide the other person towards the important matters is an important consultancy skill, and an essential one if you are going to lead seminars or workshops.

Initial Diagnosis

All this will lead to an initial, tentative diagnosis of the problems or issues facing the client. It will not, probably should not, lead to a definitive solution, because the information that the consultant will have will be necessarily limited. There will not have been enough time to be more thorough, and in any case you should be paid once the detailed work starts.

Approaches

From that initial diagnosis, possible approaches will usually suggest themselves, but in some cases it may require more effort and investigation, possibly brainstorming with colleagues or associates. If a suitable approach does not manifest itself, you should question either whether you have enough information and therefore need another meeting, or whether you are even competent to take on the work. If you are suitably equipped to handle the project, then the best way forward to the next stage should quickly become clear.

Whenever possible, you should use your discussions with the prospective client to test whether your ideas sound valid. You should also be exploring, gently, whether the approach you have in mind seems reasonable and is likely to be acceptable to the client. This can be walking a tightrope with a complex problem — if you expose ideas that do not seem valid to the client, then you harm your standing with the client. Conversely, if you do not share your thoughts you will appear lacklustre and without understanding. So you have to test your ideas in ways that allow you to change direction if they do not work for the client. You may be right and will come back to such ideas when you get into the detailed work and can demonstrate their validity. But first you have to win the work, and this requires winning the confidence of the client.

Some clients will expect you to face them down at an early stage — they may be testing your confidence and self-belief. Or they could simply be cussed characters who like browbeating people. That can only be your judgement at the time. Comfort yourself with the thought that if you genuinely disagree with the client and find that your ideas are not acceptable to them, you were probably not going to have the necessary personal relationship to do your best work anyway! Life is too short to work with clients who you positively dislike. I try not to do so, but I have worked with several awkward clients who I did not like but who I did respect — that is a very different matter.

Objectives

As you refine your initial understanding and possible approaches, you will be able to set out some objectives for the work. This will become important when you get to the stage of proposals and terms of reference. Even with initial studies you should have personal objectives for yourself and for what you want to achieve on behalf of the client. They will be your reference points for how well you perform at each stage.

Roles

As you understand the problem and likely approaches, you can start to determine the respective roles of you, the consultant, and the client. The client should do as much of the work as possible — that way they keep their costs to a minimum, thereby maximising the return on the investment in consultancy. By doing much of the work themselves, clients will get more 'ownership' of the solution and will be better placed to take the work forward when the consultant finishes. As a consultant, you should not be happy to do the routine clerical work, data collection and research — let somebody who will learn from the experience perform those tasks. Use your highly developed skills where they will count most — on analysis, interpretation and problem-solving. That way you also continue to learn and further enhance your skills.

Scope Definition

Having got a feel for the nature of the problem, the objectives, the way it should be approached, and responsibilities, then it is possible to start defining the scope of the work. This may have been done to a large extent by the client themselves, but you should validate the nature of the project and its boundaries using your own experience. At that stage there will be a need to explore and agree the definition with the client so that it can be used as the basis for a formal proposal and, after negotiation, the engagement letter or contract.

PROPOSAL AND CONTRACT

Frequently it will be necessary to break the project into two main elements. This is especially so where it is large or the nature of the real problem is not well understood by the client. In such cases, there must be an initial short diagnostic survey by the consultancy to get a better understanding of the problem. This simply involves following the steps from initial diagnosis to the scope definition, as outlined above, but in greater depth. The duration of such a mini-project will typically be quite modest, usually only a few days, although in complex situations it may be more.

This should provide the subject of a formal proposal and engagement letter, with the objectives being to define the scope of the main piece of work to follow. The scope of such a survey should be easily defined as it has very limited terms of reference.

Once the scope for the main work has been agreed, by whatever means, then a formal proposal should be prepared. In my own consultancy practice, Solidus, we adopt a fairly standard approach, which I have used for many years in various organisations. It works whether it is a brief one-page letter for a simple survey or a major project involving several people for many months — the amount of detail will vary accordingly, but the structure remains broadly the same.

The structure we use is as follows:

1. *Executive Summary* — essential if the proposal is more than a few pages long. It will be the same structure as the main proposal but with only the key details or financial totals.

2. *Benefits* — we always try to set out the business benefits to the client of doing this work and using us to help them. It gets them in the right frame of mind and stresses that we are an investment opportunity to improve their business, not simply a cost that they need to keep to a minimum.

3. *Background* — this is our understanding of the problem as a result of discussions with the client or as a result of a diagnostic survey. This feeds back to them in our words what we believe they told us about the problem, to show that we appreciate the issues.

4. *Objectives* — we make the objectives clear and in terms of objective performance measures. We do not want doubts at the end of a project about whether the objectives have been achieved. We want to be able to go through the objectives in the original terms of reference with the client and sign each one off as achieved. It is important for both client and consultant that both parties can see their exit route from the project, as it is in the interest of neither party to be locked into an indefinite commitment.

5. *Our Approach* — sets out how we will undertake the work and the methods that we will use (formal or otherwise). This may include a programme of work and even a timetable if that is not set out separately in the next section. It will be detailed enough for the client to see how we are going to do the work, but it is not a recipe that they can take away and follow without our help. Sometimes it is necessary to give more away but this is usually only the case in major projects. The programme may well change in any case as the work progresses and other ways of achieving the required result become obvious.

6. *Timetable* — simply a schedule of when the work will be undertaken or an outline project plan. Again it should only be as detailed as is needed to show the client when the benefits will be achieved. The detail will change as the project progresses.

7. *Consultant's Role* — we are specific about the responsibilities that we are taking on. This reduces the possibility of argument about who should do what, especially when the consultant is working in collaboration with staff from the client organisation.

8. *Client's Role* — again, we do not want room for argument so we detail what we expect the client to achieve. This will include what the client must provide in the way of facilities, staff and other resources. If at this stage tasks can be defined that the client's staff will need to perform to a suitable standard and timetable, then we will make this clear.

9. *Consultancy Team* — we explain who will be on the consultancy team and give a brief summary of relevant experience. This is to reassure the client that the team they meet is the team that will do the work. One of the things that clients most dislike is to agree to use a consultancy firm as a result of meeting one group of people, only to find that their work is being undertaken by a largely different group. As has already been illustrated, consultancy is about personal relationships, so the client should meet and buy the team that will actually do the work — we make it clear that this is the case. This is a strength of the small firm and the independent consultant — they do not usually have a separate high-level sales team.

10. *The Fees* — we make it clear what the project will cost and if necessary how these costs are distributed. We set out how expenses and other costs will be handled. Even if the work is charged at a daily rate we will give an estimate of the amount of time and the costs involved in doing the work, and make it clear that we will not exceed this figure without prior agreement from the client. Clients do not like surprises, nor do I, so we make this section suitably comprehensive. We will always give a total. It looks sneaky not to and it insults the client's intelligence to think that they will not bother to add it up. Clients need to know likely costs for budget purposes and for cost-benefit analysis. You do not want a client who cannot afford to pay your fees. Finally, the all-important billing and payment arrangements: again we like to make it absolutely clear who will do what and when. On our side we give the billing timetable and set out the payment schedule we expect the client to follow (and we are strict about it — late payment, the work stops). Be completely open in this section.

11. *Summary* — we may include a summary of the benefits and explain how they justify the costs. In other words, we do the cost-benefit analysis so that the client does not have to. We always aim to make it easy for the client to buy our services.

That point about making services easy to buy is important. If there is anything in a proposal that a client does not understand, it is a potential obstacle to completing the sale. So make the proposal absolutely clear with no room for doubt or uncertainty. They will either like it or not — then you can start negotiating on the detail.

DIAGNOSIS

The first stage of any consultancy project is one of diagnosis. This will be true even if the client has done the necessary detailed work. A consultant should not duplicate work already done by others, but you should validate it for yourself, as you will be expected to stand by the diagnosis.

The aim of the diagnosis should be to come to a conclusion so that the full work programme can get under way with clear objectives. However, the consultancy team, which may include client staff, should not respond simply to symptoms but should seek to identify the real, underlying causes. If necessary, the diagnosis phase should continue until those causes are sufficiently understood. Everyone in the team should avoid jumping to conclusions, but base any action on complete and accurate diagnosis.

As data is collected and processed into information it will answer some questions and raise others. This will mean that the diagnosis is an iterative process that refines understanding with each loop. With good diagnostic skills the consultancy team will move steadily towards a clear statement of the problem and the key issues.

Data Collection

Diagnosis requires information, which comes from data. So a key step is to collect data that may be relevant to the problem. That data collection should be associated with some form of problem-solving strategy. A key point is to identify the questions that need to be answered so that suitable data can be collected. In some cases the data will not be available, and alternative strategies must be followed, which may include sampling instead of using data that has already been collected for other purposes.

Frequently data will be available from other sources, in which case it may need to be extracted and reformatted into a form suitable for the work in hand. Increasingly these days this will involve using personal computers to manipulate the data. This is another skill that all consultants should seek to develop. Refer to the 'Resources' section below for a brief overview of possible sources.

Analysis

Collecting data is only the first step, as it is of little use until the information is extracted from it. This analysis stage is where consultants really start to bring their experience to bear. Knowing how to use data effectively is essential and most consultancy specialisms need it to a greater or lesser degree. I cannot think of a consultancy specialism that does not need data. Of course, there are consultancy roles that may not in certain circumstances. But as consultancy is about achieving change there has to be some way of establishing that this change has been achieved.

Therefore all consultants should be competent information analysts. And they should be able to cope with structured and objective data such as timings, costs or activity measures. But there will also be a lot of subjective data such as opinion or text-based information that does not lend itself so easily to the many analytical techniques appropriate to predominantly numerical data.

Consultants should familiarise themselves with the tools that are relevant to the data that their specialism will need or generate. If you do not have these skills, then team up with an analyst who does. There is a strong case for all consultants having some background in mathematical and statistical analytical techniques. But there are usually ways of measuring and monitoring change in a reproducible way in most activities that apparently only lend themselves to subjective opinion. It requires imagination and an ability to think laterally.

Research

There will also be a need to bring in data and other information from outside the organisation. Part of that will come from your own experience, but you will also need to investigate what has been written on the type of problem that you are examining. For instance, has anyone met a similar problem and documented it? Again, your own library will probably have some background research into matters such as best practice, comparative performance across the industry, or alternative techniques.

It may be necessary to use other research sources. This is where those resources identified in earlier chapters come to the fore. Libraries and on-line services become essential — I use one or other several times a week for a variety of research purposes. Here we are looking for anything similar to the problem with which we are faced and a description of how it was handled — just as a doctor when faced with unusual symptoms will refer to the relevant specialist texts. In extreme cases a doctor will hand it over to a (medical) consultant, just as the client manager has done with you. But the buck need not stop with you — if the problem is particularly intractable you can refer it to a specialist consultant who will help you get over the barrier to progress. That is only an admission of failure if you cannot make progress in the work without that specialist support. Remember the key consultancy judgement — 'Am I competent?'

An example from my experience illustrates what I mean. I had been retained to troubleshoot a client's computer systems, which had been poorly implemented. Most of the work was straightforward for someone with my background, supported by the helpdesks for the hardware and software. There was a problem with some specialist communication equipment that linked two offices. I did not have the expertise to solve it, so I called in a communications specialist with whom I had worked in the past. He quickly sorted the problems out and walked me through it so that I understood it sufficiently to negotiate with the supplier as necessary. (By the way, his fees came out of my own, as it was due to my lack of knowledge that I needed to use him. If I had anticipated a significant role for additional technical support I would have explained the fact and included the fees for it in my original proposal. In this case I had not.)

Deconstruction

Often a problem will be too big to grasp in its entirety, in which case it has to be broken down into manageable elements. But bear in mind that the interactions between these elements must be considered in the final diagnosis, so it will eventually have to be rebuilt into a whole.

Each problem can then be explored until its workings are fully understood using the techniques described here.

Analogy

Analogy is a useful approach to both diagnosis and problem solving generally — do I know of another problem that looks similar? It has to be used with care as it can result in false conclusions. But as a starting point for further investigation, it can be invaluable The analogous problem can often be from some completely different discipline, as it is only a starting point to get to grips with the symptoms. Remember, analogy is not about finding exactly the same problem, but a problem with some similar characteristics to the one under investigation.

I use it all the time but I take great care to only use it to lead me into new approaches to my investigation. It might for instance suggest what data I need to collect or examine. It is not the answer until it is proven to be such.

Interpretation and Problem-solving

Put together, these provide interpretation of the data and lead to possible solutions, when combined with creativity and imagination.

Synthesis

Having taken the problem apart to make it manageable, it needs to be reassembled and considered in the round. In particular, you need to examine where the various problem elements overlap and interact. In life, as in business and systems, we do this deconstruction and synthesis all the time. Consider how businesses are organised: they are broken up into separate functions, one could argue in a fairly arbitrary way. This is to make the scope of individuals' roles manageable, as is the case when deconstructing the problem into convenient pieces. But the business is an entity and no function operates in complete isolation — or rather, no function *should* operate in complete isolation although in some organisations they seem to try. The Manufacturing department needs to know what Sales have sold so they can plan what to make, Finance needs to know what has been delivered so they can invoice the customer and collect the money, and so on.

So synthesis looks at the parts of the problem that deconstruction misses, to ensure that each part is considered and that some common parts are not treated differently in the analysis of different sub-problems.

By pulling all of these approaches together, a diagnosis will be made. It may be that after one run-through, there are more questions than answers. That should be the case if the problem is not trivial. In which case the diagnosis process returns to collect new data and facts about the problem to answer the new questions. This continues until a reasonable diagnosis is achieved and can be demonstrated. It will need to be kept under review as more information becomes available during the next stages of the consultancy process. It may well be that the diagnostic process will need to be re-invoked on parts of the problem where the initial assessment does not stand up to the detailed scrutiny of later phases. The techniques are exactly the same, except that at the starting point you now have more knowledge of the problem (and what its causes are not).

RESOURCES

You will also need to consider the information and other resources available to you. If you have worked in a large consultancy or corporate body you will almost certainly have had access to some sort of library or other assistance in finding the information you needed. You will also have had access to specialist expertise in many areas. Out on your own, you will need to replace that in some way. You will need to find libraries that can provide the sort of information you will need. That information will not just be related to your consultancy interest but to general business and market trends. As you will see in Chapter 6, you will need to do market analysis and research into potential clients on an ongoing basis. You therefore need to find a convenient library or libraries that cover both business and your technical field.

In most major urban centres the central public library will contain much of the general business information that you will need, but as we have found it is not always in the most useful form. It may also be lacking in detail. You may find that the local Chamber of Commerce may be more appropriate — check it out before you commit to joining. If you are a member of the Institute of Directors and can get to London easily, then they are a valuable resource for business information.

However public libraries are not particularly useful with regard to state-of-the-art technical knowledge — their budgets and space are limited and they cannot afford to keep up with developments across all areas. I use my local university libraries which issue a borrower's card for a modest annual fee — that gives me access to the latest thinking in my fields through books and especially the expensive academic journals that I could never justify buying.

Some professional institutes may provide information services to members. You should make yourself familiar with what they provide and the costs. Certainly you should get any journals to which you are entitled — make sure you read and file them. They are part of your personal development and a research resource.

In most fields there are some key journals, magazines and newspapers that you should read as a matter of course. Many of the magazines and newspapers will be on controlled circulation which means that, if you qualify, you can get them free — make sure you do. There may be some important journals, possibly academic, which you should aim to read. They will be expensive, but if you use them I would strongly suggest that you subscribe. They will ensure that you will be aware of the topics that will be important in the future. You should aim to stay ahead of your competitors and your clients.

Bear in mind that, although these journals are expensive, one good idea from them that leads to new work will pay the subscription many times over and they will be deductible against tax as a business expense, so you save straight away!

We must consider the much-hyped Information Superhighway. Despite the excessive enthusiasm, it is a useful resource. I have used the Internet, World Wide Web and CompuServe for several years. Used sensibly, it is not expensive, and indeed I have got enough work as a result of being online to pay for several years' use.

My main use is of CompuServe, whose forums or discussion groups are managed so that there is proper behaviour and no personal abuse. Advertising is only allowed in designated advertising sections so that the general user can avoid it if they wish. Because of this controlled environment, I find it more useful. I use it a lot for resolving problems with software — often I can have a problem in the afternoon, post a message on an appropriate forum (most major software products have a presence) and when I get to work the following morning there is an answer.

The Internet contains two resources, apart from e-mail. *Usenet* houses news groups where discussion takes place, much as in CompuServe forums. Unfortunately, most are not moderated so the quality of the discussion and behaviour can be poor. I have therefore tended to avoid it, although there are moderated news groups that are worth joining.

The World Wide Web must surely be known to most readers by now. It has mushroomed in recent years. It was originally conceived as a way for researchers to collaborate across the Internet by linking their documents to those of others, providing a relatively seamless whole. Originally it was purely text-based, but it is now very much graphical in content. Most major organisations and a lot of small ones and specialist groups now have their own Web Site. The increased use of graphics has made it attractive to advertisers; many sites are little more than an alternative advertising medium. But there are useful sites and a lot of valuable information. Use a search tool on a key word and you may get thousands of references. Because of the graphical content it can be slow to download information — fortunately the sites that contain the most information tend to use graphics sparingly. For example, my company uses it to search for press coverage of companies and industries in which we are interested.

I am surprised how many would-be business people do not have the most basic information about the business sector that they are entering. And I see it from potential consultants in on-line discussions asking for sources of products, or asking the most basic questions about the field in which they intend to operate. They show their lack of basic understanding of business and their field by asking for information that should be at their fingertips if they wish to become consultants. If they are demonstrating that lack of credibility to me it will be spotted by all but the most gullible potential customers. You need to be on top of your specialist subject with a sound business knowledge if you are to survive as an advisor to other businesses.

If your specialism is such that you need a laboratory, workshop or similar base, do not underestimate the cost and difficulty of setting one up from scratch. I know someone who had the responsibility of setting up a complete workshop for a new research and development organisation. Identifying the need for lathes, milling machines, etc. was easy. The biggest problem was all those little things that such workshops (and labs) acquire over the years — non-standard nuts and bolts, the offcuts of unusual materials, etc. You simply cannot go out and buy them, even if you could predict the need for them. An established workshop or laboratory has drawers full of such odds and ends. It took that particular workshop several years before it settled down in that respect. It will be the same for you if you are starting out on your own and do not already possess these facilities.

You need to think through the resources that you will need and find out how you can best meet those needs. The list above is not exhaustive — your specialist field will have its own particular requirements. There are some useful addresses in the Appendices at the back of the book.

CREATIVITY

Creativity and imagination are a very important part of the best consultancy work. There is much that it is routine in providing advisory services, but to gain real business benefits, new approaches are needed. Managers should be producing continuous improvement; otherwise what are they doing?

As part of most consultancy assignments, there will be opportunities to improve performance in the short term, and these should be taken whenever appropriate. But the main thrust should be to make major improvements that, ideally, will lead to some degree of competitive advantage. How long that advantage lasts will depend on the nature of the improvement and on the industry. For example, new products in the financial services sector give no more than a few weeks lead over competitors. Sustainable competitive leads only come from continuous innovation, fuelled by creative thinking.

Creative thought needs a prepared mind that is willing to accept new ideas. The truly creative individual is prepared to be different and to consider ideas that may appear strange or even weird on the surface. A colleague who considers me creative described me as 'intellectually different' because of my approach. I took it as a compliment, as he used the same phrase about his wife, who is highly successful in her own right.

There is considerable debate about whether creativity is an intrinsic or a developed skill. I suspect that it is like many human skills: it is partly basic aptitude coupled with practice and development. I believe creativity can be encouraged, as I certainly had the sort of upbringing from parents and some of my teachers that nurtured and rewarded original thinking. Part of the secret is to get away from the attitude that an idea is 'silly' or 'daft' — all ideas have some merit, even if they cannot be brought to practical fruition. The silly idea may be a step along the way to the big idea. I believe creative ideas do not spring, fully formed, into existence but come about from a series of steps and connections to other concepts. Some of those connections will be made by a subconscious mind that is receptive and well prepared.

One final point: creativity is not about being different for the sake of it. True creativity comes from new insights and should, certainly in a business context, be explicable. In the arts, similar insights may not be so easily explained but there is a similar problem with false 'creativity'.

Preparation

So what sort of preparation is required? As a starting point, begin by being born to creative parents who encourage you to think laterally. Unfortunately, we cannot make that choice and may well be mature before we appreciate the importance of creativity to us as individuals. So the first thing we need to do is to accept that we need to become receptive to all ideas, even those that appear harebrained at first consideration. We need to be open to following them through to see where they lead before setting them aside. No idea is wasted, but a huge proportion will not be exploited;remember that they are seeds of other ideas. I find that when I have an idea for a book, an article or whatever, that it generates many other further ideas. If you open your mind to ideas, then you should find them flooding in and you are on the way to developing your creative talent.

As part of the consultancy process you will be collecting facts; this is a key to generating ideas. I believe ideas arise from connecting the facts of the problem under investigation and all the other knowledge that the individual possesses. Some of that will be from one's professional career but much will come from all the other details one has assimilated over time.

To make connections, to have a bright idea you will need to work at it. You will need to order your findings, possibly in many different ways, and to look at them from all angles. You will probably need to add external information from research about the problem by looking at what others have done in similar circumstances and whether it worked or failed. Those research findings must be incorporated into your analytical structure.

But do not confine your research to the problem in hand. To be creative you must have a lot of influences and be able to make connections that have not been made before. That means that you cannot know what information will be important or even useful. So read widely and beyond your professional sphere. Keep your mind open to ideas from other people, especially those from outside the area of study and do not rubbish them. Accept them, understand their thinking and file it away. Ideas and approaches are not fixed, so be prepared to lay them aside; do not become so wedded to one thought that your mind becomes closed. A closed mind is the greatest possible block to creative thinking. Challenge everything in a considered way, as there are no absolutes.

Above all you have to believe that there is a solution. You may not know what it is or even what it might look like. You cannot be wholehearted unless you believe that you will get a result eventually.

Effort

Being creative is hard work but in my view it is also great fun. You have to work at it and be prepared to give it the time. Creativity need not be isolating; you do not have to pursue it alone. I frequently work with a colleague and once we get into it we can spend hours generating new ideas and approaches. Frequently we will start off by kicking ideas related to one client around, and by the end of the session we may have a possible solution to that and often several ideas for other clients. We will then examine those ideas in more detail or put them to the back of the mind to mature further.

I find it important to jot down new ideas in a notebook that I keep for that purpose. It is too easy when the creative juices are flowing to forget ideas that may be useful at another time. So by keeping a few, very brief notes I can trigger the thought process that originally spawned the idea and follow it through at a more appropriate time.

Brainstorming is a useful approach in a team situation and should be familiar to any potential consultant. But there are a few basic rules:

- No ideas should be demeaned. However unsuitable an idea may seem, it may provide the germ of ideas that will turn out to be even more appropriate.

- No individual should be allowed to take over the discussion.

- All individuals should be treated as equals, whatever their position in the organisation.

Don't force the issue. If ideas do not come then it probably means that the mind is not properly prepared or it is simply not ready to produce ideas. I often find that, when I have a report to prepare, it cannot be forced. As long as I do the preparation work conscientiously, there will come a time when the words will just flow onto the page. But until that stage is reached, trying to write it is a waste of time, as it will not work — I will invariably throw away the few words I do produce. Mind you, having an imminent deadline can help!

Incubation

Let the subconscious mind work by allowing time for it to sift through all the information that you have thrown at it. This is a key stage in the creative, and problem-solving, process. The mind is very good at sorting out and structuring complex data, if allowed to do so. From time to time, you may want to add some new findings or to actively consider what you know. That will help jog the process along, but do allow time for the mind to work.

Be prepared for insights at any time; we have all sat up in bed in the early hours with the answer to questions that have been troubling us all day. But you have to be careful not to lose the bright idea, so when it pops into your head write it down or make a verbal note on a dictating machine. The worst feeling is waking up in the morning knowing you had a good idea but unable to remember what it was. You need to get yourself organised so that you do not lose the moment — those ideas are very valuable.

Insight and Ideas

Creativity is about numbers. The more ideas the better. One idea will generate another and each one needs to be considered because you cannot know immediately which are the valuable ones. Many ideas will be unsuitable or unworkable, but do not reject them prematurely. Think them through and keep at it until you find the ones that might work and put them aside for more detailed consideration.

Ideas, or even innovation, are not themselves the solution. They just provide the starting point for a lot more hard work to turn them into useful business benefits. Believe it or not, ideas are relatively easy. As the inventor Thomas Edison said:

> Genius is one per cent inspiration, ninety-nine per cent perspiration (Thomas Alva Edison c.1903, quoted in *Harper's Monthly Magazine*, September 1932).

So for creativity and innovation to work, we need to connect ideas from which will come yet more new, and hopefully even better, ideas. The more ideas the better. It is a numbers game, because most ideas will not stand up to close scrutiny, but will have served their purpose by providing a step along the way and the seeds of other more suitable concepts.

Do not stop when one suitable idea arrives — there may be a better one behind! Make a note of it and carry on generating ideas. Leave evaluation until a little later.

Evaluation

Once you have a set of ideas that seem superficially workable, they will need to be examined in more detail. Evaluation of ideas should be separated from generation, as time is needed to get over initial enthusiasms so that their validity can be determined by more sober analysis. It is very easy to get locked into a train of thought or to become too wedded to a particular idea. That must be avoided in the appraisal of the alternatives.

It is essential that the assessment of ideas, and their associated approaches, is conducted in a thoughtful and objective way. Emotional attachment to one's 'babies' is a common failing, especially amongst people for whom creativity does not come naturally and ideas generation is hard work. Because they have fewer ideas there is a tendency to give them too much value and credence. Ideas are like fish fry — very few will grow to maturity, but the deaths are necessary to allow the strongest to flourish. If you only produce a few ideas it is very likely that none of them will survive scrutiny; that is why I stress the importance of wading through a large volume of ideas to get to the one gem.

So be clinical about your evaluation until you have the one or two ideas, from the many, that might work. Because the real work starts here.

INNOVATION

A lot of so-called consultancy has become standardised and concerned with doing rather than advising. Consultancy, for me, is primarily about advising — the other approaches are worthy services, but for me do not constitute consultancy. Unfortunately, by becoming standardised and with the growth of 'journeyman' consultants, there is much less innovation than there should be.

Too much consultancy is derivative — it worked for client A, so with minor modifications it will work for client B. Incremental improvement is important, but it is really the role of everyone at the client organisation as part of their day-to-day jobs. They may need outside help from time to time to remind them of what they can do, but this should not be the bread and butter of consultancy. Consultancy should be about new ideas for each customer, based on an understanding of their needs combined with an outsider's innocence (and cynicism).

The problem is that true creative thinkers are rare and, combined with the rarity of perceptive and bold managers and directors, it is no wonder that most organisations are destined to be followers rather than leaders. But that should not stop them trying because without innovation, all such bodies will be slowly but surely falling behind their leading competitors. You will never catch up if you do similar things six months after the leaders.

So as a consultant, do not be afraid of generating and promoting new ideas — just be sure that they will work and that you have a client who can implement them. And remember, you are also a businessperson, so you should be innovating in all aspects of your own business (not necessarily all areas at the same time!).

If as a consultant you are not a creative thinker, then team up with someone who is and can understand your ideas and your clients' needs. Bounce the problems off them and let them generate the ideas, then use your analytical, research and management skills to turn those ideas into practical business propositions.

You can also work on improving your creative skills — there are books and techniques that help the process. As with everything, practice and hard work goes a long way. Just having wild ideas is not innovation. You have to be able to carry them through, so you must develop the idea through research, analysis and implementation — that is innovation.

But you can make a major contribution by making other people's ideas work, even if you are not yourself creative. There are many examples of people who spotted an individual's creative ability and then used their own organisational abilities to allow it to flower to mutual benefit — take, for example, Brian Epstein and The Beatles. In fact, many a successful creative genius did so only through the support of a wealthy patron. And, on the other side of the coin, Edison employed (some say exploited) many people to help with the perspiration part of his innovations; without doing so he could never have been so prolific in bringing ideas to commercial reality.

So innovate, even if you need to find someone else to generate the new ideas in the first instance.

To be creative — indeed to be a good consultant — you need to be widely read and to have understood what you have seen. That breadth should exist, not just in your own technical speciality, which should be both wide and deep, but across the whole of business and other areas that may have some impact, albeit indirect, on your work. This could include science, technology, social policy and politics (not just national but global politics). The world is getting smaller, so you should be aware of how people in other countries are rising to the challenges you face in your own market. They may be doing innovative things from which you can learn. Be interested in all aspects of the world around you — you never know what may trigger that big idea.

Creativity and good advice come from being able to interpret all this information and make connections between apparently unrelated elements. For example, the structure of the Carbon-60 molecule was understood because one of the researchers, a chemist, had an interest in astronomy. Many years before he had modelled the night sky onto a ball for his son. He had built it from hexagonal and pentagonal panels and the resulting sphere had 60 vertices — the Carbon atoms. He made the important connection and was able to show a possible structure for 'Bucky Balls' which they could then test and subsequently prove.

The same is true in any field — the ability to make connections is central to creativity, which is essential to innovation and development.

So, having stacked up a handful of ideas, the real work begins: to develop them into fully workable solutions with all the potential problems resolved. In a consultancy context, that means the technology is identified or created, the people issues are addressed, the costs and benefits are known, the investment is viable, the risks are understood and there is a will to take it forward. Many ideas will fall at various stages during the development process, so again we need to be able to generate enough so that eventually we will find one approach that will survive all the challenges thrown at it. That may then be the solution.

OPTION AND INVESTMENT APPRAISAL

At each stage there will be options as to future strategy, each of which must be evaluated, and eventually a preferred approach chosen. Such option appraisals should be based on an objective assessment and the final choice must be justified in an objective way that could be explained to outside auditors if required.

One should always consider the option of doing nothing in exactly the same way as the other options. It will provide a benchmark against which the other possibilities can be measured. It is very easy to bias the assessment towards or against any option to reflect instinct or political acceptability. This should be avoided at all costs. The same rules should apply to all the options, and demonstrably so.

You need to identify all the costs that will be incurred in implementing the proposal. And when I say all, I include all those incidental ones that tend to be ignored as they are lost in operational budgets and therefore do not fall within the budget for the project in hand. Typically these include many of the lifetime costs, such as continuing or remedial training or training for new staff. They include maintenance, consumables, revisions and upgrades to the procedures or systems as needs change with time.

But there are other costs that tend to be missed during the implementation phase of any project. These might include the costs of the extra work that falls on people other than the project team itself. This includes time lost for training, attendance at briefings or other meetings, or due to disrupted work patterns of those called on to provide information and other support to the project. Then there is often the need to run the old and new working practices in parallel, as one gradually replaces the other. And do not forget management time outside the project time — this will be at all levels within the organisation, including the board. All this means that there will be a need for temporary staff and/or overtime, which is often grossly underestimated when planning any process of change.

All of this leads to opportunity costs that must be considered. Cost-benefit appraisal could fill a chapter on its own. As there is no room here for such a detailed explanation, the reader who wants to know more should seek out other sources. There are some in the Additional Reading appendix.

Benefits also tend to be oversimplified — the intuitively favoured option usually being overstated and the less favoured strategies underplayed. Benefits should be measurable. And where particular results do not produce a monetary value, there may be alternative strategies.

There will always be costs that are inadvertently missed or otherwise ignored and these can mount up to a significant burden on many projects. So some form of contingency has to be built into the budget. This should also reflect the risk of the approach. The contingency should be realistic, not simply a notional figure used to bring the budget to a convenient total. And this figure should not be used to fine-tune the cost-benefit analysis in order to confirm the preferred approach.

Discounted cash-flow, internal rate of return and net present value are important tools for any investment appraisal. A consultant who is making recommendations that involve more than trivial expenditure should be familiar with these and other techniques. They are well covered in any book on financial management, including those aimed at non-financial managers.

If you are unfamiliar with these techniques, you should not be advising clients on anything requiring expenditure! Which also means you should not be a consultant, as it is difficult to conceive of a consultant doing anything that did not involve the client spending money — even if it is simply your fees.

REPORT

All management reports should have a one- or two-page executive summary at the front. At least one large firm I know binds the summary on the outside of the report so that it can be removed and distributed easily. Most of the senior managers will wish to know about the main findings of the consultancy project. But they will not usually be concerned about the detail, as they will take it for granted that their colleagues who have worked with the consultant will have looked after those aspects at an appropriate level.

Even with an executive summary, the report should be to the point and as brief as possible without being superficial. It should contain enough information for a knowledgeable reader to be satisfied that the recommendations are soundly based, but it need not, and probably should not, contain enough detail to repeat the analysis contained in the report. Remember, the report should be backed up by background material collected during the project, and those notes should be available to any appropriate person who needs them.

However, some of the material may have been collected on the basis that it is for the consultants' eyes only — often the case with personal details and views. That commitment must be honoured. In which case the consultant should retain the original material and make available a non-attributable summary of the sensitive material, usually in aggregated form.

Do not pad the report or be mealy-mouthed about the findings and recommendations. Tell it as it is. There may be some need to be sensitive to the cultural and political climate within the organisation, but that should not be allowed to cloud the issues. Make your findings clear.

There are two principal points that pretty well all consultancy reports ought to address. Firstly, everything else is there to achieve the benefits and to identify and justify the costs that will be incurred in achieving that required outcome. The benefits and the required outcome must be expressed in terms that business managers will understand, whatever the functional specialism of the consultant. This is because the people who will sign off the final report will also approve the investment needed to take the recommendations through to successful implementation.

Secondly, the other side of any investment decision is the costs, and as explained earlier, these should be identified in great detail. All too often, many of the incidental costs that fall into budgets other than that for the project are missed or ignored, perhaps subconsciously, because they are not the problem of the project team.

If the recommendations include an implementation or change element, the report ought to include at least an outline project plan. This should give a feel for the implementation timetable, the phasing and the resource implications. This last point means that to properly identify the costs, the project plan would need to have been outlined in any case. It should therefore be shared with the client. In many cases, this would have been a required part of the outcome in the terms of reference for the consultancy work.

It is usual to let the commissioning manager, and perhaps others, see the draft report, so that they can make comments and ensure that it meets the brief. Any comments or suggestions should then be accommodated if they do not compromise the validity of the report. The consultant has to be able to put their name to the report and be prepared to stand by it — under extreme circumstances, in court! The sharing of the draft is not to allow the client to rewrite the report to meet their particular agenda, but primarily to allow questions of fact to be checked. There may be occasions where the emphasis needs to be modified, but this should be by consensus between the consultant and the client. You must not allow a client to browbeat you into making changes with which you do not agree. A consultant should never put their name to a report with which they are not happy.

Bear in mind that the time spent preparing the report is part of the chargeable time if you are working on a time and materials basis. I had a new consultant friend who spent half a day of very intensive work preparing a report as a result of one day of on-site consultancy, and he did not charge that time to the client. He had effectively reduced his day rate by a third by doing so. He was in a difficult position as he had not allowed for it in his original estimate; but he has learnt his lesson and will in future make it clear that there will be other chargeable time in preparation and report writing, over and above the time spent on site. It is very easy to underestimate how much time is spent on consultancy work outside meetings, which should be paid for by the client.

Finally, check the report against the terms of reference and especially against the required deliverables and objectives. The terms of reference will largely determine the format of the report and, once written, it will be reviewed to ensure that it covers all the points in the terms of reference and any subsequent variations (all in writing of course).

RECOMMENDATION

Recommended courses of action should be based on objective measures, not opinion or intuition. They should have clear and measurable benefits and the costs should be quantified.

A consultant must be able to justify these recommendations if challenged. You must also be able to accept that in many cases there will be more than one possible route to success and to explain why the particular choice was made. A consultant should be aware of the alternatives and have a sound reason for not adopting them. That said, there might be circumstances where the client prefers one of the others, notwithstanding the consultant's recommendations. In such cases the consultant has a duty to ensure that the client fully understands why it was not recommended and that the client has thought through the implications of their preference. But if the client is determined to go down a different route then you ultimately have to accept it and can only try to ensure that the client fully understands what they need to do to make the best of that choice. At the end of the day, the client is responsible for the success or failure of their organisation. All a consultant can do is to advise and recommend what they believe is best for a client at the time. Clients have to make their own decisions.

PRESENTATION

Consultants are routinely asked to make presentations of their findings and recommendation to all sorts of groups, including board members, managers and staff groups. The consultant who can present well to groups with such wide-ranging interests and needs will do much to enhance their reputation and win implementation and change management work.

Focus on benefits to the client organisation as a whole and to the members of the group as individuals. Do not focus on the features of the solution; they can be covered in other ways if required, but it is the benefits (and the disadvantages) that will concern most people. Different groups will have different needs, so it is helpful if the groups are arranged to represent people with shared interests. As the form and content of the presentation needs to be tailored to the interests of the group, the more commonality there is within the group the better. Do not try and use the same presentation with all groups — treat each group separately and respect their viewpoints.

IMPLEMENTATION

Project planning is an essential skill for consultants and cannot be learned through unsupervised client work. That expertise must be gleaned in other circumstances. But the approach is broadly similar to that described later for estimating. The essential step is a top-down deconstruction into manageable tasks with clear deliverables. From that can be identified the interdependency of tasks and the resources and time that they require. That allows the project timetable to be determined, often using computers.

All plans should have clear objectives and measurable targets, as this is the only way they can be properly managed.

Any change exercise will be made or broken by the people who are affected. If they believe in the plans they will make almost anything work; but if they do not . . .

It is imperative, therefore, that the recommendations and plans are 'sold' to the workforce effectively. Indeed this is one of the most demanding aspects of making change in organisations; the consultant who makes possible the implementation of complex recommendations will be in great demand and will earn good fees. Change management is well beyond the scope of this work. There are many excellent books on the topic.

The vital signs monitoring described later in this chapter provides a viable management approach to project management. There are many other issues that need to be considered but they are beyond the scope of this book. Again, there are many good guides to project management, some specific to particular industries, at least one of which should be on any consultant's bookshelf.

MONITORING

Being a consultant means that there are a lot of management and monitoring tasks. There is the personal management of one's diary, network and sales prospects. Then there is management of the consultancy practice and any junior staff that you may have. Last, but by no means least, is the management of work for the client and the management of clients and their staff. To be successful as a consultant means that all this management must be performed efficiently and effectively.

Cycle of Control

There is a basic cycle of control that is needed for all effective management. It all hinges around having a plan and then performing the tasks defined in it. By monitoring what is actually achieved and taking remedial action, the desired objectives should be achieved. The basic cycle of control is illustrated in Figure 5.2.

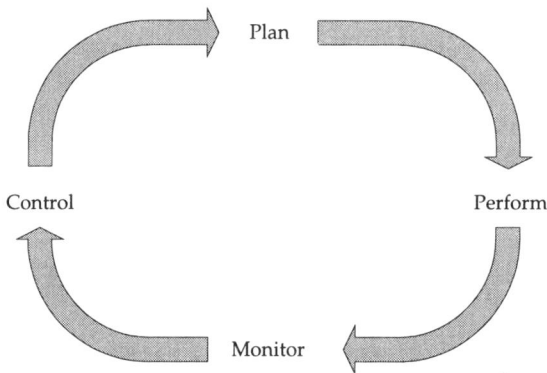

Figure 5.2: Cycle of Control

First you have to have a plan; much of this book is about creating a plan for your business. But you should plan all action and set objectives. Then you perform the plan and monitor that you are achieving the objectives. If you are under- or over-achieving, some control action will be needed and the plan may need to be revised to reflect the new realities. Let us consider each element individually:

Plan

The starting point for any management process is to have a plan against which to measure performance. And to measure performance you need to define some measures that will allow you to do so. Most managers should have heard of SMART objectives, in other words, they are:

- *Specific.* In other words they must be precise and directly applicable to the desired performance.

- *Measured.* There must be a way of determining whether the objective has been achieved. Vague terms such as 'improved' or 'better' should not be used; rather they should state which measure — sales, absence rates, scrap rates, profit, etc. — is to be improved and by how much. Better still, the objective should state that sales should be better than an absolute value.

- *Agreed or Accepted.* Different people define the objectives either way. Which is appropriate will, to some extent, depend on the culture of the organisation. Those that work by consensus will tend to make sure that they are agreed. Others with a more directed approach will seek to ensure that they are accepted, even if the individuals or groups to whom they apply do not particularly like them.

- *Relevant.* They must be appropriate to the objective and meaningful to the performance required.

- *Timed.* In other words, they should be achieved by a specific time rather than at some vague time in the future.

Perform

Once the objectives are determined and the tasks that must be performed to achieve them defined, there is a plan which can be performed. Once this plan is put into action, it needs to be monitored.

Monitor

The monitoring should be frequent and should report against the SMART objectives and associated measures as defined in the plan. The variations between the planned results and what has actually been achieved need to be examined and understood. That may require further information and more detailed analysis, which will be explored later in this section.

Control

Once the differences are understood, corrective action can be determined and taken. The aim of such action should be to get back to the plan but there will be implications for the plan as a whole. For example, there may be a need to reassign budgets or to set new targets in other areas. Whatever happens, the plan will need to be revised to reflect the new realities. However, it should not simply be amended to reflect what has been achieved — there might as well be no plan. That is not management.

The whole cycle is continuous, and although much of the monitoring is periodic (typically monthly or weekly), the process should be happening all the time. Do not try to be too subtle; management is a fairly crude art that needs to be applied in big lumps.

Vital Signs Monitoring

Fortunately, there is an approach that will make it all rather more manageable and will ease the overall management burden. We call it *vital signs monitoring*, and it owes a considerable debt to management by exception. This simply involves looking at a few key indicators to see if performance is coming up to expectations. If it is, no further action may be necessary.

Nearly all successful managers use some variation on this approach; remember, you are going to be the manager of your own consultancy business. It is highly efficient and does not rely on any particular technology — I do much of it in my head or in my journal. A successful director friend of mine swears by an electronic personal organiser — that suits him. I have worked with a consultant surgeon who used a similar method, using a dictating machine that lived in the pocket of his white coat. The secret is to find what works for you and use it conscientiously. I only use a computer to help keep track of progress for major client work and compliance recording. Hopefully, vital signs monitoring is a more complete and effective solution, suited to the rapid changes of the modern world. I have used it successfully for many years in a whole variety of circumstances, and especially now I am running a growing consultancy firm.

At first sight this sounds like a recipe for huge bureaucracy, but it is not. One has to consider how most people manage using the traditional reporting approach. They receive a large weekly or monthly report, take a quick look at the totals at the bottom of the last page and then file it in the wastepaper bin. Although such reports contain all the detail, most managers rarely look at it. They check that the totals are as they expected, and if they are, they know they are on track to achieve their objectives. They only investigate the detail if the totals suggest that something is not as it should be. That is the essence of the vital signs monitoring approach — use a few key measures or indicators to demonstrate the state of the patient and only look further if they indicate something is amiss. It has been working well for doctors for generations.

All organisations have a few key indicators of their basic health. A treasurer of a Scottish health board once told me that he was only concerned with the projected year-end out-turn against his budget. If that was on target, he slept well at night.

For each organisation or project, it will be necessary to identify the few key measures and indicators and monitor them frequently — it takes a few minutes for each reporting cycle if everything is working smoothly. The managers are not buried under a mountain of unneeded data.

It is only when there is a problem that more detail is needed, and it is then that good computer systems can really help. However, the approach also works for manual systems, because it identifies problems at the earliest possible time and therefore action is easier and the quantity of data needing analysis is minimised. Usually only the data since the last vital signs report needs investigation.

If the vital signs do not fit on a single sheet of paper (one side only!), or even better on a single page on a computer screen, then there is too much detail. Many conglomerates require their subsidiaries to report at this sort of level so it can contain sufficient information.

In a consultancy, project work tends to be both delegated and shared amongst several people or groups. Vital signs monitoring lends itself to working with such spread responsibility (and I hope authority). The vital signs for top management are very high level, but the same approach works as one moves down the hierarchy.

At each level there are appropriate vital signs that the individual or group needs to achieve if higher levels are to meet their targets. By setting individual vital signs, one can allow each person to monitor and control their own performance. That reduces the burden on their managers and enhances their role and sense of self-worth. In my experience, most people actually want to do a good job, and to be allowed to get on with it. This approach encourages and enables them to achieve that.

Each individual or group monitors their own vital signs, but a copy of the report is sent to their manager — who does nothing with it. This is because if there any problems, the junior is expected to report the reason for the problem, the action they propose to take and the expected consequences of that action. That reporting need not be bureaucratic — in most cases a brief telephone call or a quick conversation will suffice.

Only if the junior's response is inadequate in some way does the manager need to get involved. A very important aspect of this approach is that nobody should have responsibility for targets without sufficient authority to make the decisions needed for their achievement. This is simply the basis of good delegation.

The reporting is consolidated as one moves up the hierarchy so that the report remains brief and to the point (still just one page). A key consideration as to what should be included is the question: 'Is it material?' What is important to the supervisor on the shop floor may well not be sufficiently material to warrant a separate item in the report to the chief executive. That is not to denigrate the supervisor's contribution or the importance of managing the performance at that level. For the individual it tells them whether they are achieving what is expected of them. For the organisation as a whole, if each person, at each level, is achieving their objectives, then the whole business will do so.

PROGRESS

Keep progress meetings and the like brief and to the point. Concentrate on what has been achieved and what needs to be done to keep or put the project on track. Remember that project management is about minimising risk to the organisation; the cost or timetable for the work is only a part of it. Use vital signs monitoring as a practical and straightforward approach to progress control.

POST-IMPLEMENTATION

After the project is completed, the consultant and client should put together a team to audit what it has achieved. This should be directed towards improving future projects, rather than laying blame for any failures of the project under review. Ideally the team should be different from the project team, who by this point will be tired and too close to the project.

Why not use the team for the next project? It will mean that the lessons will be fresh in their minds as they plan their own project.

The review should consider what the project achieved and cost. This should be tested against the original objectives: the expected benefits and the actual costs should be compared against the budget. It might also be useful to re-examine the investment analysis using the actual figures — does it still look worthwhile?

The implementation review should highlight improvements that could be made. These can then form the first stage of the ongoing support and development of the work.

COMPLETION AND SIGN-OFF MEETINGS

Finally you should have a final disengagement meeting with the client. This serves two important purposes.

First, it gives you a final opportunity to determine how satisfied the client is with your work and what it has achieved, and to make sure that they understand what you did and how to take it forward effectively. It also means that you can learn of any problems and how to avoid them in the future, and how you might generally improve your services. Use the feedback to drive improvements — aim to make each project better than the last. Also, the client will learn how they might make more effective use of consultants — hopefully you — in the future.

Second, it gives you an opportunity to start the sales cycle again. You should not be too brazen about it — after all they have just spent quite a lot of money with you! But you should seek to keep the door open for future work with them. You might give them some free advice about where they might go next. Although they should be in your project reports, there will always be new ideas that you have had since those documents were prepared. You may also have noticed issues or problems that need addressing, but which lie outside the scope of the recent engagement; sharing those freely leaves the client feeling well-disposed towards you and hopefully when these issues reach the top of the client's 'To Do' list, they will think of you.

You should aim to finish in such a way that you can give them a call in a month or so to see how they have got on and to nudge them back on track. I try and have lunch with the key people a month or two later to see what is happening — again I keep it as a social event, but sow a few seeds. Remember, it is easier to keep a client than to win a new one. If the relationship worked, there is a good chance that the next project from the client is yours without having to compete for it. If it is, do not take it for granted and abuse the relationship. Make sure the price and everything else is keen. They have made it easy for you; so make it easy for them by sharing some of your savings from the reduced sales effort with them.

SUMMARY

Most consultancy specialisms work to a similar generic process. The details may change and obviously the technical knowledge and sources are different, but the essential process is the same.

All consultants will need to work through broadly similar stages in identifying a suitable solution to the client's needs. Some of the work may be done by the client and validated by the consultant, or indeed vice versa. The consultant should aim to provide innovation to give a real competitive gain rather than simply incremental improvement, which should be the remit of operational management. Warmed-over ideas from previous clients will not do proper justice to the current client — they need real value and real benefits that can be measured.

First there has to be an initial diagnosis and analysis phase to understand the problems and to identify possible strategies for their resolution. That must be followed by further research and analysis to determine possible approaches. These have to be examined in detail and alternatives considered through a process of option appraisal. The favoured solution then has to be subjected to a detailed investment appraisal to ensure that the money is being spent in the best way possible.

PART 3

THE BUSINESS OF CONSULTANCY

CHAPTER 6

MARKETING

Marketing is not the same as selling. The sales process follows on from the marketing strategy, which will have put forward views on how and where the services are going to be promoted. But marketing is more about identifying customer needs and ensuring that they can buy products and services. Marketing therefore is primarily about research and analysis.

OBJECTIVES

The purpose of this chapter is to help you define your market in terms of both customers and the products that you offer.

Therefore the main objectives for the chapter are to help you:

1. Understand marketing and how it differs from selling;

2. Understand the needs of potential customers;

3. Identify the consultancy products and services to be offered;

4. Identify the likely market in terms of possible customers;

5. Assess the possible ways that those customers may be reached;

6. Consider the promotional possibilities and the suitability of advertising;

7. Develop a marketing strategy that combines all the above;

8. Understand the sales and buying processes for advisory services;

9. Stress the importance of targeting effort by suitable qualification of possible clients;

10. Decide whether third parties will provide support that you will need and how to recognise charlatans;

11. Pull all of this together into a plan of action.

CLIENTS' NEEDS AND WANTS

The first question any provider of services should address is: 'What do customers need and want?' All too many new businesses and some declining businesses start with: 'What products do I have to sell?' In the latter case you might be lucky to find that there is a market for those services, but it would only be luck. Success comes from providing products and services to customers who have a need, a desire and the ability to buy them.

The questions that you must answer are:

- What do customers really need?

- What do customers want to buy? This may not be the same as what they need!

- What will they spend on those needs and wants?

- How can suppliers get those products to them?

Once you have answered these questions to your satisfaction, you can begin to look at designing your services to satisfy the prospective clients' desires. It is no good offering products that you think are a good idea if there are not enough customers willing to buy them.

Change

Change is a key factor in determining whether a client needs consultancy support. If there is no change requirement, then the existing management should be able to cope. However, change is an inevitable part of providing products and services, whether for profit or not. Small and incremental change again should be manageable by an organisation's existing staff.

To create a need for outside advice, an organisation usually needs to be contemplating a significant change that it faces only occasionally. This may include a routine change such as finding new offices or replacing a computer system, for which it is not worthwhile retaining the necessary expertise on a permanent basis. Clients use consultants for this kind of work, when needed.

But there are also other changes that may justify the use of specialist help. These would include a change in the regulatory framework in which the organisation operates. In recent years there has been a trend by governments to privatise or deregulate industries — the opportunities and changes that spring from such actions may cause organisations to seek outside help.

Other changes that often cause organisations to look for consultancy help include mergers, new technology, departure of key personnel and new or changed competitive pressures. This is by no means a definitive list, but it shows that organisations are facing change of all kinds all the time and there will therefore be an ongoing need for occasional advice.

Needs

Successful businesses meet their customers' needs, and the better they do it, the more successful they will be if they have got their pricing right. You need to start by identifying services that clients need and then consider how you might provide them. Far too many, perhaps most, small consultancies work the other way round. They start by saying 'what services can I offer?' and then try to find clients for them. In starting any business venture, the customers' needs come first in the planning.

Having identified what clients need, you can address what skills you have available to meet those needs. If you have the necessary expertise, you have the beginnings of a business opportunity. If you do not, you have to question whether consultancy is a sensible choice for you at this stage of your career — perhaps you need to go away and develop expertise that will be in demand. In that case do not consider what the needs are now, but look to the future and determine what skills will be needed and in demand when you have completed your training.

Wants

What a customer wants may be very different from what they really need. To do the best job, you have to meet needs and help the prospective client to express their wants in terms of their true needs. As an example, I was called in by a six-partner professional firm to help them select and implement a new computer system to improve fee-earner productivity. They had expressed both a want, the system selection, and a need, increased fee-earner productivity. If I had taken them at their word, I would have replaced a satisfactory computer system that was simply not being used effectively. Instead I showed how they could use their existing equipment to manage staff time and expenses. Furthermore, I showed how they could improve their productivity by changing their working practices. As a result, instead of spending £50,000 they spent just £10,000 and saved a further £40,000 on staff costs in the first year alone. They met their real needs, not their imagined wants.

Value

Whatever you look to do for a client, you must give them value and they must perceive what you offer as value. If the customer does not see the value in what you are offering, you will never sell your services to them. Nor indeed should you try because that will not build long-term trust and mutual respect — you need that if you are going to get repeat business (the best kind).

So a key question you must ask when designing your products and services is: 'What benefit will the customer get from this — and will they value it?'

WHAT IS OUR BUSINESS?

As a consultant you will be advising clients to adopt good business and other practices. So practise what you preach and plan your business properly. Do not cut corners, but start with the basics. If you are not totally familiar with them, you are not ready to embark on an independent consultancy career. Being a professional means being so in all aspects of your work.

If you are equipped with the skills and basic techniques to be a consultant, you should be familiar with the most basic analytical techniques. Even if you are offering technical skills you should still be familiar with basic business and management practice. The techniques described below should already be familiar to you, so I do not intend to describe them in great detail.

PEST Analysis

PEST analysis is about examining the environment in which the organisation operates, and is an important starting point for developing the marketing strategy.

Political

First, the political environment needs to be considered. This includes the tax and statutory framework in which the organisation operates. Amongst the issues that will need to be investigated are the applicable regulations.

Also, political factors will determine what attitude the public sector will have towards their own use of consultants. Sometimes consultants are in favour, at other times they are not, and a consultancy firm must be sensitive to such changes if it offers services to government, government agencies and local government.

Economic

What is the state of the market in economic terms? Is it growing or shrinking? Are prices high or low (which will depend on demand along with other factors)?

Economic factors also include the availability of raw materials and skills — in times of growth it is not uncommon to find that people with important skills become difficult to recruit. From time to time, this has been a particular problem with, for example, computer-related skills. As with any shortage, the price (wages) goes up, which will have an effect on prices and costs.

Infrastructure too will have an impact on the business — can you get the goods and services to the customer effectively? Are suitable communication systems such as telephone networks and high-speed data links available? All will have an impact. And if you do not drive a car, can you still get to your clients by public transport? There also appears to be a possible trend developing to discourage the continued expansion and unthinking use of the motor car — this is a political trend that may have an impact on infrastructure.

Social

An organisation does not operate in a vacuum; it is part of the community in which it operates and serves. That means there are social and environmental expectations of the business, and these days the organisation must consider its ethical standpoint.

A business must also consider its impact on its community and to what extent it is going to be involved with that community. This can be at two principal levels: firstly, as a good neighbour by not creating noise, pollution or other disturbance, which should not be too much of a problem for a firm of advisors. Secondly, to what extent is the business willing to go beyond that and take an active part in enhancing the social environment. This can be done in a variety of ways: for example, providing work experience to youngsters or the long-term unemployed, supporting local initiatives or charities with money, facilities or active support — there are many other possibilities. Some may be more appropriate than others for a consultancy practice.

Most established professional firms do some 'honorary' or *pro bono* work, where they do not charge fees for work that supports community or charitable activities with which the business leaders have sympathy.

Technology

The technology factors include all technologies that impact on the operation of the organisation conducting the review. Obviously as a consultant you may have a technology field in which you advise, such as information technology, food processing, or whatever. The nature of that technology and the pace at which it is changing will have an effect on the demand and nature of the consultancy services used. This must be reflected in the marketing plan.

But there will also be technology issues around the operation of the business. This may be as simple as whether the business needs a computer or colour printer. There are many other considerations — for example, data communications such as mobile telephones, computer networking and the Internet. These are all changing rapidly and will have an influence on how the business is organised. Many consultancy firms are moving to various forms of 'hot-desking', home-working or teleworking, or even building virtual consultancy firms.

Anybody planning a business needs to be aware of all such technology factors that will affect the environment in which the business operates and the way both the firm itself and its customers will use technology in their operations.

SWOT Analysis

Anybody planning to form a consultancy practice who does not know what SWOT stands for and how to use it should think again. They are seriously under-equipped to be a consultant. This is probably the most basic analysis technique used in planning of all sorts and everyone running a business, not just a consultancy, should be familiar with it. It should be a routine and familiar exercise.

As it should be second nature to any would-be consultant, I will not cover it in any detail. It must be noted that many issues could fit into several of the headings. That is unimportant; more important is how you respond to what the SWOT analysis is saying about you and your business.

Strengths

These are the strengths of the business or individuals under consideration. Strengths are the answer to questions such as:

- What do we do well?
- What are we good at?
- What special skills do we have?

The strengths should be considered in the context of the customers' needs or the opportunities explored below. And above all, they should be the result of comparison with competitors.

Weaknesses

The weaknesses are those aspects of the business where we may be lacking. These may be anything from skills gaps, lack of finance, unsuitable premises and equipment or simply lack of market knowledge. Again, this should be compared with competitors.

Opportunities

What opportunities do the environment external to the business offer? These opportunities may arise from changing regulations, new technology, withdrawal or failure of competitors, or any number of other reasons.

Threats

Threats are the reverse of opportunities and are the answer to the question: 'What challenges do the external environment pose?'

The next step is to plan the business strategy to align Strengths to take advantage of the appropriate Opportunities and to minimise the risks associated with the Threats. Alongside that you need to mitigate the Weaknesses by addressing them or operating in parts of the market where the weaknesses will expose the business to less risk.

Many people approach threats and opportunities first, as they will tend to determine the strengths and weaknesses that are relevant. Also, threats and opportunities are usually outside the direct control of the business, whereas the business should be actively managing its strengths and weaknesses in response to the external environment and competitive changes.

InSPECT

At Solidus, we have developed PEST further and turned it into InSPECT. We believe innovation is the key to our success in all aspects of consultancy, business and management. InSPECT builds creativity and new ideas into the analysis process, and helps us define where we are taking Solidus.

I do not propose to describe how we use it in detail — you need to find the tools that are right for your work culture. We work with it in a similar way to PEST and SWOT, which we also use. The main elements are innovation, social and political issues, environmental considerations, communications and technology.

Innovation is so important it comes first in our list. We believe that a real competitive edge is not possible without genuine creativity. Unfortunately genuine original thinkers are rare, so if you can embrace innovation and real creativity on behalf of your clients then you will give them real benefits. We seek new ideas and ways of doing things as a routine part of our client work.

The place of innovation is all-pervading. It tends to be associated with technology, but this should not be so. Innovation can be in the product, its production, administration, the organisational and management structures or even the very nature of the business. Many of the real business successes have come from major re-thinks about the industry itself.

Social issues need to be considered, as no organisation operates in isolation from the community it serves or in which it operates. For example, environmental considerations are now more important than a decade ago, in large part because of demands from those communities. Do not forget that there is a set of social issues within the organisation.

Political issues will always have an impact on even the most insular of organisations. They impact on the regulatory framework, tax, bureaucracy and even the nature of advisory services that are required. A change of government in a foreign country may have an impact in your home area, through your customer or supply chains. Consider what happened to the Western defence industries when the Berlin Wall came down.

Economic environment is obviously crucial to what strategy businesses adopt. It changes the nature of services bought — there will be fewer organisations investing in new technology or growth strategies when the economy is in a downturn.

Communications issues play an increasingly important role in the widening global economy. Information can travel around the world in fractions of a second — I routinely correspond with people all over the world, most of whom I have never met. Some of us will collaborate and do business together without ever seeing each other.

But it is not just telecommunications that will have an impact on strategy. The road and rail network, air travel and access to ports will help to determine what business you are in, where it is located and how your products and services are delivered to the customer.

Clearly if you are a consultant based on a Scottish island, you will adopt a very different business strategy to someone who is based in Central London offering similar services.

Technology is important in many areas of business strategy. It can be the technology used in the product, in its manufacture or distribution. It can be technology used in support functions — for example, the on-line services we use to research markets and to collaborate on projects with remote colleagues (here, it overlaps with communications). The only requirement should be that it should serve an appropriate business need rather than be technically led.

We use InSPECT in many different circumstances, but especially when analysing new markets and industries for ourselves and also when developing business strategy for clients. It is only part of a wider set of tools that we use — each consultancy practice needs to develop a set of techniques that are appropriate to its work. However, it should not follow them slavishly — remember that innovation is the key to success. Remember: 'if the only tool you have is a hammer then everything looks like a nail!' Use the correct tools, not just the standard techniques that you have to hand.

MATCHING SKILLS AND CLIENTS' NEEDS

Marketing

Marketing is not the same as sales, and it is a fundamental prerequisite for a successful business of any kind. It has to start as soon as the business idea is first mooted, because almost everything else follows from the understanding of customers' needs, the identification of which is a key part of marketing.

Marketing is not the glossy, glamorous work that is often associated with the stereotypes usually based on advertising agencies. It is to a very large extent a laborious desk-based job where time is spent on research and analysis. A lot of the other marketing time will be spent in libraries extracting data for analysis from directories or, if you are fortunate, the information that results from other people's research and analysis. Many market reports about industries are published, but they tend to be expensive, reflecting the amount of hard labour involved in their preparation — they will only be available in the better business and academic libraries. However, you will still have to spend time interpreting what it all means for your business.

So find and explore your local business libraries, university, college business and management libraries and any other libraries such as trade associations or professional institutes with libraries that serve your specialist field. Once you have decided which you are likely to use, get a reader's or borrower's card. You will need it for your market research, to read the more expensive journals, and for general research on behalf of clients and for your other projects.

Marketing people talk about the 'four Ps'. This is shorthand for the key issues that a marketing strategy must address.

Product, Place, Price, Promotion

Product

The product or service (it is still a product in marketing terms) must meet the needs and wants of the customer. So the supplier must first research what the customer needs, how they will use the product and other aspects of the product's nature, such as frequency of use, and the product can then be designed accordingly.

Unfortunately too many businesses, especially small and start-up businesses, start with the product and then try to sell what they have designed or made. They then wonder why it such a struggle to get established. That is ignoring marketing completely!

Place

Where is the product going to be made available? Where and how is the client going to find it so that they can buy it? What is the distribution channel? This is discussed in the next section, 'Finding Clients'.

Price

When considering price, one should be thinking in terms of the complete cost to the customer of acquiring the product or service. It is not just the selling price, the day rate in consultancy terms, but also the costs incurred by the client in finding and briefing the consultant, the consultant's expenses, the project management time, etc. Often, the basic selling price will only be a small proportion of the cost to the customer — those costs must be included, as they will provide much of the cost resistance to buying the product.

Promotion

Promotion is about how the customer is going to be made aware of the product and the benefits that it will provide. Promotion is often the only part of the marketing mix that many businesses adopt.

FINDING CLIENTS

Your biggest challenge will be finding clients. If you are leaving an existing consultancy practice or business service company, you might find that some clients may want to go with you. However, you will have to look carefully at the terms of your employment contract and probably take professional legal advice before agreeing to take them on. A new business cannot afford to get involved in a legal dispute — in fact, such disputes are to be avoided at all times. In 16 years running a consultancy, I have only once instructed a legal advisor to act on my behalf, and that was for a supplier who had failed to properly deliver what had been ordered; that matter was resolved satisfactorily after an exchange of letters and faxes.

Most of the clients for your practice will have to be new ones. Where are you going to find them? And how are you going to let them know that you are open for business? How are you going to encourage them to use you instead of their existing advisor, or to use consultancy at all? You need to address all of those issues if you are going to win any clients. And without clients, you are not a consultant!

Advertising

Advertising is not really a viable option for any but the largest advisory firms. It needs a consistently high level of expenditure and the returns on the investment are, at best, mixed. No doubt many advertising agents will disagree, but I was discouraged from spending money in this direction by an advertising agent friend. My own experience in a variety of firms also confirms the dubious effectiveness of most such promotion.

When used by small firms, it is usually a sign of no imagination and an avoidance of getting out and selling their services. I know I have used it in exactly that way. But I am afraid it is no substitute for most of the other options.

Salespeople

Good consultants can sell. They have to. They have to sell the first project and they have to sell follow-on work to existing clients. And above all, they have to sell their ideas and recommendations to the client and their staff all the way through assignments. So why employ sales staff?

Remember, consultancy is about personal relationships. Clients buy the person, not the firm. How can a salesperson do that? One of the main complaints raised by consultants' clients is that they sell with one team and then send in a different team (usually less experienced, but not always) to do the work. Clients feel cheated. So a salesperson has an uphill battle.

Few consultancy firms have staff in a purely sales role for just these reasons. They expect their senior consultants to be able to find potential clients and sell to them. The earnings of such consultants are generally dependent on what they sell rather than on the work they do — they have junior staff to help with that in any case.

Salespeople do not really work in consultancy. It is an expensive lesson to learn. If you are going to start a consultancy firm, be sure that you are prepared and able to take on a sales role; it cannot be delegated.

Direct Mail

Personally, I do not like direct mail — 'junk mail', as it is often known. I get a lot of it and most of it does not get anything like the average eight seconds of attention. Much of it is thrown away unopened.

Unfortunately, I cannot think of any way of doing without it. Many of the other methods of promoting a practice start with some form of direct mail. Even if you want to offer a free seminar on new regulations in your industry as a way of reaching potential clients, you have to use direct mail to let them know about it!

However, you can avoid getting lost in the crowd. We achieve better than typical response rates with most of our mailings, because they are highly targeted to a small group for whom we have identified their special needs. Our successful mailings tend to express strong, sometimes forthright opinions, which strike a chord with our high-level target contacts. They are not the usual simplistic selling documents with which we are all familiar.

We do a lot of research and planning, and then usually send out less than 100 letters — more than that and the letter has to become too general. For example, a campaign to gain us entry into an industry that was new to us went something like this:

- Initial mailing was very strongly worded and very critical of the industry concerned. We sent out 75 letters over four weeks, and followed up with a telephone call to about 50. We got a response from about 60 per cent — that is, we spoke to the chief executive or other director in detail about the issues in the letter. We did not count the straightforward 'thanks but no thanks' responses. We got meetings with three of the organisations at a high level and were asked to prepare two proposals — one general one and one for a specific piece of future work. The third meeting required a follow-up meeting after further work (it was with one of the top four organisations in the industry), where our ideas were to be taken to a wider audience within the potential client organisation.

- As a result of that experience, we wrote to the top 20 organisations again with ideas developed from our improved understanding. As a result, we had high-level meetings with another three of the top six organisations, one of which asked us to prepare an outline proposal illustrating the approach we would adopt with a specific problem that they faced.

- Our presentation to our original top-four contact was successful and our ideas have been dispersed among relevant divisional heads. As a result, we are going back to discuss a particular problem and our approach to such a project.

- We will follow up with the middle tier of organisations in the near future with an offering addressing their particular needs.

- As well as the possibility of work with these companies, we now have several high-level contacts within the industry with whom we are on first name terms. We can now call these people directly to share ideas or to check whether our thinking is valid. We are now moving from direct mail to networking within this industry. One piece of work from the larger organisations could well pay a consultant's salary for a year. We would be very disappointed if we did not achieve at least that much.

- Furthermore we can now use much of the same research and campaign approach with another related industry which shares many similar challenges. We can reuse letters and background papers with very little revision — it all adds to efficiency.

Some writers on direct mail recommend printing your message, or at least your name, on the outside of the envelope. As a busy recipient of such mailings, I welcome that — I can then file it in the waste bin without opening it! It saves me time. There are several training and seminar companies whose mailings *always* get that treatment; they mail me most months so their response rates must be awful.

My advice for direct mail is not to go for quantity, but aim to make each item really work. That means researching the industry and the targets, and giving the letter a strong but justified opinion. Above all, make sure that you are sending it to a named individual and that you have names, title and form of address correct — ring each one up if necessary.

In the United Kingdom, the Royal Mail publish a guide to direct mail — it should be in every consultancy firm's library. Much of the advice is aimed at large volume direct mail, but there is much solid advice that is applicable to the highly targeted approach appropriate to the small professional firm.

Networking

Successful consultants are well connected, not through an accident of birth but through consistent hard work over many years. They recognise that it is not just what you know but who you know. You never know when someone you met years before will become useful. I have had work appear, apparently out of the blue, as a result of a conversation or meeting several years before.

As with all forms of marketing and promotion, you will need to be persistent and keep up with contacts, even when you are busy. It is all too easy to let contacts fall away through neglect. Unfortunately, you never know which ones may bear fruit at some time in the future. So keep them active — at the very least, they should all get a Christmas card or equivalent once a year. Apart from that, you should aim to find at least one other reason to be in touch each year. A good opportunity is if they appear in a newspaper or trade magazine as a result of a move or promotion — a short hand-written note of congratulation will hopefully create a warm feeling. But do not make such notes a selling exercise, otherwise you will lose the benefit of the personal tone. Making contact every six months is probably about right for a casual contact, and every three months for a relationship that is closer or more active. More often than that may seem intrusive unless the relationship is very close — a regular client or associate.

Some people feel that active networking is about being pushy and forcing yourself on people you barely know. Certainly, some people do that but they will find it counter-productive. Instead, be yourself and be sensitive to the other person and to the circumstances of your meeting. For example, do not talk business at a social gathering unless the other person starts it, then keep it brief and more about them than you (but make sure you get a suitable message across). I tend to be rather low-key about these things, as I am not particularly outgoing with strangers. On the other hand, I have a friend who will get his business card into the hands of everyone in the room within half-an-hour — at least, that is how it seems. He is a much more ebullient character than me and that is his way. Mutual friends regard both of us as good at networking; we just do it differently. So the secret is to be yourself, to work at making and keeping contacts in your own way.

Do not just look for contacts who are potential clients. As your practice grows, you will also need to be able to call on specialist expertise that you do not have in-house. Far better to work with someone you have already met and perhaps worked with at a mutual client's firm. If you know someone, the risk of using them is much lower, as you will be aware of their strengths and weaknesses. Also, such associates may need someone with your skills to undertake some work for a client of theirs.

Other contacts may simply be a source of information: you may be able to call them to ask about their industry or some other matter on which they will have an insight. Access to knowledge is a key aspect of being a consultant and your network of contacts is an invaluable source. Remember to be generous with your knowledge in return — nobody wants to feel that the traffic is one-way.

You can help the relationship by being genuinely interested in what people are doing. People like to talk about themselves so give them the opportunity. Do not force yourself and what you are doing on them, otherwise they will feel that you are taking advantage of them. Make them feel as though they matter to you. If you are a natural networker, they will, and even if you are not, they should still be important to you. Be genuine.

Do not rule people out because they do not seem to be relevant to what you are seeking to do. The direction from which referrals and other valuable nuggets come can be surprising. Whilst it may be unlikely that you would use someone directly or that they would provide you with services, they can still be valuable in other ways. You may think that you will not have much use for a mole-catcher, and probably will not in a professional relationship. But you might find in casual conversation that a potential client is having problems with moles — it would be very valuable to suggest someone who can help. I have found work as a result of helping a possible client out in a similar way. Value everybody you meet — to be a natural networker, you must be genuinely interested in people.

As your network grows, it will become harder to remember who knows what, when you last called them and why, what they are doing, or even those important personal details such as the names of their partner, children or dogs. Keep a note of them and update it. And read it before you call them — make sure you are up to date.

Referral

The best business comes from referrals, but you cannot get referrals until you have clients. It is something to work on as your practice develops. You should encourage your clients to mention or recommend you to their business contacts.

Whilst writing this book, I asked several consultant friends how most of their new clients heard about them. In all cases it was primarily from other clients or by word of mouth from business associates — the network again.

So reputation is the key to success in the consultancy business. It is so valuable that you have to nurture and protect it as much as possible. The old saying that you are only as good as your last project is very true. Reputations are hard to earn, but so easy to lose — one bad project can undo many years of work.

A new client calling to tell you that you were recommended to them by a business associate is a real fillip. It really makes you feel good! But it also imposes a responsibility to the referrer — they have put their judgement on the line for you so you must do a good job to confirm that trust. Otherwise you not only harm your reputation but also that of the person who recommended you. As we have indicated from the start, the consultant, even the so-called independent consultant, does not operate in isolation with only responsibility to themselves. There are many whose lives they influence and there is always the responsibility that goes with that.

Self-promotion

A consultant's reputation is built on several factors other than simply doing good work for clients. That is certainly important and will eventually bear fruit through referrals, but it is a low-key reputation. It will not of itself generate new work or make it easier to sell to new clients, especially if you regard client confidentiality as sacrosanct and therefore do not drop names.

Most very successful consultants are also good at self-promotion. This may vary from the high profile where the individual is regularly asked their opinion on television, to a quiet respect in a particular industry niche. But it all helps the consultant sell themselves.

A public reputation cannot be built overnight. As with all success, it is usually the result of a considered plan and a lot of hard work. There are many books on self-promotion, but some of the main approaches are discussed below.

Have an Opinion and Share It

Probably the single most important part of self-promotion is to have an opinion and a willingness to share it. It should be well founded in knowledge and understanding of the field, rather than simply a rant against the status quo.

The extravagant outburst may achieve short-term celebrity, but for business success a longer-term view is needed. Opinions may be forthright, even controversial, but they should be well considered and well argued if you are going to be given the opportunity to air them often enough for your name to be recognised.

Having a name that appears in the press or on television gives you credibility way beyond what is justified. Clients are surprisingly impressed by people who have had articles, or better still books, published. This is probably because many people aspire to be writers and never managed to get anything published — I must admit that, even after three books and many articles, I still get a huge buzz from seeing my work in print.

However, it is not desperately difficult to get into print if you are a competent writer. The big challenge is to understand what particular editors need. You need to review the newspapers or magazines for which you wish to write and understand their style, slant and content. Do not try and replicate what regular columnists produce, but provide a different viewpoint on the same issues. Challenge their thinking and arguments in a reasoned way and keep it brief and to the point. They definitely will not use stuff that is obviously intended as an advertising puff for your business.

Remember, this is not about bringing in immediate work; that is the role of other promotion tools. This is about professional credibility and name recognition. It is about making it more likely that your letter is read and that the potential client will want to meet you. This is part of your long-term strategy for business development.

Letters — Don't be Afraid to be Controversial

The easiest way of getting published is via the letters pages of trade journals. The secret is to pick a topic on which you have a definite view, and preferably one that is in some way controversial or unusual. You should then argue your case in the most succinct way possible. If you are going to have a high success rate at getting letters (and later, articles) into print you need to develop a style in which every word counts. You need to make an editor's life as easy as possible; the less sub-editing your letter needs the more likely it is to be published. Stick to the message, do not try and push your services — even if the letter is used, that will usually be edited out. Finally, keep it brief — 250 words or less — as longer letters are rarely published.

If you can start a debate via the journal's letter pages, then you are on the way to developing a reputation as someone who has an opinion worth hearing. After a while you may get to the stage where your opinion is sought by those writing feature items. Once you reach that stage you are on the way to becoming a minor celebrity and if you keep working at it your opinion will continue to be sought.

Articles

There is a huge demand for well-written articles on pretty well all business, technical and organisational issues. This is especially true where they are based on best practice or state-of-the-art developments.

If you can write on such specialised matters in a clear and entertaining way, you will be in demand. As explained in the earlier section on letters, you need to understand what editors need and make it easy for them to use your writing. Remember, there are several key points that need to be considered when preparing articles for publication:

- Do not try to compete with the regular columnists — they have a contract and a brief to fulfil. If you write the same sort of things, your work will not get a second look. You need to add something different, so be original but make sure it is appropriate to the intended readership of the magazine. Analyse the non-regular features to see what sort of material is used.

- Make sure what you offer has not been covered recently. If you can, get hold of the feature schedule. It is usually made available to regular contributors and advertisers so that they tailor their work to the theme of each issue.

- Make sure your article is of the right length and style. Again, this is a case of making it easy for the editor to buy your work. Editors have to fit articles in and if you analyse them you will find that they tend to be of certain word counts, often based on multiples of, perhaps, a quarter page.

- Look for regular features that lend themselves to outside contributors, such as a case study or notebook section which covers specialist topics. Tailor your offerings to these sections and your chance of being published will be much improved.

- It may seem strange, but most magazines are designed for advertisers rather than for readers. They are actually shaped the way they are to attract readers of a particular profile to suit advertisers. With few exceptions, profits arise from advertising revenue rather than bookstand and subscriptions sales. That is why most trade journals are on controlled circulation with free subscriptions to qualifying professions — that way they can guarantee the nature of the readership to advertisers. Understand that and you will start to understand the intended and actual readership and can plan your offering accordingly.

There are several points about submission and presentation of articles. Generally, I do not write articles, or books, on a speculative basis. I only write when I have an editor interested in buying the article. My time is too valuable to do otherwise. But that said, when I started out I did write speculatively to establish a track record. I send a query letter with a synopsis of the article, explaining why it is appropriate to the magazine. I no longer send an example of my previously published writing, but I did initially and I would recommend you do so to start with. I send examples if they are interested in the article and ask for such examples to reassure them that I will deliver.

As far as presentation is concerned, there are many books on writing and presentation for publication. I would suggest that you buy or borrow a couple and follow their recommendations. The main requirement is to print it, double-spaced, on one side of the paper; these days I would also send it on disk in plain text format or in a word-processing format; discuss this with the publisher.

You will also need to consider whether you are going to be paid to write. If you merely want to gain credibility through publication, then you may be prepared to write without a fee. I regard the income from writing as part of my general income stream and I therefore expect to be paid properly for such work. If it is worth publishing, it is worth paying for. Also you owe some duty to those who write for a living not to undermine their markets; after all, you would not be happy if they offered your clients free consultancy!

Academic Papers

Academic papers are not really a viable route for most consultants. If your market is with small and medium-sized businesses, they will never see them. Even professional managers rarely read academic journals, so you will reach a very a very small audience through this route.

Also, you need to bear in mind that the lead time for publication of such papers is many months. So only pursue this route for personal satisfaction or if you have aspirations to move into an academic role in due course. In that case they will stand you in good stead.

But for general reputation, they will give little credibility, unless you are a member of a university department with a strong reputation in a particular field. If you write enough over a long enough period it may help your business credibility. But if you can get enough work published to do that then you are probably already a member of an academic department and consultancy will be a sideline.

Bear in mind that many managers are very suspicious of what they see as 'airy-fairy' academic ideas and prefer more practical approaches. So articles in the trade papers that they read will be preferred.

Books

Once you have had a few articles published, your thoughts may turn to writing a book, but it is a different scale of project altogether. Few people ever sit down and write a single piece of work of 65,000 words or more. That would be a huge consultancy report — something around 300 pages, in which case it would usually be a collaborative effort.

In my arrogance with my first book, I thought it would not be much different from writing a big report. I can only say it is a much bigger task. When I am writing a report I can usually carry most of the detail in my head — I know what I have written and where the relevant paragraph is. I also know what I need to add and where. With a book, I found I could do that up to around 30,000 words or so. Then over a single writing session I lost that overall feel and had to rely on notes and my structure plan — it was quite striking and it brought home to me how big a task writing a book is.

Because of that, I would not recommend writing a book on a speculative basis. Put together a chapter structure, what competing titles exist, details of the target readership and why your work will meet their needs. And of course say why you are the person to write it. Send the proposal to a commissioning editor, by name, of a suitable publisher. Give them at least six weeks to read it before calling them to find out what they thought of the idea. If the idea is good, you will find a publisher, so do not give up if the first one turns it down — review it, reprint a clean copy and send it to the next publisher — make sure it matches their interests and that they have not published a similar title.

Again, there is plenty of guidance available on getting a book published. Before you start, even on a proposal, get a set of proposal guidelines from your preferred publishing houses — they will give their recommended format and will ensure that you cover all the essential points. Ask for it at the same time as you find out the name of the commissioning editor for the type of book you intend to write. Remember that publishers have quite small staffs, especially on the editorial side, as much of the detailed work is sub-contracted. So do not feel over-awed at calling publishers. I have always found them very pleasant and helpful people to deal with.

Becoming a 'Guru'

Once you have begun to develop a reputation as a minor celebrity, you may get invited to speak at conferences and other meetings. You should encourage such invitations.

The number of speakers needed for these events is staggering. Remember, it is not just academic conferences; there are many more internal conferences held by major businesses and other organisations, all of which will need speakers. Most of them will use at least one external speaker, often for the keynote address, to support their own internal presentations.

Institute meetings, etc. Depending on the nature of your consultancy business, there may be institutes that would appreciate you speaking to them on your specialist field. It will not be directly profitable, as the best you can expect is a free meal and, just possibly, some expenses. You should stress to the organiser what the cost of you providing such a talk would normally be but that you are waiving your fee (or donating it back to the organisation) because you share their objectives, or whatever.

There are many directories of professional institutions in your library and you will be aware of many of them through your professional life. Write in the first instance to the headquarters and they will be able to provide a list of branch secretaries or pass on your details on to them.

You should probably have two talks of different length — say, 20 minutes for a lunchtime meeting and 40 minutes to an hour for an evening meeting; you can always extend it with questions and answers. I believe the content should challenge the audience's views gently, but there should be much with which they can agree — after all, you want them to feel that you are a kindred spirit with whom they could work.

Always have something compact to leave behind. It needs to be compact so that it can be slipped into a pocket or handbag. If it is any bigger it is a nuisance and most people will drop it in the waste bin at the first opportunity. Also, if it is slipped into a pocket or bag then it will probably not resurface until the recipient next uses the jacket or bag — that will provide a reminder and a second opportunity to reach them when it may be appropriate.

Run seminars/workshops. Many consultancies run free or inexpensive workshops or seminars as a way of reaching potential new clients, and this can be very effective. This is particularly useful if you are trying to find clients from small and medium-sized businesses.

Probably the most successful exponent of this type of meeting was a tax consultant who specialised in value added tax. At the end of his half-hour slot he had the audience queuing to discuss their problems with him and he always got new business from such meetings.

He started with the caution given by police officers when arresting someone, and continued, for half an hour, by frightening his audience (usually small business owners and directors of larger businesses) witless with the commitment that they were making when they signed the returns to customs and excise. He then added to the pressure by demonstrating the authority that Customs and Excise have (in the UK, it is greater than the police!) and their willingness to use those powers. He made the police and the inland revenue look like woolly liberals in comparison. He then finished with a photograph and the crash of prison gates slamming. It frightened me and I had seen it several times!

Personality or Celebrity

As you develop a reputation within your industry or specialist field as a 'guru', then you may be noticed by the general media. How useful you will be to them will depend on the nature of your expertise and opinions. If your experience is in an esoteric technical area, the opportunity to become a celebrity is limited. But if your knowledge is of interest to the general public, there may be the potential to develop the celebrity status so that it takes over from your professional services as your main source of income. But for most consultants, the opportunity lies rather closer to the minor celebrity status, where you appear on business programs or science and technology documentaries.

However, even such a role will make selling your services much easier through increased credibility, and people will want to meet you because you have been on television. It may even allow you to increase your fee rates. But you will still have to deliver value for your clients. As we have already said, reputation is a fragile flower and the press loves to build people up and then knock them down. The media loves celebrities with feet of clay — so once you become visible, you will have to watch your reputation even more closely.

Be Visible

The aim is to be as visible as possible. So any opportunity to state your opinions and promote yourself should be considered. There are few situations that you should avoid, but there may be some groups with whom you should not be associated.

I would suggest that you avoid political parties and lobbying groups. Being associated with such organisations means that their opponents will not use you — do not reduce your options. My view is that, whatever your political beliefs, a consultant, indeed any businessman, should be apolitical for just such reasons. However, that is a judgement that you will have to make for yourself.

Public Relations

Even if you decide not to promote yourself personally, you may want to use the press to publicise the achievements of your new practice. As with personal promotion you should not expect to get work directly from such publicity. Rather it is a long-term plan to create awareness of the practice in the minds of possible customers. By so doing, you will be more likely to get the opportunity to sell to them and will have more credibility when you do meet.

Public relations can be a two-edged sword. If you go public on orders won or customers gained it can have unfortunate side effects. If you let it be known that you have won a substantial order from a major client, you will find that you face more competition. It will seem as though all your competitors are trying to get to your customer. This will have two results: you might well annoy your customer by going public and exposing them to the unwanted attentions of other advisory firms, thereby creating extra work for them. Or you may lose your customer because they perceive that your competitors have more to offer.

I now take the view that my client list is strictly confidential, as it is possible that my customers may not want it known that they are even using consultants. For competitive reasons, most will not want it known why they are using external advisors. I never offer clients' names, although I will, with the client's permission, give them out as references if asked by a new client. Even then it is not often — references are usually not requested.

Open Tenders

Open tenders look like an easy option for the small consultancy which is struggling to find new business. Here is a potential client who is advertising that they need consultants! All you have to do is ask for the tender documents, prepare a proposal and the project is yours. Wrong! Open tenders are the most competitive work you can go for.

Think about it. Every consultant in the market sector knows about it. Some may have worked with the particular organisation; indeed they may have helped define the project requirements. Others will have worked for similar organisations on similar projects. If it is advertised it is usually a large project, so the big firms will be interested and the advertiser itself is likely to be a major, probably public-sector organisation, with strict procurement rules.

All that means several things:

- A lot of proposals will be submitted.

- Many will be highly professional — as of course will yours.

- Differentiation will be difficult.

- The cost of preparation of such proposals will be very high. Typically there are at least five days' work for a senior consultant (or equivalent) to prepare such a bid. Often it is much more

— on occasions I have been part of a team that spent a week or more preparing a response to such open tenders.

- Credibility will be a major issue.

- The client will be seeking to minimise risk as much as trying to choose the best. Therefore they will tend to choose the larger, more established firms.

- Most proposals will get a cursory glance at best.

After an initial enthusiasm for chasing this sort of work I have become much more selective in my approach. You should only bid for this kind of work where you:

- Are already working with the client in other areas and they need to go to open tender for procedural reasons, e.g. public sector procurement. In such circumstances, you might be well placed, quite properly, to have an informal discussion as to whether it would be worthwhile bidding. After all, they already know you — they may be able to save you wasted work where they do not think you large enough or do not have suitable experience. In such circumstances, do not force the issue or you will lose other more suitable work in the future.

- Have very special expertise in the field — do not fool yourself, it would have to be very special.

- Can very closely match the requirements — again, be honest and read between the lines; will they want the security of a larger or more specialist firm?

- Know or believe that they have preference for small, local firms. One major national business based north of Leeds regards Solidus, in Nottingham (100 miles away) as local. What they meant was that we are both provincially, not London, based.

All that said, I would still sometimes send for the bid documents where the work was suitable, as it will provide valuable background research and may enable me to identify opportunities for other work in the future. Until you have seen the documents, you will not know how closely you meet the requirements or whether there are any special requirements that bidders must meet. It also gives a feel for the sort of proposal that is expected. Chapter 9 looks at the tendering process itself in more detail.

ACTION PLAN

You need to get into some serious analysis of potential competitors, customers, their needs and the services that you can provide. Treat it as a pilot consultancy project and adopt a professional approach to it.

1. Undertake PEST and SWOT analyses — determine an outline for the nature of the business and customer requirements. You may need to do further research to identify competitors and what they have to offer and to find out what potential clients are really after.

2. Determine the 4 Ps for your practice.

3. Work on your promotional strategy. Decide how you are going to let prospective customers know about your services and how they can buy them.

4. Put together a plan for your self-promotion. How are you going to raise your personal profile and professional credibility?

5. Start to develop the targets that you wish to achieve.

SUMMARY

First we considered clients' needs and wants and how they are frequently different. Change was identified as a key reason for potential clients needing consultancy support. So recognising when industries and organisations are facing significant change is a first step in marketing strategy. Services can then be tailored to address the needs created by the change.

But services can only be matched to client needs when we are clear about what our business is and what our capabilities are. It is no good identifying a marketing need if we cannot respond to it. So any consultancy has to investigate what the market wants, and what it is capable of, and to target those areas where there is real (not imagined or desired) overlap. Find and play to your strengths in the context of what is happening in the real world.

Identifying and reaching clients is not about advertising. That is expensive and only works when customers are ready to buy. It is not sufficiently well targeted for most consultants and does not usually give value for money. Also, as consultancy is essentially a people-oriented profession, salespeople are less effective than they might be; in most cases, clients buy the individual consultant, not the firm. So consultants have to do their own selling.

Direct mail with appropriate follow-up will be an important approach for the new practice. It should be highly specific to the needs of a very well-defined group, or even individual prospects. It has to attract the client's interest and demonstrate where the client will gain benefits. But as you become established, more and more new work will come from referrals through existing clients, from contacts made through your networking efforts and from your self-promotion.

As you develop your network and your personal standing, you will be increasingly recognised as someone with ideas and professional credibility. Clients who have a need for advice will then start to search you out. But it is a long, slow process, especially if your specialism is not particularly uncommon. You will then have to work harder at explaining and demonstrating why clients should use you rather than your competitors — the difference may be quite subtle and will ultimately come down to your personality and ability to develop a rapport with prospective clients.

Open tenders appear attractive but are not the panacea for the new or small practice. The work they offer is usually large-scale and will tend to favour the large established practices who have experience of such big projects. The not-inconsiderable time involved in bidding for them is probably not worthwhile for the independent consultant.

Marketing is not selling. It is about matching the consultant's skills and expertise with clients' needs and expectation. And finding ways to reach the customer and to deliver the service at a mutually beneficial price.

CHAPTER 7

FEES, PRICING AND COSTING

It is all too easy for the new consultant to set their fees at an unrealistic level on the basis that they will charge more time than is probable or by simply picking a day rate out of the air. This chapter sets out a structured approach to establishing the baseline for fee setting. Once the costs and possible income is understood it will then be possible to use that knowledge to set a fee rate based on what the market will bear and what the consultant needs to meet their aims.

By adopting this approach, the advisor will be able to monitor their new business against targets that they need to achieve to meet their business objectives.

OBJECTIVES

The aim of this chapter is to enable the reader to establish their costs and the price they need to charge to be viable. The objectives therefore are to:

1. Appreciate the difference between fixed and variable costs;

2. Consider the assumptions that must be made;

3. Show how to calculate the break-even day rates;

4. Use those break-even rates for management and for setting realistic prices.

UNDERSTANDING COSTS

Right from the start in any business, you need to understand your costs and the income that you need to meet those obligations. Without understanding your costs, you cannot establish the viability of your business or set fee rates that will allow you to stay in business. There are essentially two components: fixed and variable costs.

Fixed Costs

Fixed costs are all those costs that will be incurred even if no work is being done. These fixed costs can be changed but not at short notice. These would typically include:

- Premises, electricity, etc.

- Cars and other vehicles

- Training

- Office equipment, computers, photocopiers, etc.

A further property of fixed costs is that they do not vary as workload changes, except when the load exceeds the capacity of the costs when there is a steep increase in the fixed cost under consideration.

All the real and potential fixed costs should be identified — none should be ignored, however small. There are many costs which, although tiny on their own, in combination will be significant. So it is important to include them all and then add an additional element as contingency for all those costs that have been forgotten.

Make sure you include:

- Cost of office premises, including rent (or notional rent if freehold), rates, insurance, allowance for maintenance, etc.;

- Administrative staff — in other words employees who are not charged out directly against client work;

- Maintenance and replacement of fixtures and fittings — chairs, desks, lighting, etc. — and of office equipment — computers, software, etc.;

- Postage, especially for promotion, which will usually form the largest part of mailing costs;

- Telephones, including mobile telephones — make a generous allowance for call charges;

- Subscriptions to professional institutes, Chambers of Commerce, etc.;

- Accreditation fees;

- Training courses;

- Legal, accountancy and other professional fees;

- Books, journals, online services (e.g. Internet service provider);

- Insurance: property, employee liability, professional indemnity, premises, contents, business disruption, vehicles, third party liability, etc.;

- Depreciation of capital items such as cars, computers, special equipment, etc.;

- Expenses for travel that is not associated with clients — for example, to exhibitions, on courses, to see suppliers, etc.;

- There are a whole raft of other costs, some of which will be specific to the field in which you will be operating (laboratories, workshops, specialised equipment, etc.).

These costs mount up very rapidly and, as a rough estimate, even without being extravagant, they can easily exceed the employment cost of an experienced consultant for even a small one- or two-person practice.

Variable Costs

Variable or direct costs are those directly associated with the cost of providing the service (or manufacturing and selling the product). They would typically include:

- Consultants' salaries, including those of the owner-consultant;

- Costs incurred in travelling to clients, subsistence and hotel accommodation when working away from home;

- Cost of entertaining clients — do not go overboard, but you will want to have lunch with clients, or the occasional round of golf or similar social connection with long-standing clients;

- Material costs involved in preparing and delivering reports, etc. This would also include courier services, photocopying or printing services specific to client work.

- Production costs (research services, photocopying and printing service);

- Sub-contract staff, associate consultants;

- Sales costs (preparation of proposals, whether successful or not, selling time).

These splits are not absolute and different people will treat them in different ways. I have a colleague who argues very strongly that all costs should be considered as direct costs. His main reasoning for this is that variable costs and gross profit margins tend to be managed rather more closely than overheads. This is because direct costs are someone's responsibility, whereas fixed costs tend to be a shared pot with no single person holding responsibility for managing them, so they tend to be higher than strictly necessary. The argument is an interesting intellectual exercise, useful for making a point but not widely accepted by the accounting profession.

Also, this list of cost elements is not definitive but should be used as a basis for identifying your own list. Do not underestimate them and make sure you include all the little things, as they soon mount up.

There is plenty of guidance available. There are many books on starting a business or covering finance for the non-financial manager that will cover this area in more detail. All small business owners should have one on their shelves. Many colleges and other bodies will also provide courses of all types covering finance and the broader aspects of business start-ups. Again, the new consultant without experience of all disciplines of running a small business would be well-advised to go on some courses even if it turns out to be largely revision — learning these skills 'on the job' could be unnecessarily risky. And anyway, you will need to put all your effort into developing the fledgling business, so you must be on top of the administrative aspects from day one.

DETERMINING THE BASE RATE

We need to consider how to assess the minimum acceptable level of income that is needed to break even and determine a base charging rate for achieving that income. The calculation is simple once the fixed and variable costs have been identified.

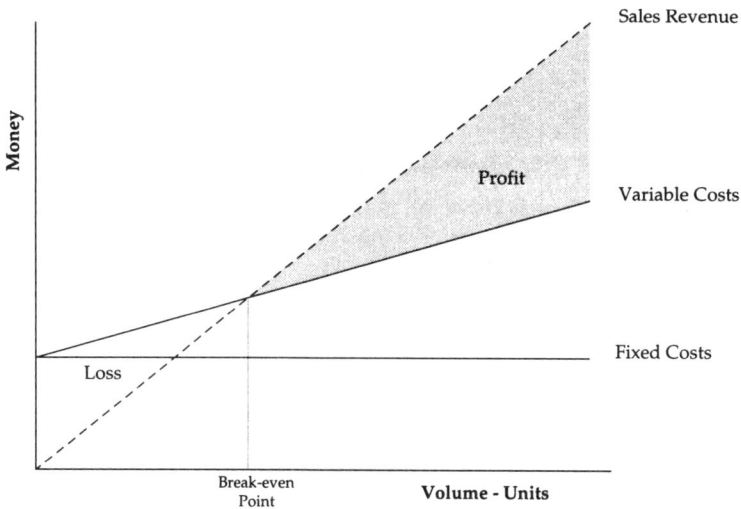

Figure 7.1: Break-even Diagram

There is one further element that needs to be determined: the number of hours (or days) that you will be able to charge to clients. Once you have taken out weekends, statutory holidays, annual leave and an allowance for sickness, most people end up with a working year of less than 2,000 hours. Most principal consultants who have administrative and sales responsibilities find that 1,000 hours is a realistic limit of chargeable time. Some years, more will be achieved, but it will, over time, tend towards an average of that sort of figure. After discussions with many consultants in a variety of consultancy specialisms that 1,000 hours was the consensus figure for chargeable hours.

As a new consultant you may need to work even fewer chargeable hours in the first year or so as you build your client base. Do not be too optimistic — that figure of a thousand hours comes from the experience of dozens of well-established consultants — you are very unlikely to consistently do any better. Even when I worked for a large professional firm they did not generally expect their principal consultants and partners to achieve more than 1,000–1,200 hours. And they had a support set-up that removed a lot of the day-to-day administrative burden from their shoulders. As a small firm or individual consultant, you will have to cover that administrative role from your working time.

It is very easy to be a busy fool, so be realistic on the amount of time you will be able to bill. Remember, we are concerned at this stage about producing revenue to cover the costs and generate sufficient personal remuneration for those in the business. If you underestimate the number of hours that you can achieve, you will have higher prices, but that is not necessarily bad. If you are then successful in billing more time than you estimated, you will make higher profits, which can be distributed to the owners and staff.

Overestimating the hours to be charged to clients and then not reaching this target will result in the business not earning enough revenue to meet its costs — an uncomfortable position, as you have to reduce personal drawings and may even have to lay off staff. This is a much worse result than underestimating billable hours.

So err on the pessimistic side, and do not be tempted to increase the hours to reduce the break-even price. If a lower price is needed, try to achieve it by reducing costs, especially the fixed costs such as extravagant cars, larger offices than strictly necessary, etc.

It is my experience that most individual consultants tend to under-price — they often seem to feel that, because they work from home, they are not 'proper' consultants. That is not the case: the only criterion that should matter in setting fees is the value given to a client and what the target client can afford. It should be remembered that many senior consultants, even from big firms, effectively work from home much of the time. Do not be apologetic about the way you are organised; that is entirely your decision, as long as you are professional in your dealings with clients.

Surprisingly, increasing prices will often result in increased revenue, even though fewer hours are worked. A colleague doubled his fees overnight, including to existing clients, and did not lose any business as a consequence. Similarly, my hairdresser increased her charges by 20 per cent on my advice and lost one marginal client out of more than 100. It would seem that clients often put higher value on us than we put on ourselves.

Costing Your Time

We now need to do a little calculation to determine our daily charge-out rate.

So far we have established F, the fixed costs, and V, the variable costs. We have discussed the number of hours, H, and from that we can determine the number of chargeable days, D, that we expect to achieve.

There is one other element that we need to consider. Profit is often forgotten in owner-managed businesses because it is not properly understood. Profit is not the reward for someone's time but for the use of their capital. It is partly to compensate for the opportunity cost of lost interest, but also for the higher risk of venture capital. So if an owner provides both capital and time, they should receive both a return on that capital from the profit and a salary for their work.

Profit also has another role: the long-term development of the business. Without profit there can be no reinvestment, and the business will decline or will need further capital injections. This is an all-too-common scenario for small owner-run businesses, as they are under-funded because of a shortage of initial investment and especially the lack of reinvested profits over time.

So we also need to consider P, the profit percentage rate in our costing. The level of profit that should be planned is more problematic. I would add somewhere between 15 and 35 per cent, but the actual figure will need to reflect interest rates, risk, the amount of capital investment, etc.

Now that we have all our variables, we can begin the calculation. Firstly:

$$D = H \div 7.5$$

The figure 7.5 is the number of working hours in a day (you may wish to use your own figure, perhaps 7 or 8, depending on your view). For our initial suggestion of 1,000 hours and 7.5-hour days, this gives 133.3 days — I would round this down to 130 days or 13 days per month. This ten-month year takes into account holidays, Christmas breaks, etc., which effectively leaves only ten months of the year in which to work the chargeable time. This is a personal approach to keep things simple.

So you calculate your day rate, R, as follows, from the required turnover, T:

$$T = (F + V) \times \frac{(1 + P)}{100}$$

where P is the required profit rate as a fraction;

$$R = T \div D$$

This rate is then the *break-even* rate. It is not necessarily the price that will be charged, but it is the lowest price that you can afford to charge. Anything less and you will be subsidising at the expense of earnings and profit.

Hygiene Factors

Having established your overall costs and your break-even price, you should now rework the calculation on the basis of a worst-case income. You need to establish what you absolutely *must* achieve to survive. These levels of income and costs are the *hygiene factors* — at this level you can keep your business healthy, albeit uncomfortable.

You need to deduct all the costs that can be shed in both the business and your private life. What is your personal survival budget if you cut out all the extras that make life pleasurable, but are not absolutely essential? These would include social activities, the weekend bottles of wine, holidays, new clothes, non-essential travelling costs (do you really need to use the car to go to the post box?), newspapers, etc. We all have many of these costs that make life more enjoyable, and many that we have simply accumulated over time. It is surprising how much many of us can remove from our personal expenditure without doing real damage to our quality of life.

The same is true of the business. What costs can we remove or avoid incurring in the first place without damaging the business and its development? Do we really need that new computer, faster printer, new car, or to stay in four-star hotels? Do we need secretaries (they are a fast-disappearing breed), or even offices? Most established businesses develop a thickening waistline with unnecessary costs — it usually takes a downturn in business before anything is done about it. Indeed reducing costs is a common consultancy role, so practice on your own business first!

Turn it into a weekly or monthly income target and do not increase your expenditure until you are exceeding that level of income consistently — and then only as absolutely necessary.

You should also work out your cash-flow projection on the basis of the hygiene factors. That way you have SMART targets that are easily monitored — with a one-person consultancy, you will probably be able to do so in your head.

With the number of chargeable days required each month established, you have most of the key factors that you will need to monitor and stay on plan.

Now you have established your hygiene factors. That is the level of income at which you can survive, albeit at a slightly slimmed-down lifestyle. As a new consultant the priority is to establish a customer base so that you meet your hygiene factor.

Setting Fees

Now you know your costs you can start to think about setting fees. Firstly, they have to cover your costs — if they do not then you will go out of business, sooner or later.

Secondly, you need to understand what the market will bear. If the market rate is less than your costs, then you have a problem and should re-examine your costs and reduce them so that they are less than the acceptable market rate. Otherwise, you will have to find a new market that will sustain the rates that you need to charge. Until you are established, I would suggest that minimising costs is easier than increasing rates on any reliable basis. So cut out all unnecessary costs and then cut out some more — if you really want your practice to fly, you will find ways of doing so.

Even if you can charge high rates, you should keep your costs to a minimum until you have an established bank balance. Consultancy work is 'feast and famine', and there will be periods where income is tight and you will be grateful for having kept your costs to the bare minimum.

The break-even day-rate calculated earlier should be used as a baseline below which you should not go when setting prices, or indeed when negotiating with clients. It is worth bearing in mind that many consultants, myself included, do not usually negotiate our fee rates; they are fixed, but we will negotiate on the scope of the work and the respective roles of client and consultant, to make the price acceptable to the client.

MARKET FORCES

Consultancy is one of those markets where a low price is not always a benefit. Over many years, I have seen as many consultants who have lost market share because they were too cheap as those who have lost because they were too expensive. Clients want to have the comfort of knowing that their consultant is good, but they have no real way of telling — so they fall back on other signs. If a consultant routinely charges high fees and has been in business for many years, then they must be good if they continue to get work. It is a bit like perfume and other luxury items — part of the benefit is in the exclusivity that comes from a high price.

However, consultancy is somewhat different in that, having sold a project to a client at a high price, the firm must deliver an appropriate level of value to justify that price. Only by doing so will the practice get repeat or referred business from the client. But if you have the skills, you can afford to do a good job if you are getting high fees — a bit of over-servicing and free added value is less painful to the profits.

However, different sectors have different thresholds of acceptable fees. The small and medium-sized enterprise market generally cannot afford to pay as much as a major multinational. Even then, there are exceptions; some smaller businesses like to be associated with 'the best' (as they see it — often, read this as 'expensive'), and are prepared to pay for such top names. Many small businesses do not like paying for what they see as extravagant cars, offices and other trappings of an expensive lifestyle — they know it comes out of their fees.

The public sector is a bit more variable. People who work in the public sector tend to be uncomfortable paying for what they see as extravagance and they often have quite a low perception of what constitutes extravagance. There is a strong tendency to be risk-averse, so often they will still choose the big names because they are 'safe' choices, even if they are expensive.

So you need to understand your prospective clients to decide what will be acceptable to them. Pitch your prices at a high enough level, but not so high as to cause them to reject you without consideration. Pitch your price at a level at which there is some resistance. If you do not get asked to negotiate on your fees, then you are too cheap and in danger of missing out on the better work. We will consider negotiating on fees and related matters separately, as there are some key issues at stake.

As a general rule, the most uncomfortable market to be in is the medium-scale market. That is where the competition is fiercest, because that is where the majority of businesses aim. It is difficult to establish yourself in this market if you want a reasonable income from consultancy. You are selling a strictly limited resource: your time. As a consultant that limits your earning power, even in a small firm. Traditionally in a professional practice, the fee-earning staff cover the overheads and the owners draw their fees as income. So the price you charge determines your maximum earning power. A low price means low maximum income. Most small and medium-sized firms do not feel that they can compete with the big firms with major international reputations.

They cannot. Or more correctly, they cannot across the breadth of industry and functional expertise. But in recent years, there has been a major growth in the number of small, 'boutique' consultancies that operate at the highest level. but in niche markets; they have adopted a focus strategy. They aim to do one particular form of consultancy very well and they can compete with the big firms. Indeed, many of the most successful boutique consultancies have been formed when complete specialist teams have moved out of the big firms.

CHARGING BASICS

However you decide to charge, you must keep it simple to make it easy for the client to buy. Do not put obstacles in the way of the client signing the contract by creating doubts about the cost in their minds.

Clients should do an investment appraisal on the project before deciding whether the returns are satisfactory. If they cannot be sure about what they are going to pay, then they cannot make that judgement. They may then choose to go with someone who is more expensive, but who has provided a degree of certainty about what they are selling. That is why I try to include all predictable expenses in the day rate so that there is minimum uncertainty about the future bills — clients seem to like it.

Day Rates

This is the traditional approach and is sometimes called 'time and materials'. Charge the client by the day, often with a minimum unit of half-a-day. There is no standard definition of a day; it can be anything from, say, 6 to 16 hours (or more). Some professional advisors (accountants and solicitors are particular examples) usually charge in units of a fraction of an hour — 15 minutes, or even less. Disbursements and other expenses are then charged on top at cost or even at cost plus an administrative charge.

Clients are often uncomfortable with such an approach, as it makes it difficult to budget and appears too open-ended a commitment. There has been a trend towards using day rates, but with a clear estimate of the total time and expenses that are likely to be incurred. Whilst this is still open-ended in practice, at least the client has a likely cost on which to base a judgement. Any consultant who has the client's good at heart will not hit the client with a bill that is over the estimate without giving good notice that work is taking longer than expected and making suggestions as to how the client might mitigate the cost overrun. The client should always be given a way of keeping the cost affordable —

perhaps by changing the scope or doing more of the work themselves. In the worst case, they should have the option of aborting the work at the earliest possible opportunity if it is going to overrun. However day rates are used, the client is taking the risk on cost and should be in a position to manage the budget.

Time and material assignments will normally be billed at the end of each month on the basis of the work undertaken in the month. Payment terms will then be due on whatever basis was agreed in the contract. Such terms are subject to mutual agreement and can be varied to suit the project in hand. There is no fixed approach.

I even know of consultants who bill in advance, so that the first payment is due at the end of the first month's work. In that way, they improve cash flow and are never owed more than a month's fees by clients. Needless to say, many clients are not keen on such an approach. Billing at the end of one month for work done, with payment due by the end of the next month, is probably the most common form of terms and conditions.

Fixed-Price Contracts

With fixed-price work, the consultant is taking the financial risk. That means the consultant must have a very clear view of the scope of the work and the ability of the client to deliver their part of the project. It also puts considerable onus on the consultant's planning, estimating and project management skills.

The terms of reference should make the respective roles of the client and the consultant very clear — if the client does not perform, then the consultant will want to recover their additional costs on the basis of their normal day rate (or whatever basis is agreed in the contract).

Results-Based

Results-based consultancy is probably one of the best ways of achieving exceptionally high charge-out rates. The downside is that the consultant takes all the risk, so it is not generally applicable. For results-based fees to work, there has to be a readily measurable outcome over which there will be little argument and on which the consultant can have a direct impact.

The consultancy practice planning to use results-based fees must not be in a position where they require other parties to achieve their targets. The results must be in the sole control of the consultants.

This approach is attractive to the client, in that they are passing the risk of using consultants on to the consultants themselves. If the consulting firm is not sufficiently confident that they can deliver the required results to put their money on the line, why should the client? However, if the consultant is successful, they will get a bigger fee than if they had worked on a day rate — that is their reward for taking the risk.

I encountered an example recently where a tax consultant worked with an organisation on a results-based fee. He saved the client £700,000 in the first year and took a fee of 10 per cent. The consultant had spent about a week on the work, so he had earned around £2,000 per hour! But the client had clearly benefited and had had excellent value, even excluding the fee of £70,000 — a tenfold return on investment in a few weeks is excellent by any standards.

The client had accountants, internal and external auditors and others who had been unable to realise that saving — it was only the consultant's knowledge and expertise that had made it possible so quickly. To be fair, the client was delighted and did not quibble that the work took so little time. As similar people have said, it is not just the few days of work that are being bought by the client, but the many years of training, research and study that made it possible to do the work so quickly.

By the way, that consultant will get a percentage, albeit much smaller, of savings made in the second and third years as a result of the changes to the accounting practices that he put in place as part of the original work. Nice work if you can get it!

Of course, when thinking about charging results-based fees, remember that you need to pay your practice overheads and your mortgage. Often results-based fees will not be realised until some time after the work is completed — sometimes as much as twelve months or more. During that time, you will still have payments to make, so only do it if you are supported by other income until the fees appear. Many results-based fees are therefore actually a mixture of a day rate or fixed price at a reduced rate, with the results element being a bonus. In that way, the cash flow is improved and the risk is shared. In such cases, the shared risk means that the final bill will lie somewhere between that of a traditional price and the purely results-based fee.

Retainers

Some consultancy roles work best by using some form of retainer. This is particularly appropriate for facilitative and more occasional services that are needed little and often. For instance, when acting in such a role, you and the client may want their staff to be able to call you without having to worry about getting approval for the expenditure each time. That would be an unnecessary burden. By making a commitment to pay for a certain amount of support over an extended period, the client can get a competitive rate as you have the comfort of having a secure income stream with regular payments. This helps the consultant minimise the impact of the 'famine and feast' associated with project-based work.

Usually the agreement is for a typical minimum level of support each month, often expressed in days. Any work exceeding that agreed level can be handled in one of two main ways. The extra time can be subject to an extra bill at a day rate, usually the same as the retainer day rate. Or it may be carried forward and balanced over a longer period — say, quarterly — and if there is still excess time used, then a balancing bill will be raised. If the retained amount of consultancy is not used up over the period, the consultancy benefits as the client would not usually get a refund — that is the risk they take by making a commitment to pay at the lower rate. The client also benefits by knowing that the consultant will be available to them at the agreed level.

This is a guideline to the typical approach. There are many variations. Some retainers are merely to ensure that the advisor will be available when needed; all time used is charged at an agreed rate. I have seen cases where, if the time used was less than an agreed level, there would be a refund to the client at the end of the accounting period used for balancing the time. Refunds rarely happened, because the client, having made a commitment to use the consultant, found it easy to do so and used them more often than they would have if they had had to authorise the expenditure each time.

As a consultant, I am fond of retainers, as they smooth the otherwise bumpy cash flow and give great comfort in that there is an underlying income, even in quiet months. I worked for one firm where, for a period, most work was on a retainer basis; this meant that business was generating income from regular monthly payments. With project work, the cheques were much more erratic, even though the turnover was much the same — but the bank charges and administrative costs were higher.

Others . . .

The payment bases described above are only a few of the possibilities. And each of them is subject to many different variations. There is a wide variety of other ways of being paid — I have even seen barter used, although how it is accounted for in the books I am rather less sure. Other possible approaches include some form of equity stock through stock options or similar methods. Work with the client to find the most mutually beneficial arrangement.

At the end of the day, the billing and payment terms must suit two requirements. They have to be affordable and manageable by the client, so the simpler they are to understand, the easier it will be for the client to buy your services. Secondly, the payment terms have to provide you with just rewards for your time and expertise and to provide a cash flow that will allow you to meet your financial commitments.

Expenses and Other Issues

Many consultancy firms charge expenses such as travelling and subsistence in addition to the day rate. Some even charge secretarial time and other support services separately. I prefer to include routine travelling, support and subsistence expenses in the day rate or the fixed price. I do charge for exceptional travelling, such as air tickets, hotels (unless they are part of the routine costs), or specialised/excessive support.

I have never been asked to detail my expenses. In part, that is because most of them are built into the day rate and therefore already agreed. But even where there are additional chargeable expenses, I have never been asked — mainly, I believe, because I detail their nature in the engagement letter and I ensure that they are reasonable. Indeed, I will usually agree what constitutes a reasonable level — type of hotel, airline class, etc. — in advance. I usually use the client's standard mileage rate for travelling by car.

However, some clients may wish to see receipts, so you should be prepared and able to justify the expenses. Expenses certainly should not be loaded or excessive. I might include a glass of wine with a meal in the evening, but I would certainly not include any more than that.

Where possible, it is probably better to let the client arrange and pay directly for exceptional expenses such as rail and air tickets, hotels, etc. This serves two purposes. It gives the client some control and comfort that the expenses are being incurred at an appropriate level (I would suggest on the same basis as the client's directors and senior managers). It also reduces the consultant's administrative burden and the need to fund the expenses from working capital. Indeed, to encourage clients to pick up such costs directly, some consultancy firms add charges of up to 15 per cent to cover administrative costs.

Travel time is a difficult issue and there seem to be almost as many approaches as there are consultancy firms. This is discussed in Chapter 11, but you will have to come to your own conclusions, depending on the nature of your client base and what is accepted practice in your field. If you are giving value and are being reasonable with the time being charged, clients tend not to query the actual figure — but that is definitely NOT a justification to load the time on the bill.

DO NOT BE TOO CHEAP!

Cheap consultancy is not valued by the client, so they will frequently not carry it through to implementation. Clients who are driven by price will be the most demanding but will give little in the way of help or job satisfaction — they are to be avoided. The same is true of grant-aided consultancy — personally I avoid it, but I know of some consultants who are happy with it and the clients it brings.

A colleague working on his own was doing quite well, but although he had a blue-chip background and only wanted to work part-time, he was earning particularly low rates. On my advice, he went back to his clients to discuss the benefits he was providing and doubled his rates overnight — his clients recognised that the benefits they were getting easily justified the increased rates. We are now working together and in the process of increasing rates by another 60 per cent — his rates will have trebled in three years. There is no point in being a busy fool — earn more per day and work fewer days if you only want to reach a particular income.

ACTION PLAN

This action plan will help you to establish a costing for your new practice and allow you to prepare the other financial plans.

1. Work out the fixed costs for your practice; allow some contingency for unidentified costs, but do try to quantify as many as possible;

2. Work out your variable costs, including your own salary, and do not forget costs such as social security, taxes, etc.;

3. Decide on your assumptions about chargeable hours, profit rate, etc. Do not be too optimistic on what you can achieve;

4. Calculate your break-even day rate and use this as a basis to set the actual rate you will charge. From that, calculate your planned income which will be higher than the break-even figure you originally used;

5. Prepare forecast profit-and-loss accounts and balance sheets;

6. Prepare a rolling twelve-month cash flow forecast;

7. Determine your hygiene factors and other vital signs for monitoring and control.

SUMMARY

Before launching a consultancy practice, you will need to set your prices. Although prices should be set on the basis of the value of your service to the customer and with reference to what the marketplace will accept, it is necessary to understand your costs.

There are essentially two main groups of costs: fixed costs, which are incurred whether or not you do any business; and variable costs which are (largely) dependent on the level of business activity. The distinction is not absolute, but there are accounting conventions that tend to suggest which costs go where. However the costs are treated from an accounting point of view is largely immaterial as far as the costing process is concerned. The important thing is to understand how the costs and business activity interact so that a break-even price can be established.

As well as understanding costs, there is also need to make a few assumptions. Perhaps the key one is the number of chargeable hours that will be achieved in the year ahead. Typically for a sole consultant or a senior consultant in a small practice, the number of chargeable hours will be around 1,000 in an average year. This seems to be largely unaffected by the consultancy specialism or the country in which the consultant operates. In larger practices, the target chargeable hours for a senior consultant or partner is probably closer to 1,500 hours, but they have more administrative support, and in some cases more customers 'walk in through the door' — they do not have to be found.

In many small firms (not just in consultancy), the owner-manager tends to treat their salary and business profits as the same. They often do not build their salary into profit. This is a serious mistake as it means that the business is not generating funds for re-investment or as a return on the capital employed. Profit should be added to the costs before establishing the break-even day rate, so that the business will generate the funds it needs to develop.

From all that, it is a simple matter to calculate the minimum day rate that will meet the business's commitments. That should be used as a baseline below which other factors should not cause the price to fall. These other factors include the state of the market, the customer value being provided; competition should then be the arbiter of the final day rate that is adopted, with the pro-viso that it must be higher than the break-even rate.

When setting prices, it must be borne in mind that, to a very large extent, consultancy is worth what the client pays for it. They do not give the same credence to cheap (including grant-aided) consultancy as to high-cost consultancy. Often revenues can be increased even though fewer hours are worked, by increasing charge-out rates. Professional advice is a bit like perfume: the customer needs to feel that there is some exclusivity or something special about the advisor. And that judgement is often made largely on the price charged.

CHAPTER 8

ESTIMATING

As a consultant you will frequently be called upon to estimate your costs so that the client can use them to set a budget; you will also need them yourself later for the proposal. You therefore need a consistent and reliable way of estimating the work involved in a project.

You should use experience from previous projects to refine your estimating process. So even if you are not billing by the hour or the day, you will need to record your time and expenses so that you can compare actual costs with the original (and any revised) estimates for the project. As with most management processes, it is a closed loop of plan, perform, monitor and feedback into the plan, with appropriate control action.

Bear in mind that the process described in this chapter is a generic approach based on the way I develop estimates. Your practice and approach may well be different to reflect your specific needs but I believe the process described is a sound starting framework for all consultants.

OBJECTIVES

The objectives for this chapter are simple:

1. To demonstrate how a complex project can be broken down into manageable elements for estimating the associated costs;

2. To appreciate the need to identify benefits that will allow the client to justify the expenditure on consultancy support.

KEY STEPS

The approach suggested here is that which I and many of my colleagues have used over the years. It is straightforward and easy to follow.

Define Objectives

As with all planning processes, it is important to decide and document what the desired outcome will be. What is to be achieved?

Whilst it will be necessary eventually to formalise the goals into SMART objectives with clear and measurable outcomes, at this stage a broad definition will suffice. The definition must be precise enough to determine what work will be required and what benefits will accrue to the client if those objectives are met.

Identify Benefits

From the objectives and the client's requirements it will be possible to put together some estimate of the benefits that the client will achieve. These should be expressed in financial terms, even if the benefit is not directly financial. A good starting point in such circumstances is to ask the question: 'How much would it cost using the current set up to achieve that same change in performance?' That will be sufficient in many situations to give a financial value for an otherwise subjective or, at least, non-financial benefit.

The benefits will have to justify the costs incurred in their achievement, so they are an important part of the estimating process. Unfortunately they tend to be ignored and only the costs are considered until it is realised, too late, that the benefits are not being achieved or do not justify the investment.

Decide Approach

Having set out the objectives and made an assessment of what is required, a suitable approach can be chosen. The choice of approach may well have an impact on the benefits to be achieved and even on the overall objectives, so it will probably be necessary to re-assess the rewards from the work.

Indeed, this is a feature of most planning processes; there is so much interaction between different elements and phases that there should be an iterative loop. In such circumstances it may be wise to go back to earlier steps and revise them in the light of experience from later steps, which in turn will be affected by that revision. Eventually the plans should settle into an integrated whole.

The chosen approach is important, as it will determine the work that has to be done, who will do it and the timetable. From that will come the detailed tasks and subsequently the costs.

High-level Task Groups

Most projects are too large to consider as single entities, so it will be necessary to break them down into series of more manageable sub-projects or groups of high-levels tasks. Such a breakdown may be fairly arbitrary, although experience will tend to suggest obvious groupings.

For example, on a major computerisation project I would probably break the project down into four main groups:

- *Software:* The specification selection and implementation of the programs to be run on the hardware;

- *Hardware:* The choice of computers, printers, etc., and their implementation;

- *Change management:* Handling the changes to working practices, involving users and others in the process;

- *Training:* There will usually be training needs in various parts of the organisation, both related to the new equipment and software, and also more general skills development.

With very large projects, those initial groups may need to be broken down further. It is important to note that these elements must not be treated in isolation, as they will have an impact on each other. In the example above, many of the change issues will have been identified in advance of the computerisation project and the new systems will be designed to support those changes. Similarly, the choice of software will determine, in part at least, the hardware that will be required, and so on.

Eventually, each element will be broken down into tasks that can be considered as an entity. This may work through several layers — it will all depend on the size and complexity of the project and the accuracy that is required of the estimate.

Bear in mind that there are other tasks that do not necessarily sit with the basic approach but are still essential. These include the overall project management, with the appropriate progress meetings and reporting requirements to management and colleagues outside the project team. There are also the milestone meetings and decision points where the 'hold or go' decisions should be made, along with re-examination of the business case and investment decisions. As many of these will involve expensive, high-ranking people the cost of such elements may well be significant.

Assign Resources and Responsibilities

Once the tasks are identified it will be necessary to assign resources to them and decide who is to take responsibility for the work. This allocation of resources is a key part of making the project cost effective. All work should be undertaken by people at a suitable level.

There are two key reasons for this. The obvious one is that a senior person is too expensive to use on low-level work. The second is that responsibility taken at an appropriate level raises everyone's job satisfaction. Generally people like to use their skills and their job satisfaction comes from using their training effectively — that certainly should be the case throughout a professionally run office. People who enjoy their work will do a better job. I worry when I see so-called consultants who are happy doing menial work that should and could be delegated to their own staff or to the client's people — I seriously question their suitability to be consultants. That said, there will always be times when this happens because other resources are not available and the job simply has to be done.

Resource allocation is not just about people. In many projects, there may be other resources — capital equipment, for instance — which must be made available to achieve particular tasks. There will be costs associated with such items and those costs may well be far more than the cost of the people involved — for example, the use of a pilot plant on a chemical engineering project. These costs need to be included in the estimate.

Estimate Costs by Task

In many consultancy projects, the main costs will be the time of the people involved. Each task should have its costs estimated using people with skills appropriate to the work involved. An educated guess can be made about the amount of time involved in the task, based on previous experience, which is why it is important to track costs even if they are not being used as the basis for billing.

Estimation is both an art and a science; it is based on experience, records and suitable procedures, but it can only ever be an intelligent guess. It can often mean breaking the work into increasingly refined levels of detail, but the law of diminishing returns soon comes into play. Experience comes to the fore in deciding when the work breakdown has reached a suitable level, but there is no definitive answer. It will vary, depending on the project's complexity, how similar it is to other projects in the consultant's experience, and even the purpose of the estimate.

Apart from time, there will often be other expenses that can be identified specifically for the project. These will include the team's travel costs, other specialist expertise, research materials, etc. There might be secretarial support over and above that already built into the overhead element of the consultant's costs. These must be identified for each task and added to the total cost.

Capital equipment has already been mentioned, and there may be other costs, such as materials, that need to be built in. You should know what is usual for your specialism — after all, that expertise is what the client is buying.

Total Costs

By totalling the costs for each of the tasks, including management supervision, it will be possible to arrive at an overall estimate of the cost of the project.

Estimate Elapsed Time

But the overall elapsed time can only be deduced by looking at the inter-relation between the tasks of the project. It is not possible to simply add up the time to arrive at an overall elapsed time for the work. This is important for determining cash flow, as the timing at key milestones will usually determine when invoices can be raised. This will allow the project manager to determine cash flow and when key resources will be required. It will also allow the client to decide whether the timetable meets their requirements.

These days, most people will use computerised project management to handle these aspects of the planning. Once the tasks and their relationship to each other have been entered into the system, the calculation of the timetable is a matter of seconds. This ability becomes particularly valuable when assessing the impact of changes to resource requirements or availability. The knock-on effects of a delay in one or more tasks can then be quickly assessed for the whole project.

Project Management Costs

The management costs have already been stressed but it is very easy to underestimate the project management work involved in all but the most trivial of projects. Apart from the basic tasks of ensuring delivery, there will be many ad hoc demands, such as meetings with senior management or colleagues elsewhere in the organisation, or even with different bodies such as other organisations (within the group or from outside), regulators or other interested parties.

So do not skimp on the management element of the project. You must, however, be able to justify the cost estimates, as this is an element that customers will almost invariably question. And they will usually be less effective than they promise in their own project management. So be firm about building in a proper management element.

Cost-benefit Analysis

The benefits of the work were quantified at the start, and now that the costs are known, it is possible to do a cost-benefit analysis. It may be necessary to review the benefits in the light of the more detailed knowledge of what is to be done, and therefore what should be achieved.

The first step is simply to ask: 'do the benefits justify the costs?' That can easily be seen from the two totals, with no consideration of the timing of the costs and benefits. If the costs are too high at this stage, then the investment justification for the project will not improve by applying other more sophisticated techniques.

There are usually timing difference between when the costs are incurred and when the benefits accrue. This means that the value of the benefits and costs have to be adjusted to make them comparable to take account of inflation and interest rates. Techniques such as discounted cash flow or net present value bring the financial values back to a fixed point in time. In this way they can then be compared directly. These techniques are covered in any book on finance for non-financial managers, and all consultants should be familiar with their application.

Any significant consultancy-based project should be treated in the same way as any other investment decision.

Affordability

The client and consultant can now explore the affordability of the project. If the project survives to this stage, then the estimated benefits outweigh the expenditure. The question becomes simply one of whether there is sufficient benefit to favour this project over other uses of the same money. The only other decision is whether the client can come up with the cash and the other resources at the time the project is scheduled to go ahead.

Client Expectations

The final hurdle is how the cost of the project and anticipated benefits fit with the client's expectations. Even though the project may be strictly affordable, the client may hesitate because the costs are higher than they or their budget anticipated. This may make it difficult to take the project forward despite the rewards.

In this case there are a few things that can be done to help make the project affordable.

Review Scope

One option is to review the scope of the work. With many consultancy projects, it would often be possible to have a fee range of ten to one for what is, superficially, the same piece of work, as described below. Of course it would not be the same because the scope would be different.

If the cost is too hard to swallow, even though justified, then it may be possible to reduce the depth to which the work goes. A lot of consultancy is about investigation and analysis, so it would be possible to go into less depth and still get most of the benefits. That would be one way of adjusting the scope to reduce cost. It may then be that the further detail could be treated as a follow-on project, if still needed, when the budget becomes available.

Alternatively, if the detail is important, the width of the work may be constrained by focusing on the core of the problem that will deliver the most benefit. Again, this will often produce most of the benefits whilst making real cost savings. As before, the option to consider the other areas as a future project would still exist. The results may look much the same, even though there would be a wide spread in the proposed cost.

Balance Resources and Responsibilities

If there is no mileage to be gained in adjusting the scope, then there may be a way of reducing the consultancy bill by re-balancing the respective resource input and responsibilities of client and consultancy. In many projects, the consultant is asked to do work that could equally be performed by the client's own staff at a lower cost. The usual problem is making such people available — often they get pulled in too many directions because the new work is largely additional to their existing functions.

Skill Mix

Finally, there may be some way of adjusting cost by varying the skill mix. The opportunity for doing so should be limited, as each part of the work should only have been planned for the least expensive person available with the appropriate skills. If there is room to make much saving from changing the skill mix, it would suggest that the original estimate was rather 'padded'.

It is very easy for consultants to be tempted into squeezing a little out of every part of the estimate, especially the project management and the contingency. This should be avoided. If the work involved is genuinely a best estimate, then it is foolhardy and unprofessional to reduce it. Similarly, contingency should reflect the risk of the project and the scope for missed and underestimated costs. Using it as a balancing figure is bad estimating.

Contingency

In any case, contingency should be just that. It should not be needed if the estimating and project management is good. It should be used as part of the investment justification, because it may be required to complete the work. But it should not be planned as part of the expenditure — the best estimate of the cost should exclude the contingency.

Indeed no part of the contingency should be used without a full reappraisal of the progress, likely outcome, and a revised estimate of the benefits and costs to complete the work. That should be taken back to senior management for them to make a decision on the options and a new investment case. The contingency fund should not be spent simply because it is there or to protect 'sunk' costs. That would be throwing good money after bad.

SUMMARY

Estimating is a combination of art and science. Much of the work relies on experience of similar projects and understanding why previous projects were successful or not.

There are two main components to be estimated with regard to consultancy projects. The obvious element is the cost, but there is also a need to identify the value that the client will gain from going ahead with the work, especially by using the particular consultant and their approach.

Once the overall purpose is determined, the work should be broken down into units that can be considered in their entirety. This is usually a multi-stage process. First, break it down into large groups and then break each of these down further. Costs and other resource requirements can then be estimated and aggregated to get the overall picture. The breakdown may be fairly arbitrary, as the only real need is to reduce the whole to a set of manageable tasks. Their interrelationships will be considered separately as part of estimating the likely elapsed time.

Once that has been done, issues such as affordability can be considered. At that stage the scope of the work or the split of responsibilities between client and consultant can be adjusted to optimise the investment justification.

Contingency should be considered as part of the risk assessment for the work. It should not be assumed that it will be used, and indeed the project should be reviewed before any contingency monies are released. The project should still be viable, even if the contingency fund is used. The contingency fund should not be used to fit the work to the budget!

CHAPTER 9

SELLING CONSULTANCY

Consultancy is a little unusual in that using salespeople is of limited value. Clients, to a very large extent, buy the individual consultant not the firm. Consequently clients will want to meet 'their' consultancy team at an early stage in the purchasing process.

The sales process is almost as much about gathering information and finding out what the client needs as it is about actually selling the service. It is also about educating the client, as consultancy is a service that clients do not generally buy often. Therefore, they need to be guided to what a consultant can do and what is needed in their particular circumstances.

So the sales process tends to centre around a mutual agreement of what is required rather than the consultant 'selling' the service to the client.

OBJECTIVES

The objectives of the chapter are to:

1. Understand how to prepare for meeting new potential clients;

2. Appreciate the importance of all meetings, especially the early ones, both to establish the consultant's suitability and to understand the client's needs;

3. Stress the importance of making it easy for the client to buy the consultancy service and eliminating obstacles to the sale;

4. Understand the typical procurement process for advisory services.

EARLY MEETINGS

There is an old cliché that says that you only have one chance to make a first impression. A successful first meeting is an essential precursor to making a sale to a new customer. Success at the first meeting will not guarantee that you will get work from the client, but it will mean that you still have a chance. A good first meeting that does not lead to an immediate assignment will leave the door open to future discussions — remember that you chose consultancy as a long-term career.

Be Prepared

If you have followed the advice given so far, you will have done some initial research on your prospective customers. Now that you have the chance to meet them, you need to extend that research and ensure that you know as much as reasonably possible about the customer, their business, markets and industry. Being prepared shows that you are professional in your approach and that you will not be wasting the customer's time by asking obvious questions about their business.

It is not difficult to get a good feel for a major business, as there are many resources open to you. Most information you will be able to get via your personal computer from online services. If you do not subscribe to search services already, you should — it will save you time and money. But do not forget the more traditional routes, such as your local business library — there is a wealth of knowledge there.

Research Financial Performance

The most basic information you should obtain is recent financial performance. If the business is incorporated, then it will have to file accounts; these are available online through various providers. Even small companies' accounts are available, although there may be little else available on them.

Whatever field of consultancy you are in, you should know how the business is performing. This will have a major effect on what they can afford to do or indeed what they should be doing. It will also tell you whether they can afford your fees — a rather important factor!

Annual Reports

If the organisation is a public company or a public sector agency, it will produce an Annual Report. They are usually freely available and I often ask for a copy when I set up the first meeting.

Apart from the previous year's accounts, the chairperson's report and other comments will outline the company's strategy for the future. This is an important insight, especially when linked with your knowledge or research of the industry in general. Surprisingly, it is not uncommon for them to be at variance with each other. That in itself says much about the organisation.

Sales Literature

You should also get hold of product and service literature so that you will know the potential client's products. Again, you should not be asking for such basic information at the first meeting, especially as it is so easy to get hold of the details in advance. Knowing the services offered prior to the meeting allows you to use the meeting to explore how those services fit with corporate strategy and your understanding of the direction the industry is taking.

Press Coverage

If the organisation is small, there may be little press coverage available, and you might have to browse the local papers and business magazines.

However, if the organisation is substantial, there will be information available online. Most of the major newspapers now have their back issues on the World Wide Web and these can be searched. This will provide press release information from the company itself, as well as independent analysis of their performance and comparison with the rest of their industry. This all contributes to the overall picture.

Contacts' Comments

You may also have contacts who know the organisation or the industry and will be able to provide some insights. Your network will start to demonstrate its value here, especially if your contact can refer you to someone else, perhaps with the company concerned itself.

You may need to treat this information with some caution, as some of it may be from competitors of the company in which you are interested or from people who are otherwise dissatisfied with them. You need to understand their relationship so that you can put their comments into context. That said, such sources can sometimes provide information that is not otherwise available.

Know Your Message

Whether you are working alone or as part of a team you should be clear about what message you want to get across. Part of that message will be who you are as a firm, what you have achieved and why you believe you have something to offer the potential client. This is essential as part of establishing credibility, which will then be confirmed by how you handle the rest of the meeting.

You will need to explain, perhaps in some detail, what you know about the clients and their challenges, and why you can help. This will have to be in terms that differentiate you from the many other consultants that the client may know. You will have to walk a tightrope between assuming too much, which means you appear to prejudge the solutions, and being too vague, indicating a lack of knowledge about the client and their industry and thereby not offering anything of real interest. You will need to give enough away, but no so much that the client does not need to use you. All that has to be planned and rehearsed in advance.

As a team, you will also need to have agreed what you are prepared to give away or what commitments you, as a firm, are prepared to make. Everyone who attends these early meetings should have a clear reason for being there. No one should say anything or make promises that come as a surprise to their colleagues. All too often, sales people will promise things that technicians are uncomfortable with or technicians will say things through lack of commercial awareness, undermining the sales message.

Have a Strategy

You should have a strategy for the meeting, especially if you will be attending with clients. You will need to be flexible, but you should decide who is to do what and what role each person is to take. But you should also be flexible and in a position so that any-one can take on any role — one of you may have a bad day or may not click with one or more of the potential customers.

Have an Achievable Objective

Before you go into a sales meeting, you should have a clear idea of your minimum objective. A first meeting may simply have the aim of developing some mutual understanding and laying the foundation for making a fuller presentation a week or two later.

The eventual aim should be to get to the stage where you are asked to prepare terms of reference for a particular project, per-haps through a series of meetings.

We recently had a series of meetings with a new client in an industry where we had little specialist knowledge. After our ini-tial research and approach by mail the process was:

- An initial 'getting to know' each other meeting; for us, to un-derstand why the client was interested in what we had said in our letter; and for them, to discover if they could work with us as people. Our aim was to return with a more specific presen-tation agreed on at that first meeting.

- After further research we made a presentation and our contacts at the client firm agreed to put it to several of their colleagues. Our aim was to reach a meeting to discuss specific projects for which they had requirements. We did not achieve this at the meeting but we were subsequently invited back to do just that.

- We met the directors responsible for the area to be explored. Our aim was to be invited to do the work, or at least to make a formal proposal with draft terms of references. We were asked to make the proposal.

- After an exchange of correspondence, we were asked to meet to discuss finer points of the engagement letter, and our aim was to reach agreement on these issues. That is what we achieved and we were also able to agree the timetable for the work.

- The next meeting was the start of the project and a long-term relationship that has resulted in regular work from this one client.

Establish How Long the Meeting is to Last

It is important to know how long the client's representatives have for a meeting. If they do not suggest how long it should last, then you, as the consultant, should set a time limit. The aim should be to make it slightly shorter than you would ideally like. That will keep you to the point and ensure that you do not overstay your welcome. It will also help prevent you talking yourself out of the work — I have seen too many jobs missed because the consultancy presentation team talked the client out of it.

Ideally, the meeting length should be established when arranging the meeting so that you can prepare for the time you will have. Bear in mind that at the first meeting, you will want the client to talk more than you do. If the length of the meeting is not agreed beforehand, then it should be established at the opening of the meeting.

Stick to the agreed timetable, unless of course the client asks you to stay on to get into more detail. But bear in mind that you do not want to appear short of work so do not let the meeting become open-ended — as far as the client is concerned, you have other things that you need to do. It will be good practice for when you are busy; at that stage, good time management will be essential to meeting your promises (you will find yourself working in all sorts of odd moments).

What Does the Client want from the Meeting?

You need your own objectives for the meeting, but the potential customer will also have their own aims. You must help them achieve these whilst still meeting your own. If you address their needs, you will earn credibility and be well on the way to turning them into a client.

The prospective client will have arranged the meeting with relatively little knowledge of you and what you do. Indeed, they may well only have a one-page sales letter to go by. The content of your correspondence will give you clues as to what interests them. Combined with your research — you know more about them than they do about you — you should have some possible ideas about why they are seeing you.

However, that understanding will be very sketchy and you cannot assume that you are right. So you need to explore the whys and wherefores as part of the initial meeting. You may well have to arrange a further meeting or some other response to meet their expectations. You should not jump to conclusions or provide instant solutions — glib answers will not be credible. You should aim to arrange another meeting so that you can present a considered and highly pertinent response. At the very least, you should ensure that they will be responsive to further information from you to address their issues. We will discuss this in more depth shortly.

Weigh up Company, Person, Culture

You should weigh up the people you are dealing with and understand the approach and culture of the organisation. You must be able to demonstrate some sympathy with the culture and, perhaps, a willingness and ability to challenge those views in an understanding way.

You may be able to do that as part of the pre-meeting research by looking at what community and other projects they support. Also, by investigating the background of the people at the head of the organisation, you will be able to get a feel for the likely nature of the organisation and its culture.

If you are invited, accept any offer to walk round the premises with the client and show an interest in what they do. And if you get the opportunity, ask the people actually doing the work about what they do. But do not be too searching at this stage; keep it to pleasantries and general background. Keep it friendly and simple.

Use such opportunities to assess the mood of staff, how well things are laid out, how busy people appear, what sort of pictures or charts (if any) are on the wall — this will speak volumes about how the company sees itself and how the staff regard it. The general ambience will speak volumes if you are sensitive to it.

If you do not get the chance, and in many cases it will not be necessary or appropriate, then you will have to make do by keeping your eyes open as you are taken to and from the meeting room. It is surprising how much you can learn by spending a short while in reception and taking a brief walk through the building. It takes practice, but learn to really see what is happening without it being obvious that you are being nosy!

Do Not Try Too Hard to Please

It is very easy to accede to every request by the potential client, but you should not do so. You are a professional and your services are valuable — do not be ashamed of that and ask for the fees that reflect that professionalism.

Also, many clients will be looking for a strong personality who can help them drive change through their organisation. They will not be happy to use someone who gives in at the first sign of outside pressure. Successful business leaders have achieved their position by doing what is necessary, and they will expect their advisors to be as strong as them. They rarely appreciate 'yes' people — there be more than enough such people within their organisation. They want people with opinions and knowledge, who are prepared to argue the merits of different views with them on equal terms — such top people often do not have such an opportunity with their colleagues.

They often want strong-minded people and will deliberately test a consultant — be prepared to say no and walk away. More than once, I have been called back and we have got down to discussing the real issues and how we would address them.

As a consultant you are being recruited for your expertise and ideas — be proud of them.

Do Not Promise the Earth

Reputation for excellence is about exceeding the client's expectations, so you need to manage those expectations. You have to be able to promise — and of course deliver— benefits that are of sufficient value for the client to engage you. But you should not promise the undeliverable — if the client asks for something that cannot be guaranteed or even achieved, then do not be browbeaten into agreeing to do so. To achieve what is asked is merely what the client is paying for, so no special credit is due to you.

Failure to meet even an unreasonable expectation (that you promised) means your reputation suffers — you failed!

The art is to promise sufficient to make the work attractive to the client as long as it is well within your capabilities, but no more. If you then deliver the extra when you do the work, you gain a valuable boost to your reputation.

Under no circumstances should you agree to any result that you cannot control. If the achievement of an agreed objective requires a certain level of performance by the client or other third party, do not put your reputation on the line. Do not even do so conditionally — the provisos will not be remembered and you will not get any benefit by pointing out to an unhappy customer that it was their fault! They simply will not accept it. Remember that as a consultant you are a professional scapegoat, so your place is likely to be seen in the wrong.

Do Not Give Things Away

At Solidus, we do very little work that is not paid for by a client. We might occasionally do a few hours of analysis to demonstrate our capabilities as part of the sales process with a potential client. But it will usually be of a form that can be reused for other similar clients. If you do not put a value on your time, why should the client? I have worked for larger consultancies that did complete client projects, free of charge, in industries in which they were trying to establish a reputation. Whilst they had some success in one or two instances, in many cases it was simply an expensive failure — the typical success rate was less than 50 per cent.

We have found that we can achieve the same result by research, analysis and creativity. We have expanded into new industries in this way, and once you start talking to senior people you will soon develop a good feel for the issues. As an admitted newcomer you can ask penetrating questions that would not be acceptable from established players in the sector.

Do not buy work by discounting your fees. If you can give the benefit that you promise, then fees should not be an issue. You should be able to demonstrate that the fees justify the benefits to the client. If they do not, why should the client use you?

But it is not straightforward; the personal tax departments of many accounting firms have a problem. The amount of work involved in preparing most tax returns is much the same. A few clients will get major tax savings, but most of the others will not — should they all be billed for the work involved? Or should they be billed on some basis that reflects the benefits achieved for the client? Perhaps the accountants should charge a modest fee for the time saved for all the clients on the preparation of the return and then an additional fee as a proportion of the tax saved? I will leave you to come to your own conclusion.

If you give discounts or do free work, the client may expect the same for all their work. If they are so price-sensitive, it is likely that there will be other problems. Also, do not discount the first stage on the promise that future work will be at a higher price. Think about it from the client's point of view. You were able to do the first piece of work at a given rate; why can't you do all the work at that rate? I do not have a simple answer because I do not believe there is one. And what happens if there is no future work? In that case you will end up doing *all* your work at your entry price.

You are, I assume, seeking to offer a quality product — do not cheapen it by covering it with 'money-off' or 'sale' stickers. Look on the High Street: the upmarket shops do not use price offers (except perhaps for an annual sale) — they are quiet, restrained, expensive and proud of it. They distinguish themselves by studiously avoiding that trap — so should you. Most successful consultancies of which I am aware never sell on price — they sell on the benefits justifying the cost. We do not meet much resistance.

Be Yourself

Providing professional advice is largely a personal service. It is about mutual trust and respect between the client and the advisor. If the people do not get along, then the project will probably not be entirely successful. Generally that problem is resolved before the contract is awarded — if the client does not feel comfortable with you then they will not engage you.

So relax and be yourself. You do not need to put on false airs and graces. Get to know the client and let them get to know the real you. I am talking about personality and sense of humour, not your life history. All through my career I have found that if you and the client can still giggle about silly problems in the early hours of the morning when you are doing an 'all-nighter', then the relationship is right. I have faced that situation more than once when acting as a trouble-shooter.

Be Prepared to be Firm

It is an old adage that 'the customer is always right' and, like so many sayings, it is at best a half-truth. Customers are often wrong and sometimes they need to be told so. Sometimes prospective clients will deliberately say things they know to be wrong as a test — they want to see if you are strong enough to defend your arguments and fight for what you believe. They may just be bloody-minded or they may need someone who is strong enough to meet the challenge they will face from their staff. The latter rarely want 'Yes' people as consultants — they have enough of those within their organisation. Such clients often want to get at the truth, which they do not believe they are getting from within the organisation.

So if your ideas and beliefs are genuinely based on good knowledge and understanding, be prepared to argue them robustly. Do not get angry; whatever you do you must retain control. Acknowledge the merit in the client's arguments, and if necessary flex your ideas, if you can do so without compromising their integrity, but do not cave in. If the prospective client does not respect you and your views, then you are never going to work together effectively, so you have nothing to lose.

But do not be too pushy, especially with regard to trying to close the sale. Understand the sales process, trial closes and the like, but use them naturally. If you have to think about it, it will be obvious that you have read the manual on selling. If you want to practise, try using the techniques when negotiating with your children — if they are teenagers it will be far tougher than most of your potential consultancy clients!

Listen

When you have won a first meeting with a potential client, it is very tempting to try to sell yourself to them. As a result you may talk too much. As an advisor, you should aim to listen more than you talk. Ask questions that encourage the client to explain the challenges as they see them, and lead them into related areas. People like talking about themselves, their job and the organisation. They will come out of meetings where they did most of the talking, suggesting that the meeting was good and useful and feeling very positive about the other person. You will rarely sell consultancy at a first meeting, so use it to research what the client says they want and to understand what they really need. Then you can prepare your presentation for a second or subsequent meeting — remember what your objective is for the meeting.

Show You Understand — Make Sensible Comments, Ask Sensible Questions

Make your questions pertinent; avoid the trivial or flippant. You are professional and your time and that of the client is valuable, so treat it as such. But a little humour can be useful from time to time — the meeting is also about getting to know each other after all.

Be Careful: Do Not Jump to Conclusions/Solutions

In an effort to impress, it is all too easy to over-estimate your own understanding or to jump to conclusions. You do not have to find the answer in a half-hour meeting; that is why there is a consultancy assignment to discuss. Remember, the client will have been thinking about the issues for some time, so it is likely that the 'easy' solutions do not work for some reason. Do not demean the capability of the client by suggesting you know what is required after five minutes. If nothing else, it will reduce your fees!

The Client is not the Same as . . .

The client's requirements or problems are not the same as those you met at a previous client firm. However similar they might appear, the client is different, the staff are different and many of the technical issues will have different nuances. If it is very similar, then you should be well placed to ask the questions that show that you understand the challenge and can bring benefits to the client.

You want to make clients feel special, so telling them that they are just like others will be counter-productive. The client will want reassurance that you have dealt with similar problems, but that they were not as interesting, complex or subtle as their particular challenge. Massage their ego and pander to their perception of the uniqueness of their problem. They want to feel loved, so show you care enough to really understand them and their problem and that you can help them with those special requirements.

Meet Promises with Regard to Follow-up

Whatever you agree to do, you must achieve it. It is the first opportunity that the prospective client will have of assessing your capabilities in that respect. Do not waste it. If you promise a paper in a week get it there in 4 days. If you promise to call them the following day, do so, whatever inconvenience it causes you.

That also stresses the point made earlier about not promising the undeliverable — whatever you agree to do as a follow-up, make sure it is possible before you make or accept the offer. This applies in the sales process probably even more than in a paid assignment. When working on procurements for clients I frequently score suppliers down for failing to return telephone calls or taking longer than agreed or appropriate to supply additional information, even prices. And I will often rule them out completely when they demonstrate poor performance in this respect. After all, if they cannot be bothered to work at the sale, what are they going to be like on delivery or support?

If you have to apologise, you have effectively blown your chances.

Keep the Door Open

Whatever objective you set yourself for a meeting, there should always be an overriding aim: to keep the lines of communication open. You need to leave any sales meeting with an opportunity to go back to the prospective customer some time in the future. It may not be appropriate to return straight away — they may have made it clear that there is no business to be done or you are not suitable. However, you want there to be an implicit 'at the present time' which leaves the door open for you to return with a different proposition.

To do that, the consultant must use the information collected before the first meeting — both specific information on the issue at the centre of the discussion and as comprehensive a background as possible on the organisation and its associated challenges. That will provide a 'hook' on which to hang some new offering in the future.

Typically, we use a first meeting with major clients to allow them to find out if we are credible and the sort of the people with whom they can do business. For our part we want to find out what are the key issues that have prompted them to meet us — such organisations rarely meet people because 'it might be interesting'. They value their time too much to waste it speculatively on suppliers. So we know they are interested in what we have to say; we need to build on that and find out more so that we can go back for a second meeting with an offering that addresses their needs in a highly targeted way. Sometimes it takes more than one meeting to get to that stage — with large organisations, the sales cycle can easily take six months, even a year.

Find Reason to Write with Additional Information

During the meeting you may be able to find a reason for writing with additional information. For instance, if you publish a newsletter you may get an opportunity to offer to send it to them. You may discover some interest peripheral to the current discussion on which you have a discussion paper or an interesting article. Do not cloud the current conversation, but note it in case the process comes to a halt — it may provide an opportunity to write and hopefully reopen a door that had quietly closed.

Finish in Good Time

As you have established how long the meeting is to last, you should aim to finish in good time so that the client can concentrate on your closing comments rather than worrying about their next meeting. Those final remarks are vital as they lead directly to the next step in the sales process, whether it be to prepare terms of reference or to agree that you will write with more details. You should summarise the key points of the meeting and make sure that the next step is agreed with the prospective client so that there is no misunderstanding.

Once that is all done, say your 'goodbyes', shake hands and leave with a genuine smile — however it went.

Leave-behinds

Many people like to be able to leave something behind — hence the need for a brochure. But you should have covered most of that ground in establishing your credentials. Whatever you leave should contribute to what was discussed at the meeting. That means it can be difficult to leave behind anything meaningful at first meetings.

At Solidus, we do not operate a standard approach on this matter, except that what we do leave is relevant to the possible client and provides thoughts and ideas that are additional to the discussion. Often we will take something 'in case', but will not leave it if the discussion takes us into areas that make the leave-behind document less relevant. We will send something more suitable through the post.

So make sure anything you use is highly relevant to the discussion and especially to any needs expressed by the client. Be flexible and do not leave it behind if it will not add positively to the meeting — it must continue to sell your services without you being there to explain it.

Typically, such 'leave-behinds' might be a brief analysis of a particular management issue in the client's industry. It would come from our own research in preparing for the initial marketing effort to the sector, but usually with some customisation to suit the client.

If at First You Don't Succeed . . .

Success comes from persistence, if the basic product or service is right for the potential customer. So you should not give up at the first failure, but you also must be careful not to irritate your contact by badgering them every few weeks. Stay in touch in a low-key way and avoid overt selling — let the opportunity arise. I have still got work from clients after four years of occasional communication.

But persistence is not just necessary with customers you have already met. New contacts need to be developed continuously, and that requires persistence, even — especially — when sales are not low. It is easy to get disheartened and give up sending those letters and making those telephone calls, but they are the lifeblood of any consultancy practice. This persistence counts, not just for new prospects but also to keep in touch with a growing network of contacts and prospective clients.

Final Step

Having left the meeting, you should not leap into your car and head straight to your next meeting or home. Rather you should find yourself somewhere to sit quietly and review the meeting and make or add to your notes — there will be several key moments. I usually go for a cup of coffee, as it provides a slightly more relaxed atmosphere than in the car in the client's car park.

In the meeting, important information will have been provided, there will have been acknowledgement (perhaps only through body language) of particular points of agreement or disagreement. You will realise that there were issues raised that you missed or points that you failed to make. Record them so that you can address them in your next meeting or correspondence.

Finally, ask yourself: 'Did I/we achieve what we wanted from this meeting — and if not, why not?'. Then you can analyse the reasons so that you do even better next time.

Remember, such meetings can be either exciting or stressful, depending on your personality. But either way, the adrenaline will have been flowing and the body and mind working hard — settle it back down before doing anything else. Those few quiet moments will help keep you healthy and earning rather than sick and worried about the lack of income. You will work better as a result.

Now you can go home or on to your next meeting.

QUALIFYING PROSPECTS AND CLIENTS

As you promote each organisation from being a possible target to a client you will have to 'qualify' them. That is, you will have to make an assessment of how realistic a chance you have of making them a profitable client. Obviously, as you move closer to that objective, you will have more information on which to base such a judgement.

To be a good consultant you need good clients, so you must select those who will allow you to do good work and thereby enhance your reputation.

Ability to Pay and to Implement Recommendations

The most important judgement is that the client can afford to pay you for your work. But it goes beyond that if you are to build a reputation. You also need clients who can afford to implement your recommendations so that you can point to the benefits that they have achieved in practice. There is nothing more frustrating than doing good analysis and producing innovative solutions, only for the client to shelve them — we all need our work to bear fruit.

So make sure clients not only have enough money to pay your fees but also to carry through the project to successful implementation.

Will to Make it Work

You need clients who not only can afford to see the work through, but who are also prepared to work with the consultant to achieve the required result. It is surprising how half-hearted some clients can be. I have even had major organisations lose complete interest in a project after they commissioned me to do the work.

A major financial institution engaged me to undertake a study for them and to come up with some recommendations as to how they could address a particular problem that they faced. After the initial meeting to hand over some documents and to meet the client's project manager, I was unable to get hold of any of the key people. Indeed, after the initial meeting I could not even manage to speak to the project manager. Normally I would have suggested to the client that we abandon the project or reschedule for a more convenient time — but I could not get hold of anyone to agree to a postponement. I got so fed up that I did the work based on the paperwork I had been provided with, and billed them. What is more, they paid for the work, so I had the consolation that I got paid for the time I had wasted chasing around after them. But it left a sour taste in my mouth — the unnecessary cost had been incurred and paid for by their customers.

It was a particularly frustrating experience, but there have been many others that have been only slightly less so. I much prefer demanding clients to those who are indifferent.

Sometimes you will suspect that the client's heart is not really in the project. You will get the feeling that the client feels this is something they ought to do rather than really believing that they have to do it. In such cases, the client's limited enthusiasm often disappears leaving the project to drift.

If this situation is even suspected, I would suggest you avoid taking it on. Nobody will be satisfied with the result and it is very easy for the client to get locked into doing work that is going nowhere. Their profits and your reputation will suffer. Be prepared and strong enough to say 'No' if the project does not look right.

Needs and Wants

Be sure that the client needs the work you are proposing to do. If they do not, they will ultimately blame you for doing unnecessary work even if it was something they said they wanted in the first place. Make sure it is a real need, not simply a desire or 'want'. If the prospective clients want particular work done, understand why; try to avoid meeting wants unless they are genuine needs.

Competence

Often clients will claim to be capable of doing important parts of the work themselves. If you as their advisor are going to be relying on them delivering satisfactory results from such work, then you need to be very sure that they will be able to complete it as agreed.

If you have doubts, or the work is structured in such a way that you are highly dependent on the client, then ensure that you have written the terms of reference so that you will be able to charge for any additional time that you may be called upon to provide.

Ultra Vires

Once in a while you may end up dealing with people who want to feel important and who will lead you on. But they may not have the authority to give you any work or to authorise payments to you. They are operating *ultra vires*, or beyond their legal power or authority. So be warned, and make sure you deal at the highest possible level.

Avoid this situation at all costs. Understand who can make contracts and the authorised budget level to which they can commit their organisation.

MAKE YOUR SERVICES EASY TO BUY

Above all else, you must make your services easy to buy. I find it staggering how many suppliers, of all kinds of products and services, actively make it difficult to buy their products, even in times when business is slow. So if you can make your professional services readily accessible and easy to buy, you will have a major advantage over the majority of your competitors.

If you make any promises you *must* meet them. This is the first test that the client can make of your performance. At Solidus, we tend to say we will put something together in a week and then get it to the client within four days. Always try to exceed client expectations, right from the start. Even when you do not want to proceed with the work, you want the client to have a positive attitude about you. Recently we turned down a project because we did not like the way the client wanted it structured. We wrote back explaining why we were not making a proposal and suggesting ways they could take the job forward without us. Two weeks later they were asking us to make a proposal on our approach at premium rates. This situation is surprisingly common.

Do not wait for clients to produce and send the contract or engagement letter. Take the initiative by sending them a clear and straightforward contract that just needs their signature on a copy to be returned to you. Make sure the language is clear and that the terms of reference for the project are easily understood. If you make it easy to understand and avoid heavy legal language and clauses, they will be much more likely to sign it without reference to their legal advisors. I am not suggesting that you try to pull the wool over their eyes or get them to avoid giving the contract proper consideration. By making the language simple and its meaning clear, they will trust their own judgement and avoid the delay of sending the contract for professional scrutiny.

Treat clients with respect and as intelligent people. Make the costs and expenses as straightforward as possible. Try to avoid hidden extras or items that may generate nasty surprises for the client in the future. Add it up and give a total cost — I have seen proposals where the supplier has deliberately not totalled the financial elements. As if the client will not do so — such tricks are so demeaning, as they say that the supplier thinks the client is stupid and will get in the way of the final sale. When I work on procurements for clients, I always put such proposals or contracts to one side and look at them only if I really have to. In any case they will be scored down heavily for not meeting the required format for the proposal — I always ask for a clear statement of total costs.

As well as making the costs clear, make sure that expected outcomes are clear. This is in the interest of both the client and the consultant. Without clear results, who is to say that the work is completed and whether it is satisfactory? All parties must be able to readily agree that the work has been completed. The consultant will not get paid unless the client believes it has been.

It will also make it possible to prevent 'scope creep'; this is in the interest of both the client and the consultant. The consultant can readily demonstrate that new work is additional and will be subject to an additional charge. The client can see that the consultant is not extending the scope of the work in order to raise additional fees. Clear objectives and well-defined required outcomes make it more comfortable all round.

BROCHURES AND ADVERTISING

Many new and even established consultants seem to feel that they need to produce glossy brochures and to advertise to get new clients. Designers, advertising agencies and advertising space salespeople will be on the telephone regularly trying to sell on the back of such belief. Resist them and your instinct to spend that money, as it will be better used elsewhere. Brochures and advertising are not a panacea — in most cases they are not even part of the solution.

For consultancy businesses, such expenditure suggests lack of understanding of marketing and how customers buy and select consultants. It is an excuse to avoid doing what is really necessary — getting out and selling the business. Customers will not walk in through the door until you have established a major reputation; no amount of advertising or general mailing of brochures will change that.

So neither are really necessary or even useful. They cost a lot of money that can be used where it works. In more than 15 years of consultancy with firms of all sizes, I cannot think of a single project that came in as a result of advertising or a brochure. They are just too general.

As a new or small consultancy you need to be very specific about what you are offering your potential clients. You need to research them, at least as a group and ideally as an individual organisation. You can then tailor your approach on the basis of an understanding of their real needs and the skills that you can offer. You will have much more success with a highly specific letter than with a general brochure. However, that implies that you will have to work at your marketing research and promotion.

If you do want something to leave behind after a meeting, then produce a one-off document that is tailored to the offer and the potential client. Show how your ideas and approach address the issues affecting the client. Desktop publishing or straightforward word-processing allows the production of proposals or other literature that is closely matched to the needs of the client and even of the particular project. You may choose not to leave it after the meeting, but to use it as part of a 'thank you' letter after the meeting — it can then reflect your improved understanding, as a result of the meeting, of the client's challenges and your suitability.

Advertising is even less useful, as it is even more imprecisely targeted than the use of brochures. For advertising to be effective, potential clients have to be looking for advisors, so the market must be relatively strong, in which case other methods will be much more effective. Advertising relies on the would-be client taking action — other techniques make it easier for the client to buy with less effort and so will work far better.

For advertising to work the consultancy will have to advertise in all the important media — magazines, newspapers and the like. And they will have to be there regularly, probably in most issues, as you will not want someone thinking 'I saw an advertisement for consultant X' and not being able to find it in the current issue because it only appears every third issue. So advertising has to be regular and frequent. A single advertisement is pretty much a complete and utter waste of money; you might as well give the money to a good cause —at least it will do some good for somebody then!

Advertising and brochures should be the last things in the marketing budget for most firms of professional advisors. I have made the mistake of trying it, for want of other ideas and effort. It simply does not work without a huge budget, and even then, it is doubtful. Save the money.

PROPOSALS

Proposals do not constitute success. At best they are a step on the way. Bear in mind that some potential clients will ask for a proposal to get rid of you, not because they have any realistic expectation of using you.

Remember that proposals are expensive to prepare; even a simple one- or two-page document will probably require at least two hours of work if you are thorough. And you'd better be thorough, because it will only get one chance to impress. A substantial proposal can easily take many days' work for a team. That can mount up to a lot of money, so it has to be good to have a realistic chance of being accepted.

As a quick checklist, satisfy yourself that:

- The client has a genuine project;
- The client has a budget and the authority to award the contract or has been asked by someone who has to seek proposals;
- The client has the will to progress the work;
- You are properly qualified to undertake the work;
- You are comfortable that the client has not already ruled you out.

Then write the best proposal you can, making sure that every word has a purpose. We will consider proposals in more detail later.

Often the best projects will be offered without the need to write a proposal; in that situation, I still write one, but I call it an engagement letter. This sets out your understanding, responsibilities and fees, and the client's responsibilities and the terms under which they will pay you (very important). Get the client to sign it as acceptance of the terms of reference for the work and you have a contract. That way there should be no misunderstanding. See Appendix E for a typical example of such a proposal or engagement letter.

BEAUTY PARADES

There has been a tendency for clients to go to competitive tenders for many more forms of advice than they have in the past. The use of these 'beauty parades' has been normal practice in many fields for a long time — especially, it would seem, for the 'creative' services such as advertising.

They have become much more common in more traditional professions such as accountancy and management consultancy. In part, this has come about because of tighter policies on procurement and corporate governance in larger organisations. Open and competitive tendering is often a requirement for bigger projects in the public-sector or where the work is being publicly-funded.

Whilst tendering for work is probably good practice, it is time-consuming and expensive for both the bidder and the client. It is difficult to get through all steps if it is to be done properly in less than about two months (longer if the work has to be formally advertised, under EU/GATT rules for public procurement).

The typical process for competitive tendering works through the following steps:

1. Advertisement seeking Expressions of Interest from firms who are competent to undertake the work;

2. Consultancy firm prepares an Expression of Interest setting out the requested information and explaining why they are competent to bid for the work;

3. Client receives and evaluates Expressions of Interest;

4. Client sends out the specification for the work to those suppliers who they accepted as a result of the Expressions of Interest and invites bids from them;

5. Bidding firm prepares a proposal, clarifying points as necessary with the client;

6. Client receives and evaluates the proposals;

7. Client asks a shortlist of the bidders to make a presentation, to provide demonstrations or to otherwise clarify aspects of their proposal;

8. The shortlisted bidders prepare presentations;

9. Presentations, other meetings and discussions are held between client and the selected consultancy firms;

10. The client evaluates the presentations and selects the preferred bidder;

11. Terms of reference, fees and other contractual matters are negotiated between the client and preferred advisor;

12. Contracts are signed;

13. The work starts.

Depending on the nature of the work, the possible number of bidders and other matters, the above process might be extended or reduced.

For large public procurements, there might be additional steps, after step 11, to agree specification and seek tenders from preferred bidders, all of whom can do the work satisfactorily. Those tenders are then evaluated, simply on a financial basis, because all other aspects of the bids are equal.

More specialised public purchasing may skip the expression of interest stage and seek bids directly — this would usually only be done where the number of competent bidders is self-limiting. Evaluating a proposal properly is expensive, so too many bids are undesirable. Where all the realistic bidders can be readily identified, there is room in the regulations for direct approach to avoid the expression of interest and advertising stage.

In other beauty parades, a shortlist of bidders to be invited to submit proposals will be drawn up internally, as a result of the client's own research. The number of bidders will normally be covered in standing financial instructions or some other policy document. Then the process will start at step 4 — inviting those selected bidders to bid against the specification. The rest of the process is then much the same as set out above.

CHAPTER 10

QUALITY AND CLIENT CARE: KEEPING CLIENTS

A reputation for quality work is essential, but the quality level required will be determined by the client.

Keeping clients means looking after them and giving them value for money. That means they must achieve real business benefits as a result of your involvement with them. Everything you do as consultant should be aimed at giving value to the customer, and from that will flow the other benefits that you seek. Customer care is the core of any business, especially a complex, people- and knowledge-based business like consultancy.

OBJECTIVES

The objectives for this chapter are to:

1. Understand the nature of quality in professional services;

2. Be able to manage quality and improve it over time;

3. Appreciate the importance and all-embracing nature of customer care;

4. Provide a positive approach to complaints handling that turns a complaint into a valuable source of feedback and new business opportunities;

5. Show that good clients make for good consultants;

6. Stress the importance of staying in touch with former prospective clients and clients themselves.

QUALITY

Quality in Professional Services

Quality is not primarily about technical matters. It goes without saying that the technical competence must be there. Customers will have their own view of what is important and they will use their judgement to determine the quality of service they have received. You must never forget that if you are to build a reputation for excellence, you must provide satisfaction based on those criteria. You need that reputation to win and keep good clients.

It is all too easy to lose sight of that — like the old joke about two surgeons discussing their day. One asks the other: 'How did the operation go?' The second replies: 'Very well. It was a complete success. Pity the patient died.' We must remember that the quality that matters is that demanded by the client, who should be able to take for granted the technical competence.

However good the technical execution, it has *no* quality if it does not satisfy the client's needs.

Non-technical Aspects of Quality

It is very common for technical specialists to see quality in their work purely in terms of the technical aspects of their skill. We can all lose sight of the fact that the customer is often not equipped to judge the technical quality. They do not have the technical skills —they are, after all, using third-party expertise. So the customer has to judge the quality of a specialist service on the basis of other factors.

There is a concept in marketing called 'product surround'. As can be seen from Figure 10.1, there are many factors that the customer will value to some extent. There are the essential core aspects of the product or service, which in many cases are technical and accepted as satisfactory by customers. But around that core there are many aspects that are not necessarily essential to the technical quality of the service and may not even be needed in the strictest sense. But they are important to the customer's perception of the quality of the service.

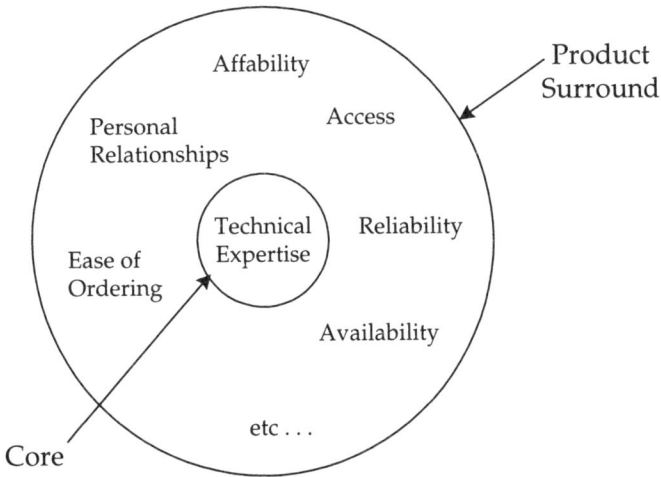

Figure 10.1: Product Surround

How many people can judge the medical competence of their doctor? I would suggest very few, so we have to choose our doctor on the basis of other factors such as their manner, the friendliness of the receptionist, the ease with which we can get appointments or how well they explain what they are doing. There are many other factors that we use to judge professionals, and the same applies to a professional advisor.

As a consultant, you need to be aware of those other aspects that the client will use to judge your quality. Also, you need to bear in mind that the emphasis will be different for different clients. For example, some will appreciate blunt advice whilst others will want their egos massaged; criticism must therefore be handled diplomatically. But there will be a large amount of common ground amongst clients' expectations:

- Timeliness: clients expect consultants to meet their commitments;

- Clarity of argument and avoidance of jargon and buzz words;

- The advisors are pleasant people to do business with;

- Ease of access: clients expect to be able to reach advisors when they want them, or at the very least to get a prompt return call;

- The fees are seen as value for money.

A few years ago, some research was commissioned on customer attitudes to professional advisors, which confirmed the above view. Affability, availability and affordability came a long way ahead of ability in the factors that were used by clients when selecting advisors. It was not that ability was regarded as unimportant — simply that it was taken for granted that established professional firms would give satisfactory advice and that the client could not, to a large extent, judge that advice at the selection stage. So it had to be taken as read, and the consultant selected on the basis of the other factors that we have just explored.

It is therefore essential to success that a consultancy firm keeps these other aspects to the fore when thinking about customer needs. The sale will be made or lost on these factors, more often than on the technical issues, as long there is obvious basic technical competence.

Management Systems

It is important to adopt an approach to client work that provides a complete paper trail of what has been agreed. Therefore by starting with a written proposal, which is converted into a formal letter of engagement or contract signed by both parties, the basic requirement of ISO 9000 for traceability is established.

Adopting a similar approach to changes to the requirements, by exchanging letters or creating an agreed change document (similar to the example engagement letter), again signed by both parties, ensures that proper control is in place.

This all provides a reference point for clarifying disputed issues and validating compliance with the agreed remit. It means that the negotiation and consultancy process will be auditable to confirm that the agreed work has been carried out.

Whilst a full ISO 9000 accreditation is not required by a small consultancy firm, the basic principles should be adopted. That is why so much emphasis has been placed on the need to document what the work is to achieve and any changes to the objectives that take place during the project. The aim is to ensure that everyone understands what is to be done, the required outcomes and the responsibilities of the various parties.

Quality Assurance Procedures

The need for review at various points in the work has already been explained. The quality assurance procedures are likely to change for each project, and should therefore be part of the project planning and management stages.

At the outset, the managing consultant should decide at what points the work needs to be reviewed and whether it should be a 'hot' or 'cold' review. If the work will commit the consultant or the client to major expenditure or risk, then the review should be hot (in other words, undertaken before formally sharing the findings or recommendations with the client) so that corrections can be made before commitment. That risk may come from using relatively inexperienced people, in which case the managing consultant should seek a second opinion on the reliability of the work undertaken. It is not fair or desirable to leave the responsibility with a relatively junior member of staff. Indeed the terms of the firm's professional indemnity insurance may be such that a partner must sign-off any opinions or recommendations before they are shared with the client.

Most projects will have certain stages where such review should take place. It may simply be the final report and recommendations. This should be planned so that it is not overlooked due to time pressures. In fact, it is in such constrained circumstances that review is particularly vital, as it is very easy to miss something important when working under pressure.

Cold review is essentially an internal process geared to improving quality through incremental improvement. It is also a valuable development tool for individuals. The work is reviewed by the consultancy firm to identify how the process could be improved or made more efficient. It provides valuable lessons for both the individual consultants and the firm as a whole.

It may also involve review meetings at various points with the clients, where findings and responses will be considered — from such meetings may come amendments to the terms of reference for the project (documented of course!). The important meeting will be the final 'wash-up' review where the work and its achievements will be checked against the documented objectives so that everyone is happy that the work has been completed.

Most importantly, both consultant and client should take away lessons for future projects — all reviews should be directed to improving practice in the future.

LOOKING AFTER CLIENTS

Treat customers as you would your friends. Most people aim to do well by friends and in return the relationship prospers. The same is true with clients: develop a warm personal relationship and go out of your way to look after them, both professionally and as individuals. It will be rewarded.

If you look after clients they will become your best marketing tool. They will recommend you to friends and colleagues and they will use you again. I have received calls, out of the blue, years after I last did any work for a client, because they had a new project and wanted to use me. As I had changed employers, they had to come looking for me — and I ended up with a major project. There was an additional spin-off as a result: I ended up doing work for other clients through my old employer who had not replaced me but still had an occasional need for my skills. All because I had built a reputation for quality and because I had looked after my clients.

Customer care therefore is not a cost, but an investment in your future prosperity. Remember that and you are on your way to long-term success.

Customer Care

Customer care should not be something that is tacked on after the sale is made and it should not be handled by a separate 'customer services' team or department. Customer care has to be built into all parts of the business, as they all have an impact on the relationship with the client. It starts by designing the services to meet clients' real needs and is continued, through the sales and marketing process, to the ongoing administration of the relationship and the performance of the service.

I am surprised how often sales people and their administrative support staff get the basics of customer care badly wrong. One would expect that sales people rely on developing a good relationship with the potential customer and would therefore be good at customer care. Yet I have often come across companies who make the buying process difficult from the start by not returning calls, showing indifference even before I tell them what I need, and failing to get literature and quotations to me as they promise.

It usually gets even more difficult when one has to deal with less customer-oriented departments — and then you reach the customer care team who seem to be there to prevent a complainant getting to the person who can actually deal with the problem.

So it is not difficult to stand head and shoulders above most of the competition by just doing the simple customer things well. Always return calls promptly, get information to the client as soon as it is requested, get proposals out on time. And then be willing to give a little bit of extra value that is not in the terms of reference. Aim to exceed customers' expectations so that they come away having had a positive relationship. And in most cases it is quite easy because customers do not generally expect very much from suppliers. They expect to have problems.

A few care issues and areas where real opportunities for differentiating yourself through your client care are described below. They will provide a starting point, but aim to provide customer care at every level of your organisation; *everything* you do must be aimed at improving the care you give your clients. You must take these ideas and develop your own culture of providing total customer care.

Complaints Handling

Complaints mean that, although unhappy, customers still want to do business with us and they should therefore be welcomed. Many dissatisfied customers will leave without telling you why — that should be of much greater concern. Consequently, you need to accept that:

- Complainants are feeling unloved — they are giving you an opportunity to show you care. The complainant needs a hug!

- Complaints tell you what is wrong with your products or service. This creates an opportunity for you to redesign them to create improvements.

- Complaints also tell you that the client's expectations are higher than what you are able to deliver. You therefore need to examine the promises you and your colleagues are making. Make sure you can deliver the benefits that you promise.

Complaints should be treated as sales enquiries. If a customer is unhappy with the service you are providing, then there should be an opportunity to provide them with something more suitable, something that will be of greater mutual benefit.

- They may be using the product or service in the wrong way or for inappropriate purposes.

- You may be able to offer replacement or additional services that better meet their needs and expectations — and even generate more revenue for you.

Complaints are market intelligence. They tell you what your competitors are doing, what your customers (and therefore potential customers) really want. You can find out:

- What your competitors are doing, how they are targeting *your* customers and what they are offering 'under the counter'.

- What your customers *really* need from your sector. This may lead to real innovation. You might even understand what they want and need rather than what you are able to sell them.

- You can understand how they are *really* using your products and those of your competitors — it will not be as you intended!

So treat complaints in a positive way and you will win more customers and increase the referrals from customers. I know of one company, not a consultancy, which makes more money from complaints than they cost them. So it is not just a case of throwing money at the problem through compensation, but understanding the *real*, underlying reasons why the client is complaining. It may be that their circumstances have changed and what they asked you to do is no longer suitable, but they do not properly appreciate this or how to approach it. Help them out.

A complaint swiftly and effectively solved is one of the best sources of good public relations — certainly better than just doing a good job because it is what clients expect. It shows that you are responsive and genuinely care about giving the client the service that they need.

Equity

Customers want to feel that they are treated fairly and are not being given a worse deal than the next customer. This is potentially a major failing of both introductory offers and loyalty schemes. The first discriminates against the long-standing customer and the second against those who have just switched — in both cases there will be aggrieved clients.

Customers' Expectations and Their Management

It is tempting to treat clients as a homogeneous whole. But they are not; they all make different demands on price, service, quality, benefits and features.

It is easy to offer custom solutions to ten customers, but when you have many more, it can become a major challenge to meet individual needs. However, as far as consultancy is concerned, that must be achieved. Each customer has to be treated on an individual basis, as they will soon spot that they are being squeezed into fitting a standard solution.

But customers can also have unreasonable expectations, and these can grow during a project. That is why it is so important that terms of reference are agreed, and that the scope of the work is not allowed to grow unchecked. Manage client expectations so that they do not become unreasonable. And, of course, the consultant must not promise too much to get the work. If you do, it will come back to haunt you.

Comparison with Competitors

Clients need to feel that they got a fair deal and made a good choice in respect of their preferred advisor. They need regular reassurance on this point. Plenty of appropriate feedback will therefore be needed, especially if they are coming under pressure through their masters asking for premature results.

Customer Greed and Selfishness

There will always be customers who are simply greedy, unrealistic or self-centred. That has to be recognised and addressed in the customer care strategy. There is a fine line between a customer simply being properly demanding and being unreasonable. And the dividing line may well be drawn differently by client and consultant.

Whatever approach to customer care is taken, that line must be drawn by the consultant. It must be recognised that not all business is good and not all clients are worth having. If the advisor is chasing new business at almost any price, then there will tend to a greater proportion of poor and often difficult customers.

Personal Relationships

It has been stressed that clients are buying a personal relationship in their choice of consultant. This must be recognised and supported as part of the ongoing client care. They want to deal with the person they chose, not the firm, and if there has to be a change of personnel they will want to be consulted. I have seen too many large firms failing to tell a client that their favoured consultant has left the firm until after the event. They then impose a new advisor on the client and wonder why they get complaints. It is a foolhardy practice — they should advise the client when the employee hands in their notice and use the client to help the consultancy choose the new advisor for that client. That way they keep a personal relationship going, without losing out to another firm.

Product and Service Design

There is a need to 'design in' customer care, not just technical quality. This includes designing the service to:

- Be easy to buy;

- Make it easy to provide support and allied services;

- Meet real need rather than perceived or stated needs;

• Accommodate change.

DO NOT BE A SCROOGE

Whilst no business should be extravagant and all should seek to be as 'lean' as practically possible, do not be mean in your dealings with customers. You should be charging a rate that allows you to give the client some small additional benefits without charging them as extras. Indeed, the little extras should be built into the budget, as should all the little routine costs such as telephone calls, secretarial support, photocopying, etc. That said, neither should you over-service a client; otherwise you are reducing your day rate and allowing the customer to extend the scope of the work without additional fees.

I am talking about the small things. If the client asks for an extra copy of a report, do not count every telephone call (unless they are expensively long international calls) or if, between projects, they ask for some advice that you can give in a brief telephone call, do not automatically charge them. Put the costs down to customer care or to practice development. They are a part of your sales costs and should be creating goodwill. If you charge for every little thing, it will make you look small-minded and will cause the client to adopt a similar approach. You could find yourself having to justify every element of you bill. Create mutual trust by not being a scrooge.

GOOD CLIENTS MAKE GOOD CONSULTANTS

Even the best consultant cannot do good work without good clients. From time to time, all consultants meet difficult clients. Often they are very nice people, but they simply do not deliver on their side of the bargain, and thereby prevent the advisor doing the job for which they have been engaged.

So what makes a good client? The answer is anybody who allows you and your team to do good work on their behalf. It is essential is to make the consultant feel needed and respected — we all work better when what we do is appreciated. It then ceases to be a chore and becomes a pleasure. And if it is a pleasure, we will work harder at the task. Much of it comes down to simple good manners; the occasional genuine 'thank you' makes a world of difference to our personal satisfaction.

On a more practical level, a good client will be prepared for meetings and will not rearrange them at short notice. Be sensitive to changes with regard to this as it may give important signals. As I write I have a good client who has become somewhat less reliable in this respect. I was getting concerned that I had done something to upset him. From the recent new work he has asked me to take on I now realise that the changes are because he is under pressure. I know he has problems with a difficult child and his role at work has also developed at the same time. He is and will remain over-burdened until he can recruit the additional staff he needs. Now I know what the problem is I can help reduce that burden and at the same time earn a few days' fees that I did not expect.

Good clients deliver what they promise. If they have agreed to do some work by a given date they will do so and will not offer excuses for being late with the work. Good clients will manage their end of the project to the agreed timetable and quality; and they will expect the consultant to do the same. By upholding their end of the bargain, they enable the client to deliver what they promised — it makes life easier for everybody. Poor clients will never meet their targets and as a result the project will slip into delay, which may well have a serious impact on the consultant's cash flow and reputation. This is a serious management problem which the consultant will have to face; hence the need for determining the capability and nature of the client right at the start. If you suspect that you might encounter this problem, you can design the project accordingly and build suitable contingency into the terms of reference. If you suspect that this will be a problem, do not under any circumstances accept a fixed price. If you do, make it clear that costs due to delays or rework will be charged in addition; you should still build in a substantial contingency!

A client can help the relationship by paying according to the agreed terms. As you will see from the engagement letter in the Appendix, I am explicit about how I bill and when I am to be paid. I should not have to chase payment, as it makes everyone a little uncomfortable and is not conducive to an equable relationship. Any time a client does not pay on time, it must be resolved as soon as possible. Often it will be a simple oversight. As a consultant I tend to work with senior people, so it reduces this problem. A quiet word with the chief executive or finance director will usually produce a cheque in short order. They in their turn do not want to upset me by not honouring an agreement. If late payment does become a problem, make it clear at an early stage that you will not be able to do further work until they settle up.

Good clients do not just accept everything the consultant says. They listen and then challenge; they make the consultant justify their ideas. With a good client, such arguments are robust, challenging and intellectually stimulating. Above all, they are fun! At the end of the day, I want the client to take action based on understanding and a belief in what they are doing — not just because I say so. It is their business and they have to take responsibility for their decisions. It does not even matter whether we convince each other of our views. As long as the views are well founded and based on sound arguments, concerted action should produce satisfactory results. In the end, a leader who understands their vision and really believes in it will make it successful. And that is what those arguments ensure: that belief and understanding are genuine and well founded. Passion and obsession can achieve a lot.

STAY IN TOUCH

As we have already discussed, client care is about developing the business in the long term. Looking after clients will reap its rewards, although some will be a long time in the future. But they will come. So the secret is to stay in touch. Once or twice a year is probably enough, so that when they need somebody, they think of you and know how to get hold of you.

Be in the business for the long term and do not make every communication a hard sell. Sometimes, it is enough just to let former clients know what you are doing and ask how they are doing on a personal and business level. Be genuinely interested.

Stay in touch with contacts and previous clients by passing on relevant information that the recipient will probably not have seen. As a consultant, you will have a different set of sources to your clients; there will be some overlap but it should be obvious where. The form of that information will be highly variable; sometimes it will simply be a couple of facts that you can jot on a compliment slip; other times it will be a whole article in a journal.

You may be tempted to simply photocopy the article and send the copy; most people will have done that at some time or other, but it is a breach of copyright. If you do not need the magazine, send the original article; if you need more than one copy, you should get permission to copy or buy reprints from the journal. Reprints are not expensive and the quality is much higher, so the client will give it more attention.

Write or call only when you have a reason — even if you have to create it. But do not make it sound too contrived, as the contact will see it for what it is. I aim to be in touch with former clients and low-level prospective clients every three to six months; more often looks desperate, while less often may allow opportunities to pass you buy.

Generally, I enjoy the company of my clients and I will try to meet former clients from time to time for purely social reasons. We will have lunch or perhaps a round of golf. We will talk about how they have progressed since I last worked with them, the changes in the business and their industry since we last met, changes we have made and just general social small talk. Usually nothing heavy, and definitely no selling. After all, they know I am in business, what I do and that if they ask I will make suggestions. If the relationship is good, and if they have agreed to meet me socially it usually is, they will raise the issue if they have any suitable work. So I do not need to push it. Keep it social.

SUMMARY

Quality is more than a technical issue. Indeed the client should be able to take technical quality for granted. The many other peripheral issues that impinge on the customer's perception of the experience *are* the quality from their viewpoint. So there must be considerable effort put into those non-technical aspects of quality.

However, the technical quality must be there, although often the client is not equipped to assess it, which is why they are using a consultant in that field. So the consultant's approach and management procedures must ensure that the client can take the technical quality for granted.

The consultant needs management procedures to agree the work to be undertaken and the benefits and other outcomes that the client can expect. These procedures must also be able to accommodate change and maintain the integrity of the modified terms of reference. Basically the procedures should ensure that there is a sufficiently complete and formal specification of the work to be performed and the outcomes to be achieved. This should leave little room for argument, but without having to detail every step along the way; a balance has to be struck. The procedure will then establish means to formally revise and track such changes to the terms of reference if the objectives and deliverables change as the project progresses.

There should also be procedures to validate that compliance has been achieved. This takes place in several ways. First, it will take place within the consultancy as part of 'hot' reviews before the work is confirmed to the client, to ensure that nothing has been missed before the client or the consultancy is committed in an irreversible way. It will also be validated after the event by cold review to learn any lessons and to improve future practice and quality. There should also be a final review with the client to ensure that both parties are satisfied that the work has been properly completed and that the client knows how to take the work forward if necessary.

Customer care is about turning clients into good clients so that you can be a good consultant. Without good clients, advisors cannot do their best work. So we need to keep the client happy before, during, and even after the project. Customer care is the core of what we do as consultants, and it is the seed that we will reap in the future. We are totally dependent on producing happy clients, because a large proportion of the best future work will come from client referral. Reputation is all.

Customer care is often poor, so a consultant who really lives to provide excellence in customer care will have a real competitive advantage over many of their competitors.

CHAPTER 11

THE PROFESSIONAL PRACTICE

One of the biggest challenges facing a prospective consultant with no experience in a professional practice is how to organise their business. Much of it is simply good business practice and should be familiar to any senior manager intending to become a consultant. However, many people from large organisations may not have been exposed to the spread of responsibilities that they will have to take on for their own small consultancy practice.

This chapter is a brief overview of the key areas that are peculiar to professional practice. It does not set out to cover the whole of small business management. There are many books aimed at small and start-up businesses, and anyone starting out on their own for the first time should familiarise themselves with the organisation of a business.

OBJECTIVES

The purpose of this chapter is to give the consultant some advice on how to manage their practice on a day-to-day basis. The approach explained in this chapter is the result of experience in developing my own practice and is also drawn from working in large professional organisations.

The objectives for this chapter are to:

1. Understand the documentation that is required;

2. Appreciate the need for time and expense recording;

3. Stress the importance of good diary and time management;

4. Understand management and accounting requirements;

5. Pull together all aspects of good professional practice;

6. Help establish quality assurance procedures for the practice itself;

7. Understand some of the issues involved in using other consultants, as employees or otherwise;

8. Stress the importance of not appearing extravagant.

PROPOSALS

Being asked to prepare a proposal is not a mark of success. It is simply a step in the sales process. Indeed, many projects are awarded to advisors without a proposal ever being required. It should be remembered that some, particularly weak, clients will ask for a proposal to avoid saying 'No'. You must be sure that there is a real project and that you have a realistic chance of winning the work before preparing a proposal.

Writing a proposal is time-consuming if it is to be done properly. Even a brief one- or two-page document will take much of a day if it is to be done properly. Remember it has to work on its own — you will not be there to explain points that the customer does not understand. Every word counts.

The format for your proposal should be designed to ensure that it provides all the essential information that prospective clients will need in deciding whether to use you. Proposals should make it as easy as possible for the client to buy your services. Some organisations try to get 'clever' and not give day rates or total costs. Others try to hide expense rates or other negative aspects of their proposal. This is foolish.

If there is a formal brief for the work, then the proposal should meet the format specified in the invitation to bid documents. In such circumstance, be absolutely strict about complying with the required format, as it is the client's most basic test of a proposal. Many will reject proposals at that stage for non-compliance, especially where there are large numbers to be evaluated in an open tender procurement. As always, make it easy for the buyer — make sure all the information they need is presented clearly, especially the total cost! Do not try to hide anything, as it will create suspicion.

There is an example of a proposal and engagement letter in Appendix E. It is brief, but properly constructed, such a document will be suitable for all but the most complex projects. I use much the same structure but with more detail, even for very large projects where no format is specified.

ENGAGEMENT LETTERS AND CONTRACTS

I have always used successful proposals as the basis of the engagement letter or contract. This means that the proposal has to be complete, as it contains pretty well everything that both the client and I want in the final agreement. Working in this way means that there are no difficult negotiations once the proposal has been accepted because it is complete and has been developed to meet both the client's and the consultant's needs.

All I usually do is to add an acceptance block for the client's signature and minor changes to the opening and closing paragraphs to reflect that the proposal has now become the final agreement.

I always require an engagement letter, as it sets out what the client and I are to do and how and when I will get paid. So even if the client does not ask for a proposal, I will prepare one, but offer it as the engagement letter. I do not start the work without a signed contract — you only get burned by starting work and then finding that the 'client' manager does not have the authority to award the contract and it is re-negotiated or refused by their boss. A lot of time and expense is wasted.

CHANGES TO THE TERMS OF REFERENCE

It is not uncommon for parts of the work to change as a result of the consultant's researches and as both the client and the advisor better understand the problem. This will mean that the terms of reference in the engagement letter will become outdated. In such cases the changes to the terms should be documented so that there can be no confusion about the new direction for the project. Leaving amendments to a verbal understanding is one of the most common causes of friction — both sides disagree as to whether the work has been completed as intended. Unfortunately, if changes in nature or emphasis have not been formally recorded, there is no valid document to go back to for clarification.

Therefore document changes or additions to the terms of reference must be discussed with the client before doing the new work. More often than not a brief letter will do. Do not get in the position of doing extra work and then having the bill queried when it is presented. Send the revised details to the most senior person involved in the contract — usually the person who signed the engagement letter. Such a letter should not come as a surprise, as the changes should have been discussed and agreed with the person concerned beforehand.

In some extreme cases, the changes to the work required will be so substantial that it is better to start from scratch with new terms of reference. In that case, the original project will be terminated by mutual agreement and a new engagement letter with appropriate new terms of reference prepared. Once that has been signed off by both parties, the work will start as a new project, although effort should be made not to duplicate relevant work that was done on the original project.

TIME RECORDING

Once a project is under way, you will need to keep track of where your time goes. Some work will be billed on the basis of time spent and you must be able to detail when and where that time went. Clients will not normally ask for that information, but some will want it occasionally, if, for example, they are surprised by the amount of time that has been spent.

From time to time there will be delays or time lost for other reasons. Of course, if it is the consultant who caused the problem then you will have to carry the lost time and should not charge it or any additional expenses to the client. On the other hand, if the delays are due to the client's failure to deliver their side of the bargain, then the consultant should be reimbursed for their lost time, especially if client delays are common and are due to their inability to manage themselves and their staff.

Keep a note of factors that caused more time to be spent than necessary — for example, if you are left waiting around for the client and their staff, failure to meet deadlines or deliver documents, etc. Be able to justify the time if there is a challenge. In my experience, if you are fair with a client you will rarely be asked to justify your time, but you should always be prepared to do so. Do not use a client's trust as an excuse to load the time and expenses to boost your profits. At best, any benefits will be very short-term and will destroy any reputation for honesty that you have. Remember also that it is fraud, with all the consequences that goes with that.

Dealing with travelling time is difficult. I know people who charge all travel time, over and above their normal time travelling to their office, to the project at 100 per cent. Others charge it at a reduced rate on the basis that they will use some of that time for working on other projects. That may be valid where the consultant can work — for instance on an airplane or a train — but is perhaps not appropriate where the consultant is driving. You will need to ask around and come to your own conclusions as to what approach is appropriate in your consultancy field — it may be defined by custom and practice.

It goes without saying that you should be scrupulously honest, with no padding of the time, however tempting. You only need to be caught once to lose total credibility, not just with the one client but with everyone else they know. Good reputations are hard to win but very easy to lose.

DIARY MANAGEMENT

Diary management is a key competency for any consultant. My diary is my bible. Not only does it contain my appointments, it also has my current and future tasks with deadlines. Of course it also contains my principal contact list and useful telephone numbers. I also use it to record details of telephone calls, to outline how my time has been spent across internal and external projects, to plan meetings and reports, even to prepare proposals. I still use a paper diary, having tried a variety of other options, because it suits my way of working. I use a computer for almost everything else.

I believe there is a cardinal rule for all consultants: never change a meeting with a client! I know many consultants who are not very strict about it, and some who are positively cavalier — I believe they are mistaken and that it represents poor customer care. Obviously there are some circumstances in which it is unavoidable, such as personal sickness, transport strikes or road closures, to name a few. But it is my belief that a consultant should not change an appointment for their own convenience, such as visiting a new client or because they have had an invitation to play a game of golf with a different client.

If you want to be strict with clients who mess you around by rearranging meetings, especially at short notice, then you, as a consultant, need to be squeaky clean and avoid doing the same thing to clients.

If you do not use a diary every day, get into the habit of doing so. And really use it to record what you do all through the day — telephone calls to make, jobs to do, costs incurred, etc. Make it really work — I could run my business from my diary with little reference to anything else.

EXPENSES

Be similarly conscientious about keeping track of expenses, especially if you are passing them on to clients. And again do not pad them out — false reclaiming of expenses is fraud. A reputation as a fraudster is not conducive to a long and profitable consultancy career.

The expenses that are to be passed on should be included in the engagement letter and the terms of reference. I usually include routine travel to the client and associated subsistence in the day rate or overall price, where it is a fixed price. That is reasonably predictable, and by including those costs in the basic fee, I can make budgeting easier for clients, which makes it easier for them to buy my services. The dislike of uncertain and often large expenses bills is one of the aspects of using consultants that constantly appears high on surveys of client dissatisfaction. So minimise that uncertainty.

On most projects, that approach will mean few, if any, additional expenses will need to be re-charged. However, if there is unpredictable travel or substantial out-of-pocket costs for other purposes, these should be highlighted in the proposal and the basis on which they will be re-charged made clear. Some consultancy firms re-charge expenses with an administrative fee of between 5 and 15 per cent. I encourage clients to pick up expenses directly, whenever possible. I suggest that clients book flights or hotel rooms themselves through their normal channels. That way they have the comfort of knowing that they are incurring expenses at similar level to those that would apply if it were their own senior staff. Quite reasonably, clients are becoming increasingly uncomfortable with consultants living at a higher level of luxury at the client's expense than would be acceptable for their own senior managers and directors.

If I need to re-charge car travel costs, I do so at the same rate that the client reimburses their own staff for using their personal car. As I tend to work with large organisations that have standard scales for motor expenses, that is easy. If I am working with small companies that do not have defined policies, I use the rates for typical cars published by one of the motoring organisations, such as the Automobile Association. I do not consider it right to expect the client to pick up the higher costs that I may incur because I choose to run a relatively extravagant vehicle out of personal choice — the client was not able to influence that choice.

At Solidus, we include secretarial and other support staff time in the consultant's day rate and do not usually charge them directly to the client. There are occasional circumstances where we might, such as when the client needs some additional resources. In that situation, secretaries, researchers or other support staff are no longer supporting the consultancy team but have become fee-earners in their own right. Clients should then be charged as for a consultant at a suitable rate, bearing in mind any additional expenses that they will incur. And of course there will be an engagement letter setting out the role and terms.

PROJECT MANAGEMENT

Project management is a key skill for most consultants, especially if using junior staff or associates. If you do not have experience of managing significant projects, then think long and hard before setting out on a consultancy career. We all make mistakes when we are learning new skills, and a new business is fragile enough without having to carry such difficulties. Hone your project management skills at someone else's expense by staying in employ-ment until you are confident!

There are many courses and books on project management to guide the novice project manager. The risks of getting a project wrong are double-edged. Firstly, the consultant can find that the project overruns and, as a result, ceases to be profitable. Secondly, there is the risk of consequential and other losses being claimed by the customer. This means that there is the direct cost of reim-bursing the client (for example, for increased insurance premiums and uninsured losses) and the indirect cost of a damaged reputa-tion.

So make sure you are a competent project manager, with the right tools and methods, before getting in too deep.

SALES TRACKING

The sales process is perhaps the most important one in your busi-ness. Without new customers you are not going anywhere. De-spite that, it is often poorly managed, especially in organisations that do not have a professional sales team. Consultants have to sell themselves; some try to use sales people but I know of none who really make it work without heavy involvement from the senior consultants themselves. At the end of the day, clients buy people, not firms.

Therefore sales tracking and management is just one of the many roles taken on by the consultant; it inevitably often gets in-sufficient consideration. There are many good books on sales management and there are frequent reviews in the computer press for client and contact management software. Look at those and set up a way of keeping track of what you have sent whom. There is nothing more embarrassing (and damaging to the pros-pect of a sale) than sending the same (or similar) direct mail to the same people more than once.

You need to have a list of potential and current clients, the main contacts there (do not forget the secretaries) and information about the company — size, number of employees, whatever is relevant to you. You then need to record what contact (visits, let-ters, telephone calls, etc.) you have had or are going to have with these clients — it is not very professional to meet a colleague at the same meeting without knowing they would be there.

I would suggest that the task of tracking sales should be computerised, as it will assist with direct mail campaigns and the like. It will rapidly become your central corporate information resource, and there is sufficient choice out there for it not to require you to develop your own.

ACCOUNTING

It is not appropriate to go into the details of bookkeeping in a book such as this. As a professional you should ensure that you are properly prepared to run a business before you embark on a career as an independent consultant.

My main advice is to keep it simple. You may be tempted to get into heavy project costing, and I would not discourage you if you have the skills and good reasons for doing so. But successful consultancy is about the bottom line, so keep an eye on that.

Remember also that a high proportion of business failures are due to lack of cash, not poor profitability in the short term. So make sure you manage your cash flow, and if there are gaps then keep your bank informed. Banks do not like surprises or sudden demands for increased lines of credit. Give them plenty of warning and they will be a lot more accommodating, as they will be reassured that you are actually managing the business and not simply reacting to events. Bankers do not like risks and risk is reduced by planning and management. Show that you are on top of the challenges.

As a small business owner, I would recommend that you keep your accounting as simple as possible so as to minimise the administrative burden and allow you to concentrate on finding new business and doing chargeable work. The one thing I would strongly urge is that you monitor your cash flow tightly so that you can identify potential problems at least two or three months ahead — that will give you time to negotiate temporary facilities with your bank and impress them with your professionalism.

If you adopt a vital signs approach to monitoring your practice, you will not need complex accounting, at least not initially.

Essentially, I manage my business on a handful of measures that I can carry in my head:

- *Number of chargeable days:* I know how many days of chargeable work I need each month to meet my targets, and what rate I should charge. This also allows me to schedule my holidays or other work, such as my writing, around my main deadlines.

- *Bank balance and invoices outstanding:* Most of my costs are regular and do not vary much from month-to-month. The few exceptions, such as tax bills or major car services, I carry in my diary, and know how much they are and when they are due, so I can adjust my cash flow forecast accordingly.

- *Prospective work:* I know what projects I can hope to get over the next few weeks or months and what they are likely to be worth. That gives me a feel for the longer term cash flow.

As I say, I normally carry this with me, but I occasionally sit down and write it all down more formally, so that I can see what it looks like and make sure that I have not missed anything. I make sure I do this when I feel things are getting tight for whatever reason, good or bad. I usually find that problems are less of a worry when I have worked through them, which also makes them easier to address.

QUALITY CONTROL AND REVIEW

Some form of quality control is an essential part of being professional and continually striving to improve your service. It is also vitally important for credibility, especially if you are a one-person band. The very small operation can often gain an edge over middle-sized organisations by having clear and demonstrable quality review procedures. A lot of multi-partner firms do not have them, and even if they do they are often not followed conscientiously. The big firms do have such procedures and generally operate them as intended. If you have good procedures that you use properly, then make sure potential clients know — it may raise questions in their mind that they will ask of your competitors. It will help you differentiate yourself from the many ordinary firms of advisors.

The consultant, and especially those operating on their own, need such review processes for their personal development and to ensure that standards do not slip. It is all too easy to become complacent and to let unsatisfactory work go out when under pressure. Independent review will help prevent such work becoming the norm.

Most professional firms adopt three main levels of quality review. There will be several different approaches within each level. The main quality review elements are hot and cold reviews and regular and occasional audits. The review should be based on the terms of reference and any subsequent correspondence between the client and consultancy firm that relates to the project.

Hot Review

Hot reviews are undertaken before the client sees the work, and is especially important where the practice and/or the client will be exposed to risk if there are errors in the work. It usually takes one of two forms, depending on the importance of the project or the firm's procedures.

Note that all review work should be about trying to raise standards and not about scoring points or laying blame. The question that should always be addressed is: 'What can we learn from this work that will allow us all to improve our work?'

Peer Review

In this case the work is reviewed by a colleague of similar status. This is to get a second opinion, to check that there are no obvious errors or omissions, that the work is complete, that all relevant issues have been covered and that it is appropriately presented. Obviously the consultant doing the review cannot repeat their colleague's work so they have to take it on trust that the work has been performed. But they can, and should, ask questions and seek clarification about how the work was undertaken and how the conclusions were reached.

The aim is to reassure both the person performing the work and the practice that nothing obvious has been missed. We have all finished a piece of work and had that uncomfortable feeling that we have missed something. The reviewing of work is to identify what is not quite right or to allay the fear by showing that it is a complete and competent piece of work.

Partner or Manager Review

Where there is a hierarchy of consultants, there is an opportunity for review by a senior or supervising colleague. In many professional firms, such a review would be required before a report or other written opinion could be sent to the client. In such circumstances it is an essential part of the firm's quality assurance procedures and it is often also a requirement of their professional indemnity insurance.

It will take much the same form as peer review, although the manager should have more knowledge of the work as they will usually have project or client management responsibility. In that case, they will usually have directed the work and discussed it whilst it was being undertaken. The manager should therefore be able to ask more and deeper questions about the document being reviewed and should be able to see any significant omissions.

Cold Review

Cold reviews are performed, as a general development and quality assurance process, after the work has been shared with the client. The aim is to learn how performance can be improved on an ongoing basis. It is not about finding fault or laying blame — the work should be satisfactory and the client happy. If that is not the case, then other approaches should come into play.

The results of reviews should not be confined to the group who undertook the work and the reviewing team. The results and lessons should be shared throughout the office or firm so that everyone can use the knowledge to improve their own performance.

Audit

Audit is undertaken after the event and many large firms use it to ensure compliance with their internal quality procedures. In such circumstances, it is usually undertaken by someone independent of the project team. Often it will be someone senior from the firm's headquarters or seconded from another office for the purpose. They will usually work on a sample of the projects chosen at random or on the basis of some risk assessment that the projects represented for the firm.

As the people performing the review are even further detached from the client than in other situations, their interest will tend to identify areas where risk could be further reduced by revised working practices. Auditors will look at the work to ensure that proper practice has been followed, from terms of reference to completion. They will examine the points where reviews were undertaken and ensure that they were appropriate to the risk to the client or to the consultancy firm itself. The focus is much more on procedure and presentation than on content and approach, although consideration will be given to such factors.

The result will usually be a report to the head of the office, indicating where they could improve their practices and compliance with the firm's standards. The auditor will also use it as an opportunity to share current best practice learnt from the audit of all offices. This will drive the development of the firm's standards and procedures and should, if properly used, lead to continual improvement of the firm's quality across all offices and teams.

Review in the Small Firm

How can the small practice and the single consultant operate such procedures? The answer comes back to the network of associates that has been developed as a result of networking. Find someone who you can trust, who shares similar standards and approaches to yourself and who can understand your work. Then come to a mutual review agreement where you review each other's work from time to time. If you operate in slightly different fields or in different markets, then the issues of competition should not arise — I have operated this way for several years with a former colleague and we are now in the process of merging our practices. I would recommend that you put the agreement in writing and set out the requirements for mutual non-disclosure and non-competition as far as the clients that are reviewed are concerned.

ETHICS, VALUES AND CODES OF PRACTICE

Ethics are a growing issue in business and public life. There seems to be a feeling that social and moral values have declined, and a growing desire to stem or even reverse the decline. There are an increasing number of businesses that are promoting themselves on their ethical and environmental stance. This is true, not just for consultancy, but for businesses in general.

Most professional bodies have a code of practice, which they enforce with varying degrees of rigour. One of the best that is applicable to consultancy is that of the Institute of Management Consultants (IMC) in the United Kingdom, a summary of which is included below. Most other institutes representing consultants have similar codes.

Institute of Management Consultants: Code of Professional Conduct — Summary

Principle 1: Meeting the Client's Requirements

- A member shall regard the client's requirements and interests as paramount at all times.

- A member will accept work that the member is qualified to perform and in which the client can be served effectively; a member will not make any misleading claims and will provide references from other clients if requested.

- A member shall agree formally with the client the scope, nature and deliverables of the service to be provided and the basis of remuneration, in advance of commencing work; any subsequent revisions will be subject to prior discussion and agreement with the client.

- A member will hold all information concerning the affairs of the client in strictest confidence and will not disclose proprietary information obtained during the course of assignments.

- A member will make certain that advice, solutions and recommendations are based on thorough, impartial consideration and analysis of all available pertinent facts and experience and are realistic, practicable and clearly understood by the client.

Principle 2: Integrity, Independence, Objectivity

- A member shall avoid any action or situation inconsistent with the member's professional obligations or which might in any way be seen to impair the member's integrity. In formulating advice and recommendations, the member will be guided solely by the member's objective view of the client's best interests.

- A member will disclose at the earliest opportunity any special relationships, circumstances or business interests which might influence or impair, or could be seen by the client or others to influence or impair, the member's judgement or objectivity on a particular assignment.

- A member shall not serve a client under circumstances which are inconsistent with the member's professional obligations or which in any way might be seen to impair the member's integrity. Wherever a conflict or potential conflict of interest arises, the member shall, as the circumstances require, either withdraw from the assignment, remove the source of conflict or disclose and obtain the agreement of the parties concerned to the performance or continuation of the engagement.

- A member will advise the client of any significant reservations the member may have about the client's expectations of benefits from an engagement.

- A member will not indicate any short-term benefits at the expense of the long-term welfare of the client without advising the client of the implications.

Principle 3: Responsibility to the Profession and the Institute

- A member's conduct shall at all times endeavour to enhance the standing and public recognition of the profession and the Institute.

- A member will comply with the Institute's requirements on Continuing Professional Development in order to ensure the knowledge and skills the member offers to the client are kept up to date.

- A member shall have respect for the professional obligations and qualifications of all others with whom the member works.

- A member will negotiate agreements and charges for professional services only in a manner approved as ethical and professional by the Institute.

- A member shall be a fit and proper person to carry on the profession of management consultancy.

Many of these points have been stressed elsewhere in this book as the way that a consultant should operate. They are most definitely best practice and are entirely compatible with running a profitable consultancy practice. Indeed I would argue, as no doubt would the IMC, that this is the only way to run a consultancy business if it is to be successful in the long term.

PROFESSIONAL INDEMNITY

It is good practice for the consultant to have professional indemnity insurance — and many larger clients will insist on it. It may be available through your professional body, but at the very least they will be able to provide names of insurers who offer cover to consultants in your specialism.

The cost of cover varies widely, depending on the insurer's experience and the perceived risk of bad advice by the consultant. So, for example, professional indemnity insurance for information technology consultancy tends to be higher than that for general business consultants.

Bear in mind that in many fields (design engineering, architecture, etc.) there will be a need to keep the cover in place, even if you stop operating in the field. This is because problems may manifest themselves many years after the original work is completed, and liability for the consequences could fall on the advisor. In such circumstances, the premiums should fall over time as the risk falls and new work is not being added — the insurer's overall exposure is therefore reducing.

You will need to shop around and find out what your consultancy colleagues are using.

LICENSING

Most professional advisory practices do not need to be licensed. The main exceptions are the legal and accountancy professions, of course. The other general exceptions are those human resource consultancies who get involved in recruiting employees for their clients or in placing staff in employment who may fall under rules that regulate employment agencies. Advice on local regulations will be available from the professional association representing specialists in the area.

PROFESSIONAL ASSOCIATIONS

Apart from the professional bodies that represent particular expert fields, such as the engineering institutes, there are also industry-specific associations. Generally speaking, consultants should belong to the institute that represents their expertise, as well as a specialist consultancy body such as the Institute of Management Consultants in the United Kingdom. There are similar bodies representing the consultancy profession in most developed industrial countries. There is a list in the appendices.

GOVERNMENT AGENCIES

It is not uncommon for government agencies to be involved in supporting consultancy through grant support and diagnostic services. The aim is usually to encourage economic activity and thereby new employment. The funds may come from local, central government or European Union development funds.

Grant support is a mixed blessing. In general, advice is worth what a client pays for it; having paid little because of grant help, the client tends to regard the advice as of little value. They therefore they do not put the effort into helping the consultant or into implementing the recommendations. The result is, the grant is wasted and the stereotype of consultancy being a waste of time is confirmed.

As a new consultant, you may be tempted to regard grant-aided consultancy as an easy source of income. This is not generally the case. The accreditation requirements mean that you have to pay fees to the accreditation service, with no guarantee of accreditation or indeed any fee-paying work. There are also annual renewal fees, and if any work does materialise, there is often a project fee payable to either the agency or the accreditation management company — this is usually 5–10 per cent of total fees, which includes the grant-aided element. In many cases, the project fees are payable, even if the consultant originates the work and recommends that their client seek the available grants. On top of that, the daily rates that qualify for grant support are frequently limited and mean that you will only be able to earn a middle management salary — you will certainly not get rich.

In fact, accreditation will not usually be available to the new consultant until they have sufficient experience and enough client references to qualify. You therefore have to do your own marketing for the first year or two in any case.

Personally, I tend to avoid grant-aided consultancy for all the above reasons, because I find it results in poor clients and gets in the way of good consultancy.

CONSULTANCY NETWORKS AND FRANCHISES

You need to be very careful about being attracted to paying fees to join consultancy networks, companies or whatever other structure they suggest. After assessment for suitability as a consultant, most promise high earnings, training, marketing and administrative support. Unfortunately, the more unscrupulous operations accept everybody, however ill-equipped for a consultancy career.

Some of these bodies seem designed to extract redundancy cheques from the unsuspecting newly redundant manager. They require payment up front for expensive initial subscription and training.

Many do not and cannot deliver on the promises of referred work or effective marketing, because as we have already discussed, consultancy is a personal service that individuals have to sell themselves. As a result, even with the proper networks, the new consultant will have to sell most of their own work. They may get some sales leads but they will have to convert this into sales themselves.

Some of the real consultancy networks have collapsed after a period of reasonable success. These have failed, usually because of internal squabbling, often over the sharing out of the best work, costs and sales leads.

CONTINUING PROFESSIONAL DEVELOPMENT

An increasing number of professional organisations require their members to invest time in their own personal development. Whether or not that applies to you as a consultant, you should be investing in your own expertise and knowledge. If you are to succeed you need to be constantly updating what you offer clients. That is what it means to be a 'professional'.

If you are interested in your work, then it should be enjoyable and be something you want to do. To be successful, consultants should be good at learning without the need to always be taught in a formal way. Someone who has the attitude 'I cannot do that, I have not been on the course . . .' will never be a good consultant.

EMPLOYING CONSULTANTS

Employing consultants and building a practice may look attractive as a way to develop the business. But there are some major snags that you will have to address:

- Consultants who come, learn your techniques, build a personal network of your clients and then move on to start their own practice, taking those clients with them.

- Senior consultants who are unable or unwilling to sell. They draw their salary but increase the selling burden on their colleagues. All consultants, if they wish to get to a senior level and earn higher salaries, need to be able to sell. Indeed, for most large consultancy firms, senior positions are only given to those that can bring in substantial new business (with very few exceptions).

- Consultants who talk a good story and apparently have good curriculum vitae but actually deliver very little in the way of value to the practice. They may be slow, disorganised, incompetent or simply lazy.

Good senior consultants will be expensive but will bring in new clients and do quality work. They should be rewarded on the basis of targets for new business and fees earned. They should share in the success, or otherwise, of the practice, and should be given the freedom and encouragement to do so.

USING ASSOCIATES

From time to time you may wish or need to work with others. If you are successful, you will run up against resource issues: either you will simply need more people with similar skills to cope with the workload that has outgrown you (and your partners) or you will need complementary skills to handle larger, more broadly based projects.

You need to be clear, before you face that situation, how you will handle such additional resources, and you must build up a network of associates with whom you would be happy to work. There are several ways in which you may work with other consultants.

Associates

Associates are treated as peers and are usually principals in their own practices. They will usually be consultants with whom you have worked in the past or who have been recommended to you by people whose judgement you trust on such matters. They will share your values and professional approach and should require little management from you — you will be able to trust them to deliver what is required to the same time and quality standards as yourself.

Because they need minimal management from you, they are the best resource even though you will need to pay them more than sub-contract staff. That higher rate will be offset by the reduced management time you will need to spend on projects using associates. Typically, fees paid to associates will be around 70–80 per cent of the fee you receive for their time. This margin will be needed to cover your marketing costs and the account management function — if this margin seems high, just consider that you will need to spend around one day each week on marketing, whatever else you are doing.

Sub-contracting

There may be circumstances when you need skills and resources that are not available through your associate network, in which case you may need to use people with whom you are not familiar who will need more management than an associate. In that case you will need to use sub-contract staff.

In that case you will have to pay sub-contract rates which will depend on the sub-contractor's skills and the demand for such skills. However, sub-contract staff will usually be less expensive than associates, as they will usually not operate as self-managing practitioners. The reduced rate reflects the extra management burden for the contractor.

Cross-referral

Sometimes you will come across work that you cannot take on. You owe it to your clients to remember the consultant's key judgement: are you competent to take on this work? If the answer is no, then you must decline the work; but if you have established a relationship with a client or prospective client then you may want to add some value to the relationship by helping them to find a suitable firm to do the work.

Suggesting a suitable firm of advisors gives you the opportunity to build on relationships with other complementary firms by referring the client to them. It may not be a full recommendation, merely a suggestion that the client talks to your contact. After that, it is for the associate firm to sell and do the work. All you need to be sure of is that they are competent to take on the work. In return, you can expect them to refer work to you on a similar basis — it is surprising how much work is placed in this way.

Building such relationships with complementary firms opens all sorts of possibilities. Apart from cross-referral, there may be opportunities for you to use each other on your respective client bases — this may be as an associate or in your own right. That is a decision for you and the principals of the associate firms, probably on a case-by-case basis.

The Solidus *Dynamic Consultancy* Model

Solidus is a small company but its range, both functionally and geographically, is wide. That is because it was designed as a *dynamic consultancy*. It is not a consultancy network or franchise, or even a shared marketing operation. Rather, it has a core of basic capabilities with layers of additional specialist support and organisations to which it provides support.

These additional layers are integrated into the core operation to a variable extent. All the associated consultants and firms operate freely in their own right, but co-operate with Solidus in various ways. Many are independent consultants who are willing to work through Solidus when we need their specialist expertise; the rest of the time they are principals in their own practices. When working on Solidus projects, all participants will work to Solidus quality and other standards and business practices, which helps create a client base with consistent expectations.

The relationship is broadly agreed in advance of their skills being needed, so that Solidus can bid for work knowing on what basis to include associates in the proposal. The only factor that might have to be checked is availability and details of particular, highly specialised, capability. A point that should be made is that the arrangement with an associated practice or consultant will be specific to that firm. Some we know work to similar professional standards and are self-managing; therefore we can use them with little supervision. Others may have excellent technical ability and reliability in their field but are perhaps less organised and therefore need to be managed more closely — our arrangements with them will reflect our extra workload. The aim is to give a consistent and high quality service to our clients.

A few associates are more closely integrated and we work together more actively. In some cases, we will work as a consortium under the Solidus banner to bid for particular work. In other cases we might actually work together on marketing and selling into completely new markets with new services. But we remain separate businesses, albeit working very closely together. Obviously, to work this closely requires a high level of mutual trust that neither party will use what they learn about each other to the detriment of the other. This trust only comes from working together over time.

In some cases, Solidus will work as the specialist arm of another firm and operate under their 'brand'. This usually happens where the client is an existing client of the associate or requires the associate's specialist expertise, but with additional skills that they do not have that can be supplied by Solidus. Almost invariably, with odd exceptions, the work undertaken is only part of a much larger project for the associate. In these circumstances, Solidus adopts the associate's practices, but by the nature of the relationship, these standards tend to be very similar in any case.

Some of the latter group may then move towards becoming part of Solidus itself. They will earn their way in by working with the existing members of Solidus to create new business opportunities and to carry them out. Over time, they may then become full members of Solidus, sharing in any profits and losses according to the level of their participation.

As the numbers at each level grow, so do the wider connections which enable Solidus to offer a broader range of services in an ever-growing number of industries. It must be said that, so far, participation in this approach is by invitation. Associates tend to be people with whom members of Solidus have worked — sometimes we find consultants who share a similar approach when we work with them at client firms. Others come recommended to us by people whose judgement we trust. So far we have never taken on anyone who has approached us to be included, and I suspect that will continue to be the case for the foreseeable future.

Whilst this approach is quite new, it is working well and we have people and practices at all the above levels.

OFFICES, CARS AND OTHER EXTRAVAGANCES

Be true to yourself; you are what you are. Do not pretend to be anything different. Superficial gloss will soon be seen by clients as just that. Remember they buy you for who you *are* — not what you *pretend* to be. Clients are not fools; do not treat them as such.

Offices are not really necessary. In more than 15 years of consultancy, the number of times a client has needed or wanted to come to me rather than me go to their premises is tiny. In any case, I would sooner go to the client, as I will learn a great deal by simply watching how their site is organised and what their people do. I would lose that valuable information if they came to me, and I would not get to talk to their staff — that also provides a useful insight into the issues.

So unless you are running training courses or seminars on a regular basis, it may well be more economic to not have offices, or at least to only have a small headquarters for taking messages and the like.

If clients do need to come to you occasionally for a course or other purpose, hire a conference room at a hotel or your local college or university. It will be cheaper overall and will get you away from interruptions from colleagues and the telephone.

Typists are a disappearing breed and secretaries appear to be following them. I would encourage any consultant to learn to type and use a word processor. All consultants should write reports and letters straight into the word processor — I have done so for many years. Overall it is more efficient, even if a secretary is used to polish the presentation. Even that is becoming less necessary with the increased sophistication of word processors.

Cars are always a big issue. Do you need to impress or should you play down your affluence? As a start-up, keep the costs down. And then aim to keep them down as the business develops. It is easier to keep the fat off than it is to lose it quickly — as anyone who has tried to lose weight will confirm. It is the same with unnecessary costs.

Clients do not like consultants who look extravagant. In this context, that means anyone who appears better off than they do. So, if you are successful, be careful about how you show your affluence. Think long and hard about the message you are giving your clients. After all, it is their money that is paying for it all.

ACTION PLAN

1. Review your plans for cars, offices, etc. Will they appear inappropriately extravagant to your likely client base?

2. Make sure that you are not taking on costs simply to look the part. It is not needed; if it is purely gloss, clients will see through it.

3. Shop around for professional indemnity and third party insurance cover. Also, as part of this process, consider membership of appropriate professional bodies.

4. Document your quality assurance procedures and make arrangements if necessary with trusted third parties for independent review.

5. Put in place your administrative procedures for sales tracking, diary and time management, accounting and vital signs monitoring.

6. Decide how you are going to cope with excess demand on resources — are you going to employ or use associates? Design your procedures and establish a formal relationship with potential associates.

SUMMARY

If consultants wish to be regarded as professionals, they must be professional in all aspects of their business. It is not sufficient to be a professional advisor. You must also be professional in your administrative practices. Indeed, I know of a major firm who won a large project to help a client sort out their problems with billing and slow payment by debtors. Before the work started, the client found out the consultancy firm had a similar problem and cancelled the contract on the basis that if the consultancy could not keep its own house in order, how could it presume to advise clients on good practice? So practice what you preach in all aspects of the business.

To provide proper control, all agreements about fees, the scope of work and respective responsibilities should be negotiated and agreed before the work starts. That means that proposals and engagement letters or contracts should be sufficiently comprehensive to remove doubt as to what it is to be achieved. Inevitably, there will be occasional changes as the nature of the problem becomes better understood. If these changes alter the scope of the work, then they should be treated in a similar way to the original engagement. That means they should be negotiated, agreed and there should be an exchange of signed letters detailing how the terms of reference are to be amended. In extreme cases, completely new terms of reference may be needed to replace the original remit. This is fundamental to the control of professional engagements.

The boring administration should be invisible to the client or prospective client, but should still be professionally managed. As a consultant you never know when you might be asked to justify an invoice — to do so requires a good record of what work was done and when, and what expenses were incurred. Similarly, a consultant should manage their time to ensure that they achieve the objectives agreed with the client and do not have to rearrange meetings because of errors in managing diaries.

There are some basic approaches to quality control that are applicable to most professional advisors. This involves reviews at critical points before the client or advisor is committed — so-called 'hot' reviews. There are also reviews carried out to check compliance with practice procedures and to learn any lessons from completed work, successful or otherwise. As these take place after the event, they are known as 'cold' reviews. These reviews, along with professional audit, can be carried out on a peer basis, by the consultant's manager or partner, or they can be undertaken by external auditors either from outside the practice or from another office. Such procedures should be put in place by all professional advisory firms, even the one-person firm.

Most consultancy practices will from time to time find themselves with insufficient resources or without necessary specialist resources for some projects. In some circumstances, these gaps may be filled by recruiting additional staff. But often it will be more appropriate, because of the occasional nature of the need, to use associates or other third parties. Any growing consultancy should have a strategy for how it will cope with such situations. Where it is likely that outside skills will be needed, then the firm should be discussing reciprocal or associateship arrangements with other possible practices and individuals. That way, the engagement consultant can discuss matters with potential clients knowing the basis on which they will be able to meet client's needs. It is far better to get these arrangements negotiated in general terms when not required rather than to try and establish them in a hurry to meet client deadlines — it weakens your negotiating position.

Finally the consultant has to balance looking successful with looking extravagant. It is a thin dividing line and what will be appropriate for one client will look excessive to another. Extravagance is in the eye of the beholder, so plan accordingly.

CHAPTER 12

WHEN THE GOING GETS TOUGH

From time to time, most businesses will go through difficult times. Small consultancies are particularly prone to variable income. Indeed, by the very nature of project work they suffer from periods of feast and famine. Such periods need to be managed to keep the practice on an even keel.

FEAST AND FAMINE

Project-based professional services are always prone to feast and famine. It is almost impossible to have a forward order book as would be possible in many product-based businesses. When a customer decides they are ready to use consultants, they want them on site straight away, however long they took to decide to go ahead.

Some firms reduce the impact of the problem by having regular repeating business. But for many consultants, that is not possible on any consistent basis. The occasional retainer-based project is the best they can hope for.

As a result, a consultancy firm must be prepared to face gaps in their income between projects. That is why it is essential to keep a steady marketing and sales effort going, even when busy with chargeable client work. The lead time for new work is often six months or more, so you cannot start when the current project finishes — you need to have started the sales cycle before the current project.

Even with consistent sales effort, there will be many occasions when the end of one project and the start of the next do not coincide. Keep money in the bank to tide you over such periods and be persistent with your marketing. If your services are sound then new work will come.

TIGHTEN UP

Obviously the first thing to do is to tighten your belt. At the earliest opportunity, begin reducing costs; some you will be able to do straight away but others will take time. Do it for both your domestic expenditure, so that you can reduce your expenses, and for the practice. Plan reducing costs further over time — you do not know how long the lean spell will last.

Over time, any business will gain expenditure that is not strictly necessary if it is doing well. As soon as the future gap in income is spotted, you should start reducing it as quickly and completely as possible. Much of it will seem trivial: journals that nobody really needs, unnecessary journeys, visits to unimportant exhibitions, hotels that are a bit more up-market than strictly necessary. All those individually small costs actually add up to a considerable sum, as you will have seen when you did your original costing. In fact, this would be a good time to compare your actual costs before and after pruning with your original estimate. Even after pruning, I bet that your actual costs are well over your original estimate, so further reductions can be made. Do it also for your personal budget — the same will be true.

KEEPING AN EYE ON THE BALL

When work is not coming, it is very easy to lose sight of your strengths and start chasing everything. Most business comes from existing clients, either directly or through referrals, so do not neglect past and present customers.

Go back to basics and re-plan the business, remind yourself why you came into it and why you were successful in the past. You may find that you have stopped doing some of the simple things, like making follow-up calls when you promised, or have stopped doing your preparation before targeting possible clients. You may have got into a 'scatter gun' approach rather than the 'rifle' approach that is needed.

It is very easy when things are not going as they should to equate high volumes of sales letters with serious effort. I have found over many years that if I send out 100 letters, I get little response but if I spend the same effort on 10 or 20 letters I get more responses — not just a better response rate but a greater number of subsequent meetings.

VITAL SIGNS

Identify the vital signs that you will need to monitor to keep the business alive. Isolate potential threats to the business, such as lack of cash, and monitor those key indicators carefully. Then act decisively as soon as they vary from the plan. Remember also that too much business can be as big a problem as too little.

PERSISTENCE

Do not give up, unless you are in danger of trading insolvently. Then you must consider your position and that of your other senior colleagues. If you do trade when insolvent, you are exposing the directors to personal risk — limited liability will not protect you in such circumstances. Most successful people who started businesses have come close to failure at some stage in achieving that success. Many have failed at least once, although failure is not a prerequisite to success. Business start-up is a calculated risk and does not have a very high success rate. You can expect to go through some lean times, especially in the early years.

But success in any field comes from focus, hard work and persistence in pursuit of a vision. Hopefully, you have all those, because if you do not, I have failed to dissuade from starting your consultancy practice. They are essential to real success and personal satisfaction in any consultancy role.

You will need to keep the sales effort going at all costs, because that is going to bring in the new work that you need to climb back to comfortable viability. It is one of the key reasons for having major gaps in the income stream and it is an area that many consultants enjoy least, so it is easy to give up on it when times are good. But you will pay the price — I make no bones about it, as I speak from experience. I am trying to help you avoid the same mistakes that I have made. It is difficult to put time aside when you have more clients than you can handle, and it is so easy not to do any practice development this week, with the genuine intention of making it up next week. A month can go by, and the seeds of a lean time, which might not show for several months, might be sown. But you can be sure that it will show, and probably at the most inconvenient time, such as when a major project finishes and there is no work to follow on. And no work means no cash flow.

Keep at the selling — even in good times you need to be spending at least one day a week on it. And on top of that you have to do some marketing to determine where the effort needs to go for new services or potential clients. On top of that you must continue networking to stay in touch with old friends, former clients and other agencies who may refer work.

AVOID DESPERATION

Whatever you do, you must not become desperate; if you do, your critical faculties will fail you. You need to be as dispassionate as possible so that you think through the problem logically.

Many years ago, I was given sage advice by a general dealer who bought and sold for a living. He told me that, when you are buying, whatever the circumstances, you must behave in a way that shows the other party you do not *need* to buy, however much you want what is on offer; and when selling you do not *need* to sell, however much you need the money. Salespeople who are desperate do not succeed. Never, ever play the sympathy card, even with long-established clients who you regard as friends — you will usually lose both relationships.

It is difficult, but absolutely essential, to stay cool, at least on the surface. Several people who I have worked with have asked me how I manage to stay so cool in a crisis — it is because I believe it is not possible to respond rationally to a situation if you lose control. In a crisis, I take action to positively slow down and record how I am going to work my way out of the problem (whether technical or business). When the adrenaline is flowing, you will still work faster than normal, even having apparently slowed down.

BE LEAN — AND MEAN BUSINESS

Once you have made the business lean, keep it that way. Even if things are going well, go through the cost reduction process and cut out unnecessary expenditure. But keep the business in mind and do not cut the heart out of it; otherwise, you will no longer be able to deliver real customer value.

It is very easy to cut costs at the expense of the long-term viability of the business. Circumstances may demand that you cut costs to the bone. But having survived such a situation, make sure that you rebuild that long-term viability through properly justified investment in capital equipment and people. And do not forget yourself and your business partners.

THE CONTRACT OPTION

In many areas in which consultants operate, there are agencies for freelance staff, the biggest of which is probably for contract information technology staff. There are similar outlets for people with most specialist skills. Indeed, at the time of writing, there is a healthy demand for interim managers to cover long-term sickness, maternity leave and gaps due to vacancies.

The aim must always be to keep some cash flow and if things are looking difficult, it may be worthwhile getting in touch with such agencies. They may enable you to get a few months' breathing space whilst you develop new opportunities. The day rates will be lower than you would charge if you were working directly, but they will usually be full-time, in which case the week rate may be comparable. And you will work regular hours, so you will usually get your evenings and weekends to work on your practice development. The downside might be that you could be away from home, especially if you do not live in a major metropolitan area or are looking for a high-level role.

In fact, for many would-be consultants, working as contract staff through an agency will be more profitable than trying to work on their own. The agencies take over much of the marketing burden and the better ones provide reliable cash flow, with no waiting for the end-client to pay. This is a real alternative for those who do not enjoy the selling part of the work and simply wish to use their specialist skills. They find the continuity of work, and income, means that they actually earn more than they would running their own practice, even if the daily charge-out rate is a bit lower.

SUMMARY

Keep your eye on the ball and when the going gets tough, focus even more closely. As soon as matters start to take a downturn, action must be taken. A key part of handling difficult times is continuing to run a tight ship, even when times are good. By building up a buffer, the lean times can be managed far more constructively.

But above all do not panic. Go back to the basics. Sit down, review the situation, make plans and then act wholeheartedly.

CHAPTER 13

FINAL SUMMARY

Well, that is about it. Now it is down to your own efforts. I hope this book has given you a feel for some of the issues and will help you avoid some of the more common mistakes. All that remains is for me to summarise the key points, and to wish you well with your new (or improved) venture.

PART 1 — IS CONSULTANCY FOR YOU?

In the opening section, we examined what consultancy involves. We came to the conclusion that consultancy is essentially about providing advice and support to clients, rather than acting as a manager or director.

We looked at why people become consultants; it is clear that we all have different motivations. One point that was stressed was that consultancy is not a career to drift into, as the personal and professional demands are considerable. Consultancy is for those who wish to tip the balance between work and home closer to work than most. It was accepted that, for the successful, the financial rewards can be high, but the real reward is the richness of the life it provides. As a consultant you need to be a polymath who enjoys intellectual challenges, achieving their aims and meeting a wide range of people in a huge variety of positions. The experience of consultancy, if you are the right person, can be highly satisfying and enjoyable.

But those rewards come at a cost, which means it is not for everyone. I will repeat what I said early in the book: admitting that consultancy is not for you is not failure; but attempting to become a consultant when you are not equipped or if your heart is not in it almost certainly will be. In any case, you are advised to stay in paid employment until you are fully prepared to go out on your own, as there will be enough to learn even if you have all the essential basic skills.

So you need to conduct an appraisal of your skills, aptitudes and interests. It is also important to ensure that you have the support of your family and friends, and that they understand what your becoming a consultant will mean for their relationships with you. Above all, consultants have to be aware of the limits of their competence — everyone has them. A consultant is employed for their judgement and the most important judgement is whether they are competent to properly undertake the work on offer. You must turn it down if you have any doubts.

A wide range of skills is required, of which the functional specialism in which you will provide advice is only a part. Such knowledge must be at a high level and it must be possible for the client to take it for granted. But to win work and perform it satisfactorily will require many different, mostly personal, skills. Clients buy consultants with whom they develop a rapport, so interpersonal skills are essential. But so is the ability to sell, to be creative, to understand how business works and, especially, to be committed and disciplined to ensure that what is promised is achieved, whatever the personal cost.

PART 2 — THE NATURE OF CONSULTANCY

In the second part, we explored the styles of consultancy. Some are essentially about providing technical advice, whereas others may work in a more facilitative role. In the latter case, the consultant works with clients rather than for them. But the aim is the same: to bring value to the relationship. The individual roles that a consultant may take are even more wide-ranging, but again the aim is to achieve business benefits for the client.

We also considered the specialisms that are offered and came to the view that there are consultants in almost all fields of business knowledge: industries, geographic regions, political, economic, management and functional fields.

Chapter 5 gave a brief outline of the generic consultancy process. Whilst there is a wide variety of different forms of consultancy practice, the basic approach to most projects is broadly similarly. The difference lies in the detail of how the work is undertaken and managed. Before any action is taken, there should be an appraisal of all possible options, including doing nothing. The option appraisal should include a detailed examination of the investment justification. Only when it demonstrates that the project will achieve an appropriate return on the capital employed should the go-ahead be given. All too often, the investment analysis is used to prove the decision is right rather than to test whether it should proceed.

A general vital signs monitoring approach to management was outlined, based on a few key measures of project health. This should all largely be revision for anyone who is ready to become a consultant. This covers general and project management and is a well-tried approach, albeit rarely used as much as it should in practice.

PART 3 — THE BUSINESS OF CONSULTANCY

Business should start with marketing. Without knowing what the customer needs and what is already available, it is impossible to design the products or services. As far as consultancy (and many other businesses) goes, change is identified as an important factor in a potential client's desire or need for professional support. Whatever the consultant decides that the client needs, there must be clear value to justify the client's investment in the consultant's fees.

We also understand the capabilities of our budding consultancy practice. We need to be able to appreciate the implications of what is happening in the business environment and relate it to our skills and knowledge to determine that what we can offer is relevant to those factors.

But in designing our services, we have to bring together what the client needs, what the market factors are and how it all interrelates with our capabilities. Only then can we put together a marketing strategy that will enable us to reach our customers, with products and services that they want and that we can deliver, and at a price the customer can afford and which is profitable for us. We also have to decide how we are going to make those customers aware of our services and how and where they can buy them. That is all there is to it!

Promoting and selling consultancy is difficult. It is not something that clients buy frequently and it is difficult to identify those who have a current need. It is possible to recognise those who are likely to have some need of outside advisors by understanding the changes in their market or regulatory frameworks. Change is a key trigger for generating a need for consultancy. It is the consultant's job to recognise those facing change and to get their name in the minds when the potential client is ready to use outside advisors.

In general, this makes advertising and many traditional approaches insufficiently targeted. Even direct mail is not ideal but is probably the best of a poor bunch for getting started. But most consultants find that, over time, more and more of their work comes from referral by satisfied clients and through other contacts who have mentioned their name. This makes the ability to network a key skill for any principal consultant — it is very much a case of the people you know rather than what you know that leads to success. It also stresses the need to keep in touch with former colleagues and clients — you never know when they might have another requirement, so you need to keep refreshing their memory of you.

As part of that self-publicity, letters and articles in magazines, seminars and public speaking will all contribute to making potential clients think of you when they have need of support. Even books provide further credibility, but whether they justify the effort involved in writing them is another matter. If you work at it you can become a 'guru' and a minor celebrity whose opinion on appropriate matters is sought by the media.

Estimating is a task that all consultants should be familiar with, and it links smoothly into project planning. It is important to be able to break down a large project into separate tasks that can be costed with reasonable accuracy. These elemental tasks may well be very similar to the task breakdown that will be produced when the project starts, although they may need to be broken down further for project management.

Selling consultancy is difficult, and it must be remembered that you are to all intents and purposes selling the person, not simply the skills. For many readers, that means you will be selling yourself, something many people find difficult; they may take the rejection personally. You will have to learn to get over that.

The early meetings are probably the most important and your aim must always be to keep the door open. Listen more than talk, use the opportunity to understand the client's real issues, as they may be very different from those stated initially.

You must have clear objectives for each stage of the process of selling to a potential client. You must also be properly prepared, with as much knowledge about the client as possible but do not use it to jump to conclusions. Lead the client through their understanding of the problem and the work involved. Above all else, meet promises and make it easy for the client to buy your services. So if you promise to send something or to call them, do so exactly as promised. Send them proposals that are also engagement letters, so that all they have to do is sign them to place the contract with you. And do not try to hide things in the proposal — it will send all the wrong messages to the client.

Setting fees is a mixture of art and science. Remember that clients who buy consultancy on price alone tend to be reluctant to allow you to do good work and will not carry the work through effectively. Use fees to position yourself with the sort of clients with whom you want to do business (assuming you have the necessary skills). In my experience, it is harder to sell consultancy to clients who pay low fees than to those who are prepared to pay high fees. Certainly, in the former case you have to do a lot more education about the role of consultants before you can start actually selling your services.

Throughout this book, I have stressed that consultancy is an interpersonal service that puts a premium on good customer care, treating people as individuals and meeting their expectations. It is important therefore to approach everything, from service design to administrative procedures, with customer care as the driving force. By doing so, you will automatically address the issues that the client perceives as important to quality. People with specialist skills, like consultants, tend to take a technical view of quality.

Their clients, on the other hand, take such quality for granted. They are not always able to assess it, and focus instead on the peripheral aspects as their measures of quality. These 'peripheral' aspects are the customer care factors, effective administration, prompt and complete resolution of problems, politeness, prompt returning of telephone messages, and so on. But that is not all there is to customer care, as it also links back to your promotional strategy through networking and staying in touch with former prospects and clients — keep giving them some value.

We also covered some of the basics of running a practice, focusing especially on quality assurance through having a proper paper trail setting out what is to be done and any changes that have been made to the terms under which the work is to be carried out. This leads on to hot and cold reviews to ensure that, not only is the work carried out properly, but that lessons to improve the quality of the work are also learned. Continuing development is a professional responsibility, both for the firm and the individual. Indeed it is often a requirement of professional institutes.

The final chapter recognised that, by its nature, the level of work tends to ebb and flow. We set out some strategies that could be adopted when there is a downturn in work. Some are good practice at all times; others are survival strategies. But the overriding message is not to give up — commitment and persistence is essential to the consultant, as demonstrated throughout the book.

FINALLY

I wish you well with your new career and I hope to hear that some of you have gone on to great things, having begun with the advice in this book. As I have already said, I hope it will help you avoid some of the mistakes I, and some friends and colleagues, have made in the past. It cannot help you to avoid the mistakes we have not yet made and recognised, and in any case I expect you will invent a few mistakes of your own. Do not let then throw you off your chosen path; learn from them and then put them behind and look to the future.

Good luck!

Appendix A

Start-up or Re-launch Programme

PERSONAL PREPARATION

Personal Assessment

Are You Ready?

The first thing you have to do is establish whether you are ready to pursue a consultancy career. Throughout this book it has been stressed that you must take a cold, hard look at yourself, your skills and personality before embarking on the demanding, but rewarding, life of a consultant.

You should undertake the personal assessment test again and be honest with yourself. You need to be sure that:

- You have the range of skills that are needed. Apart from your main field of expertise you need to be comfortable with:

  - Sales and marketing

  - Project and time management

  - Report writing and giving presentations

  - Administration and finance

  - Business strategy and planning

- You really understand that consultancy is a high-stress career with many uncertainties. Are you prepared to face the difficult times on your own? And be self-disciplined to eat healthily, exercise and make time for yourself so that your mind and body can cope with that stress?

- You are also self-disciplined to deliver on your promises, whatever it costs in money, time or unsocial hours. You demand high standards of yourself and deliver them in your work.

- You are tough-minded so that you can keep your head, whatever the pressure. You need to be able to perform when the heat is on.

- You can put your specialist experience into a wider business context.

But above all understand why *you* want to become a consultant. Really examine your motives — is your heart really set on it or does it seem an easy option to get out of an unsatisfactory job or to cope with redundancy? The latter reasons, and many like them, rarely produce committed, and thereby successful, consultants.

Support

Be sure that you have a professional network established to provide additional resources, should you be successful in winning work. You will also need a support network of people who can fill the gaps in your own expertise. As part of that, you need to have access to professional libraries appropriate to your fields and perhaps to specialists through the Internet and other on-line services. Make sure they are in place before you start out.

Family and Friends

You need to make sure that your family and friends understand what you are going to be doing and what it will really mean for them. You will be less available to them, especially at first, and when you are established you will, on occasions, have to put work before domestic and social life. Are they prepared for that and do they really understand what it means? Make sure that they do and they *genuinely* accept it. You will not perform if you are under pressure both at work and at home.

Financial Survival Budget

You will need to establish your domestic survival budget. What do you and your family need to meet the essentials of life, mortgage, gas, electricity, food, etc. Cut this to the bone, but be sure that you could live on it. Exclude all the little niceties such as the newspapers or the evening at the pub. If things get tight, it is important to know what you need to be able to draw from the business to survive — we will use this figure later to establish what the business needs to earn to survive.

Also, look at your capital resources, as this will determine how long you have to make the business self-sufficient. Very few businesses achieve a steady and adequate cash flow from the start — most take twice as long as planned to do so. You will have to survive that period if you are going to become established.

Make the Most of Your Current Employment

As a result of your initial personal assessment, you should be aware of missing skills. If you are not ready to become a consultant but still wish to do so, you should manage your existing career to prepare yourself. That may mean taking a role in sales, for example, to give you the essential selling skills or it may even mean a move to a new employer who can provide exposure and training in your weaker areas (weaker as far as consultancy is concerned). I took a job for a year to get some essential expertise for my planned move into an independent role — I stayed for three years because I was adding further new and important skills.

Often you will be able to widen your skills with your current employer if you take a positive approach and show a willingness to take on new responsibilities, even before you are paid the salary for that position. Be prepared to prove yourself first and then worry about the salary — remember you are now investing in your future consultancy practice. All the training and personal development will be well worth the effort. You never know, you may become so successful and get so much job satisfaction that you will never make the switch; so be it — you will be happy anyway!

SWOT, PEST ANALYSES

Use SWOT and PEST analysis to determine where your business opportunities lie and why clients should use you rather than your competitors. Build a plan as to how you are going to realise those opportunities and mitigate the threats and weaknesses.

You will also need to apply the same test to yourself and to any colleagues or partners in the practice.

SKILLS

By undertaking a thorough SWOT analysis on the people in the practice, you will be able to identify what skills you have and, more importantly, what skills and experience are missing. This will enable you to put plans in place to eliminate those skill gaps. That should be built into your business plan before you start to operate as a consultant.

You will probably need to undertake training and to do research and study. Some of that may be available with a subsidy, or at least at low cost, from government business development agencies and Chambers of Commerce and Trade. You will need to establish contact with such bodies in any case and know what they can offer to your practice and to your clients. The quality of such agencies can be very variable, but the best are excellent.

PREPARING THE BUSINESS

Once you have examined your skills and those of your colleagues, and prepared an overall business strategy, you will need to prepare an operational plan that you can use for the day-to-day management of your new practice.

MARKETS

As part of your business strategy you will have determined the type of client you will be seeking and what they will require from you. You will also have decided whether you are going to compete on price or by adopting a differentiation strategy. You will therefore have decided how and where you are going to position yourself in the market.

PRODUCTS AND SERVICES

By now you should be clear about the nature of the services you will be offering and their relevance to your potential market. You must remember that they are sold on their benefits to the client's business. No product is sold on the basis of its features, but on how they satisfy the customers' needs.

COSTING

You will need to establish what income you need to break even. In the first instance, calculate it based on the personal drawings that you expect to earn. That will then allow you calculate the fee rates that you need to achieve that salary and a profit for the use of the capital and to reflect the risk to it. As described in the main body of the book, you should separate your income as an employee — your salary — from your income as a shareholder — the profit.

Remember not to be too optimistic about the number of days you will be able to bill to clients. An established consultant should be able to make a reasonable income and a profit on around 1,000 hours per year. Of course, you should expect less when starting out, unless you have an initial contract that will give you more — then allow for a substantial dip when that finishes and you need to find follow-on work.

You should also calculate your worst case survival position, based on only drawing your personal survival budget described earlier. This will give you a fee rate below which you should not go, as it is not viable business. Remember that with any given client, it is very difficult to increase fee rates — even when they have suggested that they would try you out at a low rate initially.

Most importantly, you should prepare a cash flow forecast on both bases. This will give you a feel for when more cash will be coming in than going out. Make an assessment of how the income will grow, and then at least double the period to break even. It is exceptionally rare for a new business to grow as fast as originally expected, so make sure you can survive an extended business build-up. Remember, more business fail because of lack of cash than due to short-term lack of profits. Make sure you are not one of them by only drawing your personal survival income (or less) until the business has built up a bank balance. Once a consultancy business with properly structured billing and payment terms is in a period of steady workload, it should be generating cash.

ADMINISTRATION

As a new business you will need to organise various matters: These include:

- Bank accounts for the business must be separate from your private accounts, otherwise you will get in a hopeless muddle.

- Accounting procedures should be established — probably a proprietary accounting book or a low-cost computer program.

- Premises must be organised, or at least decide on the address from which you wish to operate. If you are working from home, you may consider having a post office box for business purposes.

- Stationery should be properly designed and printed on quality paper. After all, it will often be the first contact a client has with you, so make sure it looks good. A tip I recommend, especially if you have a high quality laser or ink-jet printer, is to only have the coloured part of the design printed and use your word-processor to 'drop-in' the black address lines, etc. This will be cheaper to buy and you can risk buying a larger quantity, as it will still be usable if you move or change telephone numbers — just change it in the word-processor. I have used this approach for many years and I have found it very effective, as you can use the paper for a variety of purposes.

- Telephone and possibly fax numbers will be required. If working from home, I would strongly recommend having a separate line from your home telephone for business purposes. This has several advantages: it can be answered with your business style, you can put an answering machine at night or weekends and you will not miss important calls because your teenage children are hogging it!

- E-mail may also be important to you, especially if you are likely to collaborate with colleagues or clients who are geographically spread — in which case organise an e-mail address with one of the major online service providers. Initially you will probably not need your own Internet domain — save that for when you have established the practice.

- Insure your equipment and employees for third party liability and professional indemnity. The latter will not be cheap and the actual cost will depend very much on the nature of the advice you are giving. But if you are a sole trader you could face massive damages if your advice is flawed. Consider the cost of damages if you are a consulting structural engineer and a bridge or building collapses because you made a mistake in your calculations. The damages for flawed advice in any professional field can be substantial and disruptive. So insure for it.

- Computers are now so commonplace that no serious consultancy practice should be without one for word-processing and spreadsheets. You will also be well advised to buy a client and contact management database, usually aimed at sales operations, to keep track of potential clients and the stage they have reached in the sales process. If you do, remember to register the database with the Data Protection Registrar (in the UK) or its equivalent. Buy a good printer — go for quality over the ability to print colour, if funds are tight.

- Standard document formats are a valuable way of achieving consistency of style in and through documents. Most word-processors have some form of style templates which can be applied to documents so that paragraph styles can be selected from a list (this paragraph is a top-level bulleted list, for example). Once these style sheets are set up with standard headers and footers (the black part of your letterhead, for example), you will save an enormous amount of time in achieving a consistent house style.

- Directories will be a very occasional source of leads, but they are also used by clients to check whether you are established, so make sure you have a basic entry in them. They are usually

free. In my fields, I have not found it worthwhile to take en-
hanced (and chargeable) entries and certainly not separate advertising.

- There will be many other matters to address. Make a checklist
and update it as ideas occur to you, and then make sure they
are all dealt with before you launch the business.

LAUNCHING YOUR CONSULTANCY PRACTICE

The principal task now is to let the world know that you are open
for business. However you do it, they will not be beating a path to
your door. So the initial launch is only the starting point of a lot of
serious work, most of which will not involve consultancy!

Public relations is a valuable tool when you first launch the
business, especially if you have an unusual or amusing story to
tell. If you have just returned from a solo voyage around the
world in a small yacht or have done something else noteworthy,
then use it. In fact use anything that will mark you out from the
common herd.

If you are producing something for the press, then make sure
that it is short and punchy, with all the key facts. It needs to be
well enough written for them to use it as written if they wish.
Many local papers will do so, as they have limited editorial resources. If you make your press release easy to use and pertinent
to their readership, it has a very good chance of being used.

You will also need to write directly, both to potential clients
and to those who advise them such as bank managers, accountants, or whoever. Who the relevant advisors are will depend on
your specialism. In fact, some of this contact should take place
prior to the launch, as it will be valuable market research, although you will have to temper any initial enthusiasm that may
be shown for your new service with reality. It will be much more
muted when they actually have to use you!

You may consider it worthwhile setting up a small road show
of free or low-cost seminars or workshops. These are a valuable
way of showing the importance of what you can offer. You need
to strike a balance between providing information to allow those
attending to address the issues, and creating a demand for your
services. Provide information, create valid concerns, but do not be

seen to be selling. Just let them know that you understand their fears and can help address them. Have a small buffet lunch afterwards so that they are encouraged to stay and talk to you individually. Collect and distribute business cards, and follow up with a letter or a telephone call to find out how the workshop was received, whether there was anything missing and whether it was relevant to the prospect's needs. That may then give you a starting point for the real sales process.

FINALLY

You are now on your way and I wish you every success. It will be a challenge and there will be highs and lows — so low that you may wonder why you ever set out on this route. I hope you meet some highs first, because then you will know why you chose to be a consultant and know that you would not be anything else. I have met those lows (gaps in the workload, cash flow problems, weariness, awkward clients, etc.), but I have never seriously considered doing anything else. Enjoy your new career and I hope you get as much reward, financial or otherwise, as I do.

Appendix B

Glossary

Beauty Parades

'Beauty parades' have been common practice in the creative fields such as advertising for many years, but it is only relatively recently that they have become usual in fields such as accountancy, legal advice and consultancy. Typically, several firms of advisors will be required to tender competitively for the work and will be asked to make formal presentations to the prospective client. In the past, the client would have relied on recommendations and personal preference, but the increased emphasis on sound corporate governance and the growing use of consultants has led to a more competitive selection process.

BPR

Business Process Reengineering was coined by Michael Hammer and James Champy in their 1994 book, *Reengineering the Corporation*. It involves fundamentally rethinking how an organisation delivers value to its customers. It became yet another management consultancy product during the 1990s. IT companies also jumped on the BPR bandwagon as a means of selling more hardware and software.

Cold Review

This is a quality control review undertaken after the work is completed and sent to the client. The aim is to check compliance with practice procedures and to learn any lessons from the project that can be applied to future work.

COST

Costs, Opportunities, Strengths and Threats. An analytical method similar to SWOT, proposed by Tom Lambert.

Cost-Benefit Analysis

All investment and other expenditure should be subject to an evaluation of the costs and the benefits. The costs should only be incurred if they are outweighed by the benefits. Some consideration should also be given to the timing of costs and benefits by using methods such as discounted cash flow.

CPD

Continuing Professional Development is now a requirement of most professional bodies. It should only be a confirmation of existing best practice, as any professional advisor worthy of the name should be seeking to continually improve their knowledge and expertise.

Discounted Cash Flow

Discounted cash flow is a method for determining the cash value of expenditure and benefits, taking into account the changing value of money over time. It relates all monies to a value at a given point in time. It is explained in most books on management accounting or finance for non-financial managers.

Dynamic Consultancy

A particular form of consultancy, devised by Solidus, which is increasingly being adopted in a variety of guises. The practice consists of a core of consultants who are in demand, supported by associates, usually with less frequently required specialist skills, who are brought into the practice on a project-by-project basis. They are used for their particular technical skills or as a means of coping with excessive workload.

Engagement Letter

This is simply the letter setting out the terms under which the consultancy practice will undertake a project or provide other services. It will usually include the terms of reference, the fees that will be charged and the billing and payment regime, along with any other relevant information. Quite simply, it is a contract for the provision of professional services.

Expression of Interest

In formal tendering procedures, it is common to seek expressions of interest to help select a shortlist of firms, who will be asked to submit substantive proposals for a piece of work. It is in all parties' interests that unsuitable bidders do not undertake the considerable work involved in preparing a full proposal and it will also save the client the task of evaluating inappropriate proposals. The expression of interest usually takes the form of an extended letter setting out the competency, relevant experience and available resources of prospective bidders in response to a brief description of the work. The client can then select a short list who will receive the full details of the work and be invited to submit full proposals for undertaking it.

Hot Review

Hot reviews are quality control checks that are undertaken before a report is shown to the client. These should be undertaken where the consultancy firm or the client will be exposed to financial or other risks as a result of the opinions or recommendations being made. It will usually be a peer or manager review, to ensure that the conclusions are valid and that the work has been carried out with due diligence. It is often a requirement of professional indemnity insurance.

Internal Rate of Return (IRR)

Similar to discounted cash flow, this is a way of relating the value of costs and benefits incurred over time. It takes account of the changing value of money.

Net Present Value (NPV)

As with discounted cash flow, this relates the value of costs and benefits to a particular point in time. It takes account of the changing value of money over time.

Option Appraisal

As a result of any analysis, there will be recommendations for further action. There will usually be a range of possible approaches, from doing nothing to extensive investment and change. Each possibility should be subject to evaluation of the costs, benefits and risks to allow selection of the best option. That is the option appraisal.

Peer Review

Peer review is where a colleague of similar seniority reviews a piece of work for completeness, suitability of approach and to establish whether the recommendations are sound and can be supported by the findings. It is sometimes called a 'sanity check' and is intended to give the authors comfort that they have not missed anything or made insupportable assumptions or conclusions.

PEST

Political, Economic, Social, Technology — an analysis approach similar to SWOT that looks at the factors that have an impact on the business strategy. It should feed into a SWOT or COST analysis and ultimately lead through an option appraisal to a strategic and operational plan.

Practice Development

This is the name often given to the sales and marketing effort in a professional firm. It should be on-going, whatever the workload, otherwise you will get to the end of a project and have an income gap whilst you search for new work.

Product Surround

The product surround consists of all those elements around the product that are peripheral to its basic technical performance but which have a significant bearing on the client's perception of quality. The technical validity of the consultant's work is the 'core', but matters such as the availability of the consultants, their manner, timeliness, etc. fall into the product surround.

SCOPE

Symptoms, Clarity, Options, Precise, Essential facts — an acronym introduced in *Getting the Most from Consultants* (Wilson, 1996) as a guide to defining the problem and preparing a specification for consultants. Consultants should bear it in mind when collecting information at the early stages of a project, particularly before the proposal.

SWOT

Strengths, Weaknesses, Opportunities and Threats. This is a key part of the business planning process and should be second nature to all consultants, whatever their specialism. It can be applied at corporate level and at all levels down to the individual. If you are not familiar with the term and the process, then you need to do more work before becoming a consultant!

Terms of Reference

Terms of Reference simply describe the work and the way it is to be undertaken, and will usually form part of the engagement letter or will be attached as a supporting schedule to the contract. It should make clear who is responsible for what and include a timetable and what is to be the result of the work.

TQM

Total Quality Management was a popular management issue during the 1980s. It was designed to make everyone in the organisation aware of and responsible for their part in the achievement of quality products and services.

Time and Materials

Time and materials is a basis for determining fees, as opposed to a fixed price. It is where the client pays for the time spent by the consultant and for any agreed disbursements such as travel, subsistence and other project costs. In some cases this may include printing, telephone calls, etc.

Appendix C

Useful Addresses

EUROPE

FEACO (Fédération Européenne des Associations de Conseils en Organisation)
145 Rue Royale
B-1000 Brusells
Tel.:   +32 2 223 04 13
Fax: +32 2 223 06 74
E-mail: feaco@mail.interpac.be

AUSTRIA

FUD (Fachverband Unternehmensberatung und Datenverarbeitung)
Wiedner Hauptstrasse 63
A-1045 Wien
Tel.:   +43 1 50 105 35 39
Fax: +43 1 50 206 285
Internet: http://www.wk.or.at/ubdv

BELGIUM

ASCOBEL (Association Belge des Conseils en Gestion et Organisation)
Place des Chasseurs Ardennais 20
B-1030 Brussels
Tel.:   +32 2 742 17 82
Fax: +32 2 742 17 85

DENMARK

FMK (Foreningen af Managementkonsulenter)
Norregade 7A, 4
DK-1165 Copenhagen K
Tel.:   +45 33 97 80 80
Fax: +45 33 97 81 81

FINLAND

LJK (Liikeenjohdon Konsultit ry)
Pohjantie 12A
SF-02100 Espoo 10
Tel.:   +358 9 6 76 67
Fax: +358 9 46 76 42
E-mail: ljk@co.inet.fi

FRANCE

SYNTEC Management — Chambre Syndicale des Sociétiés de Conseil
3 Rue Léon Bonnat
F-75016 Paris
Tel.:   +33 1 44 30 49 20
Fax: +33 1 42 8826 84
Internet: http://www.syntec-conseil.fr

GERMANY

BDU (Bundesverband Deutscher Unternehmensberater e.V.
Friedrich Wilhelm Strasse 2
D-53113 Bonn
Tel.:   +49 228 91 61 0
Fax: +49 228 91 61 26
E-mail: bdu-bonn@online.de
Internet: http://www.bdu.de

GREECE

SESMA (Hellenic Association of Management Consulting Firms)
c/o Inforgroup
25 Filellinon Str.
GR-105 Athens
Tel.:   +30 1 32 20 507
Fax: +30 1 32 47 948

ITALY

ASSOCONSULT (Associazione delle Società di Consulenza Direzionale e Organizzat)
via Pantano 9
I-20122 Milano
Tel.:   +39 2 583 011 08
Fax: +39 2 583 050 28

IRELAND

Association of Management Consulting Organisations
Confederation House
84/86 Lower Baggot Street
Dublin 2
Tel.:   +353 1 660 1011
Fax: +353 1 660 1717

NETHERLANDS

ROA
PO Box 85515
Den Haag NL - 2508 CE
Tel.:   +31 30 236 30 30
Fax: +31 30 236 30 70

NORWAY

NBF (Norwegian Association of Management)
c/o Akersveien 24C, pb 2608
N-0131 OSLO St. Hanshaugen
Tel.:   +47 2286 5230
Fax: +47 2220 7605

PORTUGAL

APPC (Associaçao Portugesa de Projectistas e Consultores)
Avenida Antonio Augusto Aguiar 126 - 7°D
P-1050 Lisbon
Tel.:   +351 1 314 04 76
Fax: +351 1 315 04 13

SPAIN

AEC (Asoc. Espanola de Empressa de Consultoria)
Orfila 5, Esc. 1, 4° C
E-28010 Madrid
Tel.:   +34 1 308 01 61
Fax: +34 1 308 23 27

SWEDEN

SAMC (Swedish Association of Management Consultants)
Box 7470
S-103 92 Stockholm
Tel.:   +46 8 613 16 50
Fax: +46 8 791 81 21
E-mail: alf.gluckman@mbox304.swipnet.se

SWITZERLAND

ASCO (Association Suisse des Conseils en Organisation et Gestion)
Bahnhostrasse 37
CH-8001 Zurich
Tel.:   +41 1 211 10 34
Fax: +41 1 211 10 36

UNITED KINGDOM

Institute of Management Consultants
5th Floor
32–33 Hatton Garden
London
EC1N 8DL
Tel.: +44 171 242 2140
Fax: +44 171 831 4597
E-mail: consult@atlas.co.uk
Internet: http://www.imc.co.uk

The IMC is the principal professional body for the independent consultant and smaller practices. It has strict entry qualifications for full membership, which involve a minimum of three years experience as a consultant, the preparation of a portfolio, an interview and client references. It operates a strict Code of Practice and has a requirement for continuing professional development.

Management Consultancies Association
11 West Halkin Street
London
SW1X 8JL
Tel.: +44 171 235 38 97
Fax: +44 171 235 08 25

The MCA represents the interests of the largest consultancy practices in the UK.

APPENDIX D

REFERENCES AND ADDITIONAL READING

REFERENCES

Hammer, M. and Champy, J., *Reengineering the Corporation: A Manifesto for Business Revolution*, Nicholas Brealey, 1994.

Tallentyre, S.G., *The Friends of Voltaire*, 1907.

ADDITIONAL READING

Baguley, P., *Managing Successful Projects*, Pitman/Institute of Management, 1995. (Essential project planning and management.)

Barrett, J. and Williams, G., *Test Your Own Aptitude*, Kogan Page, 1990. (Test your own capabilities.)

Buzan, T., *The Mind Map Book*, BBC Books, 1993. (An approach to making the most of your mind and abilities for creative thinking.)

Essinger, J., *Starting a High-income Consultancy*, Pitman, 1996.

European Innovation Programme, *The European Handbook of Management Consultancy*, Oak Tree Press, 1996.

Freemantle, D., *The Successful Manager's Guide to Business Planning*, McGraw-Hill, 1994.

Hamilton, A., *Management by Projects*, Oak Tree Press, 1997.

Harrison, J., *Finance for the Non-financial Manager*, Thorsons, 1989.

Lambert, T., *High Income Consulting*, Nicholas Brealey, 1993.

Lock, D., *Handbook of Management*, Gower, 1992. (A general guide to a wide range of business and management matters. Useful background for any business owner or consultant providing business advice.)

McDonald, M., *Marketing Plans*, Butterworth-Heinemann, 1995. (A marketing handbook with a fast-track guide to creating a marketing plan.)

Minto, B., *The Pyramid Principle*, FT/Pitman, 1987. (A guide to structured writing — essential reading for anyone who needs to write formal reports and other complex documents.)

Obeng, E., *All Change! The Project Leader's Secret Handbook*, FT/Pitman, 1996. (A guide to change and project management in an unusual format.)

Rowntree, D. *The Manager's Book of Checklists*, Gower, 1989. (A useful prompt.)

Thomas, B., *Royal Mail Guide to Direct Mail for Small Businesses*, Butterworth-Heinemann, 1996. (An invaluable aid to direct mail for any business.)

Turner, Grude and Thurloway, *The Project Manager as Change Agent*, McGraw-Hill, 1996. (Project management is more than a way of managing projects; it should also be geared to producing organisation change. This book provides a useful background into that aspect of project management.)

Wilson, M.P., *Getting the Most from Consultants*, Institute of Management/Pitman, 1996. (Looks at consultancy from the client's perspective. Understand what clients should require from their advisors.)

Appendix E

Sample Proposal and Engagement Letter

PROPOSAL

Commission Director
AClient Co.

Dear . . .

Consultancy Support to the 'New Direction' Strategy Group

Thank you for your time on Wednesday. I am pleased to enclose our proposal and Terms of Reference for the above project, as we agreed. I hope that it accurately reflects your needs, but if there are misunderstandings or points that need clarification, please do not hesitate to contact me so that we can resolve them.

Background

A Client has been through a series of major changes over the last three years, having absorbed several complementary businesses into the company. It has been recognised that the company now needs to redefine its strategy to fully exploit the new opportunities provided by these mergers.

The 'New Direction' Strategy Group was formed under the chairmanship of the Chief Executive, Dr I.M. Wright to lead this work. As well as the five senior executive directors of Finance, Marketing, Sales, Operations and Product Development, the group will from time to time co-opt major suppliers, long-term and prospective customers under non-disclosure agreements.

The group is required by the main board to present its strategy and detailed projections not later than 1 September this year so that the plans can be agreed and presented to the shareholders at the AGM and in the Annual Report in January.

It has been recognised that the 'New Direction' Strategy Group will need assistance in various areas, and that support is the subject of this document.

Objectives

The key objectives for the consultancy support to the 'New Direction' Strategy Group are:

1) To make the permanent members of the group aware of current thinking on corporate strategy and planning;

2) To develop a strategic planning framework for the current planning round and to use as a basis for planning in future years;

3) To train members of staff in appropriate analytical and planning methodologies so that they can support their functional heads and the strategy group;

4) To facilitate the involvement of as many staff as possible in the planning process as part of the 'bottom-up' approach;

5) To facilitate the contributions from external parties such as suppliers and customers to the 'New Direction';

6) To prepare an initial project plan for the strategy development for presentation at the April board meeting;

7) To provide other specialist advice and research as needed;

8) To provide appropriate planning tools, software, etc.;

9) Reporting is to be directly to the Chief Executive.

Our Approach

Timetable

The timetable for the work is already set by the remit for the 'New Direction' Strategy Group, with a clear deadline of 1 September with all revisions, preparation of shareholder presentations to have been completed by 17 January. There is a final review meeting of the group to document the lessons of this project and the group will be wound up immediately after ratification of its final report at the February board meeting.

However, within that strict timetable we see the work falling as follows (assuming we are engaged by 1 April):

10) Initial Project Plan	10th April
11) Staff seminars/workshops	April/May
12) Data collection/analysis training	TBA Immediately
13) Etc. . . .	

We would discuss this in more detail at the initial group meeting immediately after the contract is awarded. A complete project plan will be prepared as a result of that meeting.

Our Role

Solidus will:

- Run a strategic awareness research exercise

- Run a programme of workshops on current strategic thinking and its application to the group's role

- Provide facilitators to each project team

- Act as a link between the 'bottom-up' project teams and the 'top-down' work of the Board start-up group.

Your Role

Ensure that staff are released to attend training on the agreed dates.

Ensure that staff and other resources are made available as necessary so that the 'New Direction' work is performed in a timely way.

Our Team

Solidus' project management team will be led personally by Martin Wilson, our Managing Director. He will be supported by A.N. Other, who will act as Project Manager and provide the primary point of contact for the project. They will have specialist support from S.O. Else, experienced strategy consultant with blue-chip FMCG experience. She has particular industrial expertise in . . .

(CVs may be included as an attachment.)

Other Issues

It is recognised that time is of the essence for the performance of this work. Both Solidus and AClient will make necessary resources available to meet the agreed timetable, except where prevented by force majeur.

Our Fees

As we discussed, our fees for this work are based on the following range of rates:

- Director/Principal Consultant   £X1 to £X2

- Managing Consultant/Senior Consultant   £Y1 to £Y2

- Consultant   £Z1 to £Z2

The actual rate will depend on the individual concerned.

Because of the nature of this work, it will be undertaken on a time and materials basis. Our initial estimate is that it will involve approximately D consultant days giving a total fee estimate of £F. Due to the skill mix, this gives an average day rate of £A.

Please note that all the fees quoted include all normal travel, subsistence and other disbursements involved in our staff working on your premises in Birmingham. Other expenses — for example, visiting overseas subsidiaries, visiting suppliers or other exceptional items — will be billed at cost plus 15 per cent handling charge. We would prefer that such travel, hotels etc. be booked and paid for directly by AClient at the same level as for equivalent grades of their own staff. Any additional travel within the UK will be charged at £0.tt per mile, the same rate as for AClient staff using their own car.

The work will be billed at the end of each month and will be due for payment within 14 days. Value Added Tax at the appropriate rate will be added to all charges.

ENGAGEMENT LETTER OR CONTRACT

At Solidus we use the same basic format for engagement letters as for contracts. Once we have negotiated the proposal, which incorporates the Terms of Reference for the assignment, we merely modify the opening and closing paragraphs and add an acceptance block for signature by the client. We sign two copies and send them both to the client who signs a copy and returns it to Solidus. The contract then exists and is properly documented.

The acceptance paragraph that we use currently looks like this:

The above letter accurately states our understanding of the work to be performed and the fees, terms and conditions that will apply. We therefore wish to proceed with the work as described, and this copy, duly signed, constitutes our acceptance of the above terms.

Signed: _____   *Date:* _____

Position: _____

For: _____

Purchase Order No: _____

INDEX